Transcendental Echoes

(A Spiritual Journey of a Walk-in-Soul)

Transcendental Echoes

(A Spiritual Journey of a Walk-in-Soul)

Prabhakar Sinha

MOTILAL BANARSIDASS INTERNATIONAL DELHI

First Edition : Delhi, 2025

© Author
All Rights Reserved

ISBN : 978-81-989854-7-7

Also available at :
MOTILAL BANARSIDASS INTERNATIONAL
41 U.A. Bungalow Road, (Back Lane) Jawahar Nagar, Delhi-110007
4261/3 (Basement), Ansari Road, Darya Ganj, New Delhi-110002
Shop#. 6, 241, Luz Ginza Complex, Luz Corner, Mylapore, Chennai - 600004
12/1A, 2nd Floor, Bankim Chatterjee Street, Kolkata - 700073

Stockist : Motilal Books, Ashok Rajpath, Near Kali Mandir, Patna-800004

No part of this book may be reproduced in any form or by any electronic or mechanical means including information storage and retrieval systems without permission in writing from the publishers, except by a reviewer who may quote brief passages in a review.

Cover Design *by Satyarth Dube*
Back Cover Painting *by Ms. Anupriya*

Printed in India by
MOTILAL BANARSIDASS INTERNATIONAL

Dedicated to

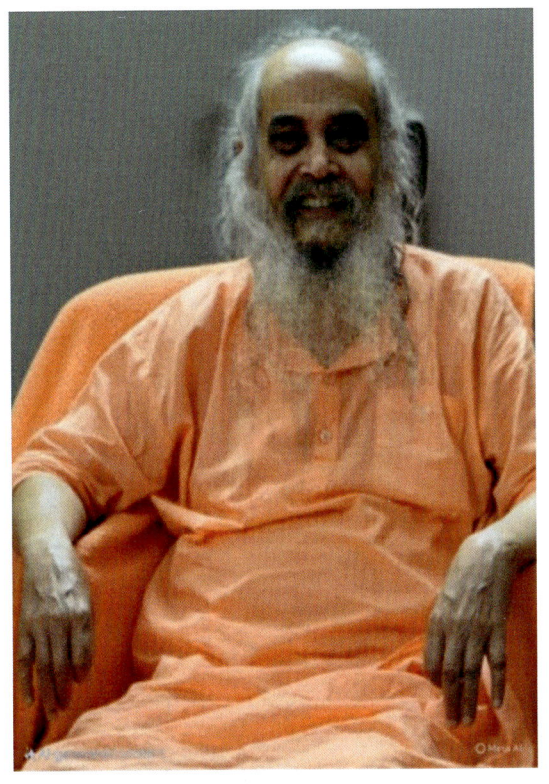

Shri Bhuvneshwaranand Giri Ji Maharaj
of
Goner Ashram, Jaipur

अखण्डमण्डलाकारं व्याप्तं येन चराचरम्।
तत्पदं दर्शितं येन तस्मै श्रीगुरवे नमः॥

The Ageless Yogi

Shri Mahavatar Babaji

The Householder Yogi

Shri Shyama Charan Lahiri

Foreword

When I look back, my life appears as my spirit's wild ride on a roller coaster-an extraordinary journey marked by soaring highs that filled me with exhilaration and plummeting lows that tested my resilience. I've experienced steep, sudden drops that left me breathless and moments of ascent that offered sweeping perspectives, each twist and turn shaping my understanding of who I am. Over nearly half a century, this adventure has unfolded across two seemingly opposite yet deeply intertwined dimensions of consciousness: one rooted in the intensely physical, where the senses, emotions, and the tangible world demanded my full attention; the other, profoundly transcendental, where I glimpsed realities beyond the material, touching the ineffable and timeless dimension. These dual aspects have not only defined the contours of my existence but have also complemented each other, revealing that the physical and the spiritual are not adversaries but partners in the dance of life. Through the interplay of these extremes, I have come to appreciate the richness and complexity of being-how each challenge and triumph, moment of pain and joy, has contributed to the unfolding of a deeper awareness. In retrospect, I see that my journey has been less about the destination and more about the evolving consciousness that has accompanied me through every rise and fall, every shadow and illumination, making my life a unique tapestry woven from both earthly experience and transcendent insight.

Born into the simplicity and quietude of a humble rural household, I found myself swept into a series of unfolding episodes that seemed to shape my destiny in ways I could neither predict nor control. As my journey progressed, I was often left pondering a profound question: was I truly the author of my own life, or was life itself orchestrating events according to some deeper, inscrutable will? Time and again, I wondered whose life I was really steering-was it my own conscious choice at the helm, or was I merely a vessel through which life, with all its mysteries and intentions, chose to express itself? With each passing year, this sense of ambiguity only deepened, and I began to perceive my existence as a mystical composition-a unique manifestation of self that transcended the boundaries of any single lifetime. It felt as though my being was woven through a great subtle fabric of existence, each birth and the silent intervals between them forming intricate patterns and connections. The joys, struggles, and quiet moments of reflection were not isolated events, but rather notes in a larger symphony, orchestrated by a consciousness far greater than my own. In this light, my life ceased to be a mere sequence of random occurrences and instead became a living testament to the interplay between fate and free will, individuality and universality-a journey shaped as much by surrender as by intention, and one that continues to unfold in ways both mysterious and deeply meaningful.

Everything I experienced in this physical body, carrying a name and identity, often felt as though it was unfolding from a pre-written script, each moment seamlessly following the next like scenes in a carefully orchestrated play. I found myself more a witness than a participant, observing the narrative of my life as it played out, with little sense of agency or control over what transpired. Events, emotions, and encounters seemed to arise and dissolve according to their own mysterious logic, leaving me to simply watch as the story unfolded. This realization brought with it a profound humility, as well as a quiet liberation; I began to accept that my role was not to direct the course of events, but to remain present and aware, bearing witness to the intricate play of experiences that life, in its infinite wisdom, chose to reveal through me.

The life I have lived, as detailed in this experiential account, has been marked by a series of striking contrasts and profound transformations. Each phase unfolded with a dramatic shift in tone, often turning deep emotional pain-moments that could have easily spiralled into chaos-into catalysts for growth and renewal. In an instant, despair would give way to hope, darkness to light, and turmoil to tranquility, ushering in entirely new chapters of my journey. Throughout these cycles, I have experienced a consistent awakening, a rising above adversity that left me stronger and more resilient at the end of every tunnel. The writing of this journey's account began well before the upheaval of the Covid-19 pandemic and has spanned nearly half a decade. Between 2011 and 2024, my life was profoundly shaped by spiritual awakenings that redefined my understanding of self and existence. Just before the pandemic struck, I received a vivid cosmic message that inspired me to embark on this project. Though the process took longer than I initially expected, I am grateful for the depth and insight it has brought. Notably, several chapters in the latter part of this account were composed simultaneously, reflecting the interconnectedness and immediacy of those transformative experiences.

In this present moment, I find myself suffused with a deep and abiding bliss, grateful for having lived a life in its fullest sense-one that has unfolded in all its unique and unpredictable forms. There were times when I was thrust into the crucible of intense physical and emotional struggle, moments so dark that my consciousness was pushed to the very brink of despair, even to the point of contemplating the end of it all. Yet, it was precisely through these harrowing experiences that I came to appreciate the astonishing resilience of the human spirit. Alongside the shadows, I have also been blessed with moments of profound illumination-those rare and precious instances when I glimpsed my true self, radiant and divine, and felt a boundless joy that transcended all worldly suffering. My journey, in essence, has been a remarkable transition: I have moved from a life oriented outwardly, defined by the shifting circumstances and demands of the physical world, to a more inwardly focused existence, where the mind is gradually internalized and the source of meaning and fulfilment is found within. This shift from external to internal-from seeking validation and purpose in the outer world to discovering peace and clarity in the depths of my own consciousness-has been both liberating and transformative. It has taught me that even amidst the greatest turmoil, there lies within each of us an inexhaustible wellspring of strength, wisdom, and joy, waiting to be discovered by those willing to turn inward and embrace the fullness of their own being.

The inspiration to write this journey's account springs from the profound celestial churning that has been a constant undercurrent in my life since 2005. Over the years, I have been propelled by an inner urge to make sense of the intense spiritual upheavals and awakenings that have shaped my journey, each episode leaving a lasting impression on my consciousness. The purpose of this book is to share, with honesty and humility, the narrative of a common householder's spiritual emergence-a journey that mirrors the timeless metaphor of the lotus blossoming from the depths of a muddy pond. My own life has been no exception to this enduring image; like the lotus, I have drawn sustenance and wisdom from the murky waters of daily struggles, doubts, and the often-chaotic realities of ordinary existence. Through these challenges, I have encountered moments of extraordinary clarity and transcendence, allowing my spirit to unfold and reveal its innate beauty. This account is not just a chronicle of personal transformation, but an affirmation that spiritual awakening is possible for anyone, regardless of their circumstances or background. By sharing my story, I hope to offer encouragement to others walking similar paths, and to remind readers that, much like the lotus, we all possess the potential to rise above adversity and manifest the hidden radiance within us.

Pure consciousness

> You saw my outline and called it familiar,
> Judged me through the mist of your own beliefs,
> Naming shadows, never seeking the source-
> Your thoughts, tangled in borrowed meanings,
> Could not reach the heart of what I am.
>
> I am not the sum of your perceptions,
> Nor the echo of your fleeting thoughts.
> Your attempts to define me
> Only reveal the edges of your own consciousness,
> Tarnished mirrors reflecting your longing for certainty.
>
> Within me, consciousness abides-unchanging,
> A bliss untouched by memory or expectation,
> A sun that rises silently within,
> Merging me with its golden dawn each day.
> At my core, the moon ascends-
> Its gentle light ungraspable,
> A mystery beyond the reach of words.
>
> I am not bound by flesh or form,
> But drift in the high, uncharted sky,

A star-bright atom, radiant and free.
Sweetness flows in the silent river within,
An inner music only awareness can hear.

I remain awake to all that is,
Yet allow you to dwell in your chosen boundaries,
Your frames of judgment and illusion.
I cannot change the course of your vision-
That, too, is woven into the cosmic embroidery
Of which I am a single, shining thread.

So, I hold to this-absolute awareness,
A lightness of being that transcends the seen,
Radiant at the heart of my atomic self,
In harmony with the vast, singing totality-
A luminous presence,
Unmoved, unchanged,
Forever one with the infinite whole.

– **Prabhakar Sinha**
Bhadrapad Maas, Shukla Paksh,
Radha Ashtami, Vikram Samvat, 2082
31 August, 2025

आरिफ मोहम्मद खां
Arif Mohammed Khan

राज्यपाल, बिहार
GOVERNOR OF BIHAR

राज भवन
पटना-800022
RAJ BHAVAN
PATNA-800022

13th August, 2025

Message

It gives me profound pleasure to have run into the extraordinary spiritual chronicle of *Shri Prabhakar Sinha*, so gracefully articulated in his recent work, *Transcendental Echoes–A Spiritual Journey of a Walk-in Soul*.

This is far more than an account of one seeker's inner transformation; it is an uplifting testament to the universal truth that the doors of spiritual awakening stand open to all, irrespective of life's circumstances or origins. In candidly sharing the luminous are of his journey–from the trials of the outer world to the serene discoveries of the inner realm–*Shri Prabhakar Sinha* extends encouragement to fellow travellers on the path and offers the reassuring reminder that, like the lotus which blossoms unsullied from the depths of the mire, every human soul carries within it the power to transcend adversity and reveal its innate radiance.

His narrative is an invitation to reflect, to aspire, and to awaken to the boundless possibilities of the spirit. I warmly congratulate *Shri Prabhakar Sinha* on this significant contribution contemporary spiritual literature. May *Transcendental Echoes* reach far and wide, touching hearts and illuminating minds, and may the author be blessed with fulfilment, good health, and success in every noble endeavour of his life.

(Arif Mohammed Khan)

Message from Swami Ram Das

।। सत्य परम धीमहि ।।
"यह तन विष बेल री, गुरु अमृत की खान।
शीश दिए जो गुरु मिले, तो भी सस्ता जान।"

"This body is a vine of poison; the Guru is the mine of nectar.
If a Guru is found by giving one's head, it is still a cheap bargain."

On a personal note, you and I have often partaken in profound and heartfelt discourses upon this sacred subject, and verily, it does seem that our souls have journeyed together along this hallowed path through many incarnations.

There exists two sovereign kinds of power and prosperity: one belonging to the outward, transient world—its honours, possessions, and fleeting triumphs; the other, far more exalted, springs from within—the immutable inner strength and spiritual wealth. To cultivate this inner power and prosperity is of supreme import; nevertheless, such divine gifts are not attained without deep self-realization, devout worship of the Divine, complete surrender of the ego, and, above all, the gracious benediction bestowed by the true Sadguru.

Most venerable Prabhakar Sinha Ji, this treatise, "Transcendental Echoes: A Spiritual Journey of a Walk-in Soul", is presented as a sacred offering to the society at large. It is designed for those noble seekers who tread the spiritual path, yearning to embark upon a celestial pilgrimage—a journey that reveals the profound message and mysteries of realms far beyond this crowded and competitive mortal sphere. May this work prove a luminous beacon, guiding sincere aspirants towards the eternal light.

— **Swami Ram Das**
Himalaya Badrika Ashram,
Uttarakhand

Message from Dr. Priyabhishek Sharma

Yet another distinguished addition to the rare and timeless tradition of Himalyan-Guru-based spiritual autobiographies - a genre graced by perhaps only a dozen works of genuine repute and enduring merit: 'Autobiography of a Yogi', 'Living with the Himalayan Masters', 'Apprenticed to a Himalayan Master', 'If Truth Be Told' - to name a few.

In **Transcendental Echoes (A Spiritual Journey of a Walk-in-Soul),** Prabhakar Sinha carries the reader along on a relentless yet poetic current, as the embroidery of his life unfolds with striking unpredictability - culminating in the sudden, lifealtering appearance of a Guru from the hidden Himalayas, at the very brink when it seemed all would dissolve into tragic oblivion.

Those deeply versed in the Himalayan Yogic path will feel an especially intimate kinship with Prabhakar Sinha's mystical revelations - whether it is his merging into the Divine Flame at the Third Eye, soaring on astral journeys through the boundless cosmos, attuning himself to the subtle resonances of *Nāda*, or dissolving into the ineffable bliss of Silence and *Shūnya*.

Works such as this are never the outcome of mere textual study or intellectual exertion; they are born of lives wholly lived in the crucible of direct experiences - forged in the discipline of rare, esoteric practices and illumined by the grace of a Realised Himalayan Master.

— **Dr Priyabhishek Sharma**
Author of the widely acclaimed
'The Himalayan Master and the Sixth Sense'

CONTENT

Foreword ... ix

Message from Shri Arif Mohammad Khan,
Hon. Governor of Bihar ... xv

Message from Swami Ram Das ... xvii

Message from Dr Priyabhishek Sharma ... xix

1. Echoes of the Divine: A Journey into the Spiritual Domains ... 1
2. Dancing with Death: A Journey Beyond Dying ... 26
3. The Sacred Himalayas: A First Encounter ... 42
4. A Journey of Shared Destiny ... 49
5. Insights into the Early Years ... 57
6. Adolescence: The Transformative Years ... 67
7. When Alcoholism Tore Family Apart ... 77
8. Celestial Control from the Sacred Himalayas ... 90
9. A Mysterious Guru from Gyan-Ganj ... 97
10. Astral Tavel to Gyan-Ganj ... 109
11. Embraced by the Narmada ... 126
12. Pashupatinath: A Gateway to the Divine ... 137
13. Maa Anandamayi: A Sanctuary of Spiritual Bliss ... 142
14. First Visit to Shri Mahavatar Babaji Cave ... 171
15. An Interface with Shri Neeb Karori Baba ... 208
16. The Quiet Mystic of Goner ... 222

17.	The Covid-19 Pandemic's Hidden Gift: A Shift in Consciousness	235
18.	Unity of Existence: The Inner and Outer as One	277
19.	A Musk Deer in the Himalayas	297
20.	Revisiting Badrinath	318
21.	And the Takeaways	335

Afterwords   349

Acknowledgement   354

Chapter - 1

Echoes of the Divine: A Journey into the Spiritual Domains

Both my mind and my ordinary intelligence gradually became aware of a transformation quietly unfolding within me, the story of which this narrative seeks to recount. It was in my late thirties, sometime between 1995 and 2005, that the first subtle signs of an unbidden change began to make themselves known. Never had I imagined that I would develop an inclination toward pursuits that had previously held no interest for me; it was as if distant echoes, foreign to the familiar language of my daily life, were softly calling me toward a new direction.

On the other hand, during this period, I was deeply absorbed in the advancement of my career, striving to achieve milestones that epitomized worldly success. Yet, amidst this outward ambition, I experienced a gentle but profound reconnection with my original self—a quiet awakening that unfolded beneath the surface of my everyday pursuits. Despite this inner transformation, I continued to fulfil my role as a householder, diligently balancing the responsibilities of family life, with my two children remaining at the very centre of my world.

During this period, driven by relentless focus and ambition, I ascended to positions of significant responsibility-culminating in my appointment by the end of 2003 as Director of a major public health program in

Uttar Pradesh, one of India's most challenging states-where I oversaw large-scale operations, managed multidisciplinary teams, formulated and implemented policies, coordinated with government and non-governmental stakeholders, and travelled extensively to engage with diverse communities, all of which allowed me to witness firsthand the complexities of public health at the grassroots level and work toward improving health outcomes in underserved regions.

Although these years were adorned with material accomplishments and professional recognition, they also brought with them a unique set of challenges that often went unnoticed beneath the surface. The relentless pace of my lifestyle and an unwavering focus on outward achievements gradually drew me into the seductive illusions of temporal success, where each milestone reached seemed only to fuel the desire for the next. While accolades and tangible rewards provided fleeting moments of satisfaction, I often found myself grappling with an undercurrent of emptiness and restlessness that no amount of external validation could truly satisfy. Yet, it was within this very whirlwind of ambition and accomplishment that the seeds of deeper reflection were quietly being sown. The contrast between my public persona and my private yearning for meaning became increasingly pronounced, prompting me to question the true nature of fulfilment. These formative experiences, both triumphant and trying, ultimately laid the foundation for a more profound exploration of life's purpose-a journey toward understanding the delicate balance between material pursuits and the enduring quest for inner contentment and self-realization.

During this time, my life appeared to be soaring-focused on material success and worldly pleasures-but beneath the surface, I was increasingly consumed by the harsh realities of the mundane world. Alcohol became a daily crutch, and by 2000, I had developed a dependency that left me uneasy without a drink in the evening. My intake steadily grew, often leading me to fall asleep after drinking without having dinner, which sparked frequent morning conflicts with my wife, Purnima. The grip of alcohol dulled my awareness and made me less receptive to her concerns.

Internally, a persistent agitation gnawed at me-a growing sense that my mind, body, and soul were drifting apart, leaving me feeling unmoored and incomplete. The relentless demands of my professional responsibilities only compounded this inner unrest, fuelling a quiet desperation for something deeper and more meaningful, though I struggled to articulate exactly what I was searching for. Amidst this personal turbulence, my attention was repeatedly drawn to a neglected copy of the Hindi version of "Autobiography of a Yogi" by Paramhansa Yogananda, which had been languishing on our bookshelf for months. Its yellowed, timeworn pages and frayed cover seemed to echo the state of my own life-battered by the passage of time and the weight of unaddressed longing, yet still quietly enduring. Each time I glanced at the book, it felt as though it was silently inviting me to turn its pages, promising solace, renewal, and perhaps the spiritual clarity I so desperately needed. In that moment, the book became more than just an object; it was a symbol of hope and a potential gateway to rediscovering the harmony and purpose that had eluded me for so long.

In the summer of 2005, after months of unbroken routine and a relentless stream of official responsibilities, I found myself teetering on the edge of exhaustion. My professional life, typically unforgiving and rarely allowing even a moment's pause, seemed to have reached a fever pitch. Yet, beneath the surface, I sensed a subtle but insistent pull-almost as if some cosmic force was gently urging me to slow down and reclaim a measure of balance. Yielding to this inner prompting, I managed to secure a few precious days of earned leave, a rare concession in my demanding career.

I chose to spend this brief respite at home in Lucknow, the city I called home at the time. There, away from the constant demands of work and the noise of daily obligations, I was able to reconnect with myself and my surroundings. The familiar comforts of home, the unhurried pace, and the simple pleasures of everyday life offered a welcome contrast to the relentless drive of my professional world. In those quiet days, I began to realize the importance of stepping back, listening to the quiet urgings of the soul, and allowing space for rest and reflection-an experience that would subtly but profoundly influence the course of my life in the years to come.

The book's yellowed pages and worn cover spoke quietly of its age and the many hands it had passed through, yet as I began to read, its content started to resonate with a depth I hadn't anticipated. At first, the journey was anything but easy; the spiritual experiences and intricate correlations shared by Paramahansa Yogananda seemed worlds apart from my own pragmatic understanding of life, almost as if I were peering into a realm both foreign and elusive. Each narrative, steeped in mysticism and profound insight, challenged my habitual ways of thinking, offering perspectives that felt simultaneously fascinating and difficult to grasp. There were moments when I found myself struggling to relate to the extraordinary events and spiritual revelations described on the pages, yet I was equally drawn in by their sincerity and the quiet conviction that underpinned every story. Gradually, what began as an exercise in curiosity transformed into a subtle awakening, as the unfamiliar wisdom within the book began to stir questions and reflections, I had long neglected. In this way, the battered volume became more than just a collection of stories; it emerged as a silent guide, encouraging me to look beyond the surface of my own experiences and inviting me to explore the deeper, more mystical dimensions of existence.

However, as I delved deeper into the pages, I found myself increasingly drawn into the blend of Yogananda's life. His upbringing in a traditional Hindu household-surrounded by rituals, meditation, mantras, and a profound devotion to gurus-began to resonate with a surprising familiarity, echoing the contours of my own rural Brahminical Hindu background. The book's rich descriptions of spiritual practices such as 'pooja', 'havana', and 'deeksha' awakened memories that had lain dormant within me since childhood, conjuring the sights, sounds, and fragrances of ceremonies I had grown up witnessing and participating in. What had initially seemed distant and mystical now felt intimately accessible, as if Yogananda's journey was gently guiding me back to the spiritual roots that had quietly shaped my early years. With each chapter, the boundaries between his experiences and my own began to blur, and I felt a renewed sense of connection to the traditions and rituals that had once been an integral part of my identity. The narrative not only deepened my engagement with the book but also rekindled a sense of reverence and belonging, inviting me to rediscover the spiritual heritage that had always been a part of me, waiting patiently to be awakened.

Gradually, as I delved deeper into the pages of the book, I felt a gentle transformation begin to take root within me. The internal restlessness that had so often left me feeling unsettled and fragmented slowly started to dissipate, replaced by a growing sense of calm and clarity. Yogananda's profound wisdom, coupled with his masterful storytelling, captivated my mind and spirit, offering a sanctuary of solace amid the relentless demands and chaos of my professional life. Each story and insight seemed to resonate with uncanny precision, as if the book itself was attuned to the silent questions and yearnings that had long lingered beneath the surface of my consciousness. The vivid narratives not only provided comfort but also sparked a deeper introspection, gently guiding me toward a more meaningful understanding of myself and my place in the world. In hindsight, it is difficult to see my encounter with this book as mere coincidence; rather, it feels as though some subtle, divine orchestration was at play, nudging me toward a path of self-discovery and spiritual awakening at precisely the moment I needed it most. Reflecting on this experience now, I am convinced that picking up this book was not just a random act, but a pivotal moment of grace-a quiet turning point that would shape the course of my inner journey for years to come.

On a serene Saturday summer morning in Lucknow, as the city slowly awakened under the golden embrace of the rising sun, I found myself sitting outside my home around 7 am, comfortably reclined in a chair and utterly engrossed in the pages of the book. The gentle rustle of leaves and the distant chorus of birds provided a tranquil backdrop, yet I was transported far beyond my immediate surroundings. The book had become a portal, drawing me into a realm that seemed to exist between waking and dreaming, where subconscious memories and impressions surfaced-vivid yet just out of reach, familiar yet mysterious. As I reached the midpoint of the narrative, I became completely captivated by the account of Shri Lahiri Mahasaya's transformative meeting with his Guru, Shri Mahavatar Babaji, set against the mystical landscape near Dunagiri in present-day Almora district, Uttarakhand. Yogananda's evocative storytelling painted the scene with such clarity that I could almost feel the spiritual energy pulsing through those sacred hills, sense the weight of destiny in that encounter, and imagine the profound silence that must have enveloped the two great souls. In that quiet morning hour, the boundaries between my own reality and the spiritual odyssey unfolding in the book seemed to dissolve, leaving me with a deep sense of awe and a newfound connection to the timeless quest for truth and transcendence.

Yogananda's account masterfully unfolds the extraordinary circumstances surrounding Shri Lahiri Mahasaya's transfer to Ranikhet, revealing it not as a mere administrative decision, but as a divinely orchestrated move by the enigmatic Mahavatar Babaji to set the stage for their destined reunion. In the sanctified stillness of a hidden cave near Dunagiri, Babaji disclosed to Lahiri a truth that transcended the boundaries of time and memory: he had been Shri Lahiri's Guru in a previous life, and this very cave was the sacred ground where Lahiri, as an accomplished Saadhak, had once delved into the depths of meditation and spiritual realization. To dissolve any lingering doubt, Babaji presented belongings that Lahiri had left behind in his former incarnation-objects miraculously preserved through the ages, waiting patiently for his return. Yet, despite the overwhelming evidence and the profound spiritual atmosphere, Lahiri found himself struggling to reconcile these revelations with his earthly consciousness. The veil of forgetfulness, so intrinsic to human existence, cast a shadow of scepticism and disbelief over his mind, making it difficult for him to accept the mystical continuity of his soul's journey or to fully embrace the Guru who had guided him across lifetimes. In this poignant moment, Yogananda captures not only the awe-inspiring nature of spiritual destiny but also the very human challenges of awakening to truths that lie beyond the grasp of ordinary understanding.

Babaji revealed that every detail of Lahiri Mahasaya's job transfer had been divinely orchestrated to ensure his timely return to the sacred cave near Dunagiri, a place of profound spiritual significance in his soul's journey. Despite the weight of these revelations and the unmistakable presence of the divine, Lahiri struggled with hesitation, torn between embracing the extraordinary destiny laid out before him and his strong desire to return to the familiar routine of his official duties. This delicate balance between divine intervention and human doubt struck a deep chord within me as I read, reflecting the universal tension that arises when the soul is beckoned toward higher truths yet the mind clings to the comfort of the known. Yogananda's narrative illuminated not only the mystical orchestration behind life's pivotal moments but also the very human resistance to surrendering control, reminding me of the subtle ways in which we all wrestle with faith, uncertainty, and the courage required to step into the unknown.

The story stirred something profound within me, awakening a sense that my own life, too, might be woven into an embroidery far greater than what I could immediately perceive. As I lingered on Yogananda's account, I found myself enthralled by the idea that cosmic forces-subtle yet immensely powerful-are constantly at work, silently shaping our destinies and gently guiding us toward the paths meant for us, often without our conscious awareness. There was a quiet thrill in contemplating how the universe conspires, through seemingly ordinary events and chance encounters, to nudge us closer to our higher purpose. Equally captivating was the narrative's exploration of the timeless bond between Guru and disciple-a relationship that transcends the boundaries of a single lifetime, rooted in an unspoken spiritual recognition and a shared journey toward awakening. The unwavering devotion, trust, and surrender that defined this sacred connection resonated deeply with me, casting new light on the meaning of guidance, mentorship, and faith in my own life. In those reflective moments, the story became more than just a tale from another era; it was a living reminder of the invisible threads that bind us to one another and to the greater mysteries of existence, urging me to remain open to the subtle guidance that may be shaping my own journey.

As I ventured further into the moving account of Lahiri Mahasaya's meeting with Shri Mahavatar Babaji, I was suddenly overtaken by an emotional intensity that seemed to rise from the deepest recesses of my soul. Without warning, tears began to pour down my cheeks, their flow relentless and cathartic, as if a dam long held in place had finally given way. My heart felt as though it were being torn open, yet within that pain was a strange, almost ecstatic sweetness-a sensation as if a fine needle had pierced my Anahata Chakra, releasing a flood of long-suppressed feeling that was both exquisitely pleasurable and achingly intense. The experience was overwhelming; I cried with a force and abandon I had never known, unable to articulate or even fully comprehend the source of my sorrow and longing. It was as though the story had awakened a spiritual memory or yearning within me, one that transcended the boundaries of time and self, leaving me raw, vulnerable, and profoundly moved. Throughout the day, the tears continued unabated, each wave of emotion washing over me with renewed vigor, refusing to be soothed or contained. My wife, Purnima, quietly observed my state with concern and tenderness, gently guiding me indoors and encouraging me to rest. Even as I lay down, the tears would not cease, and I surrendered to the torrent, allowing myself to be carried by the mysterious current of emotion that had overtaken me. In that vulnerable space, I sensed that I had touched something sacred and transformative-a spiritual truth that defied explanation, yet left an indelible mark on my heart and consciousness.

The next day unfolded in much the same way, as if I were caught in the gentle but unyielding grip of an emotional current that refused to subside; my tears persisted with the same intensity, and I found myself untouched by any sense of hunger or thirst, sustained only by an overwhelming and inexplicable urge to cry. It was as though my body and mind had surrendered completely to this tidal wave of feeling, leaving me suspended in a state where the ordinary needs of life faded into insignificance, replaced by a singular, unrelenting longing that I could neither name nor quell. Amid this bewildering and deeply vulnerable state, a persistent thought began to echo within me, quietly yet insistently, as if it were rising from the depths of my own soul: a sense that, somehow, I too had been present at that divine encounter with Mahavatar Babaji in the sacred hills of Dunagiri. The question haunted me with a strange familiarity and gravity-could it be that I was, in some forgotten lifetime, Shri Shyama Charan Lahiri himself? Although I could not claim certainty or proof, this idea resonated with an uncanny force, stirring something ancient and profound within me, as if a hidden memory was brushing against the edges of my consciousness. The boundaries between the story I had read and the emotions I was experiencing seemed to blur, and I found myself suspended between worlds, as if the past and present were momentarily intertwined through the mysterious workings of spirit. In this state of surrender, I allowed the question to linger, neither embracing nor rejecting it, but simply honouring the depth of feeling and the sense of connection it brought, trusting that, in time, the meaning behind this profound experience would gently reveal itself.

Was it truly me who once lived as Shri Shyama Charan Lahiri in a previous life? I cannot claim certainty, and I am well aware that even entertaining such a thought may be an overstatement-one for which I hope to be excused. Yet, the idea refused to loosen its grip on my mind, lingering with a haunting familiarity as the memory of that holy encounter replayed itself over and over, casting a spell that rendered me incapable of engaging with the outside world. The entire day slipped by with me confined to my bed, enveloped in a cocoon of emotion, doing nothing but surrendering to the relentless tide of tears that seemed to rise from a place far deeper than ordinary sorrow. In this heightened state, my inner vision became strangely vivid; behind closed eyes, I glimpsed faces and human forms that bore no connection to my present life-figures that felt at once distant and intimately familiar, as though they belonged to some ancient part of my soul's journey. Among these spectral presences were beings of extraordinary stature and luminosity, their features imbued with a sense of grace and wisdom that surpassed the ordinary, and one in particular stood out: a youthfully radiant figure, powerfully glowing as if a sun itself blazed within the confines of a human body. The sight of this being filled me with awe and reverence, stirring a sense of recognition that defied logic or explanation. Suspended between worlds, I lay there, humbled and bewildered, unable to distinguish memory from vision, past from present, or dream from reality-yet profoundly aware that I had been touched by something sacred and transformative, an experience that would linger in the deepest chambers of my heart long after the tears had dried.

As I lay in bed, adrift in the aftermath of such overwhelming emotion and spiritual bewilderment, my wife would occasionally approach, her presence gentle and concerned, asking me questions or simply checking in with quiet care. Yet I found myself unable to respond with anything meaningful, as if words themselves had abandoned me; I had so little to share, for I was suspended in a state of mesmerizing unawareness, my senses dulled to the world around me and my thoughts lost in a haze of unspoken feeling. It was as though my heart was crying out in a language beyond words, while my conscious mind had seized up, paralyzed by the sheer intensity of what I was experiencing. The boundaries of my everyday self-seemed to dissolve, overtaken by a consciousness that felt ancient and vast, as if it belonged not to this life but to some deeper, timeless part of my being. I could not help but think of the phenomena described in accounts of past-life regression, where individuals are swept into vivid memories and emotions from other lifetimes-though I had never undergone such a session myself, the parallels were uncanny. Lying there, I felt as if I were traversing a landscape of memory and spirit that was at once foreign and intimately familiar, unable to articulate or even fully comprehend what was happening, yet strangely comforted by the sense that I was being guided through an experience both mysterious and profoundly meaningful. In this state, all I could do was surrender to the moment, trusting that its significance would eventually reveal itself, and allow myself to be carried by the silent, transformative current that had so unexpectedly entered my life.

The sensation was as if I had been gently lifted from the familiar contours of my present reality and transported to a realm where the boundaries of time and identity blurred, and memories or impressions not belonging to this life began to surface with a vividness that was both exhilarating and deeply unsettling. Each wave of emotion seemed to challenge the very fabric of my understanding, forcing me to reconsider not only the nature of reality itself but also my own place within its vast, mysterious inter-play. The intensity of these feelings was undeniable-so palpable that it reverberated through my entire being-yet I remained unable to fully grasp what was unfolding within me or why I had suddenly become the vessel for such profound, inexplicable experiences. For days, the lingering impact of what felt like a past life memory haunted my consciousness, casting a subtle yet persistent shadow over my waking hours and infusing each moment with a sense of sacred significance. I became increasingly convinced that my current incarnation was inextricably linked to Shri Mahavatar, whose luminous image now hovered at the edge of my awareness, returning again and again as if to remind me of a forgotten promise or purpose. Although the reasons for this awakening eluded me, Shri Mahavatar's presence became an unwavering companion in my thoughts, guiding me inward and prompting a quiet, persistent introspection. It was as if a dormant faculty within me had begun to stir-something ancient and long-hidden, now awakening like a seedling breaking through the dark earth, reaching for the light of understanding. With each passing day, I felt a previously unknown realm unfolding before me, inviting me to explore the depths of my own consciousness and to embrace the mysteries that had, until now, lain dormant and undiscovered within the silent chambers of my soul.

Upon completing Yogananda's *"Autobiography of a Yogi"*, I found myself compelled to explore further the mystic life and teachings of Shri Mahavatar Babaji, seeking to illuminate the shadows surrounding his timeless presence. This yearning led me to acquire Marshal Govindan's *Babaji*, a captivating account that chronicles three profound encounters between Govindan and the Great Guru in the remote, sacred heights of the Himalayas near Badrinath. Despite the relentless demands of my busy work life and frequent inland travels, I made it a point to keep Shri Mahavatar's presence close to me, both physically and spiritually. I carefully framed two images of the Great Guru-one from Yogananda's seminal work and another from Govindan's evocative narrative-and placed them prominently in my home and office. These images became more than mere pictures; they were silent sentinels and sources of inspiration, their serene and radiant gazes offering solace and strength amidst the bustle of daily life. In moments of quiet reflection or overwhelming stress, I would find myself drawn to these sacred visages, feeling a subtle yet profound connection to the divine lineage they represent. Through this simple act, I nurtured an ongoing dialogue with the Great Guru, allowing his timeless wisdom and presence to permeate my surroundings and guide me on my own spiritual journey, even as I navigated the complexities of the modern world.

In a remarkable and almost immediate and magical turn of events, a third image of Shri Mahavatar unexpectedly came into my possession, adding a profound new layer to the sacred collection I had begun to cherish. During a visit to my office, a perceptive guest noticed the two framed images of Shri Mahavatar that I had displayed and, with a knowing glance, inquired whether I had ever encountered another, far more extraordinary depiction of the Great Guru-one that I might not yet have seen. Intrigued, I listened as they described a striking painting portraying Shri Mahavatar seated in deep meditation, but with four hands-an image that immediately stirred a deep sense of awe and reverence within me. The visitor kindly shared an electronic copy of this powerful portrayal, and from the moment I gazed upon it, I felt an unmistakable spiritual energy radiating from the image, as though it captured a transcendental aspect of the Master beyond the ordinary. This painting is believed to have been created by an individual who had the rare privilege of witnessing Shri Mahavatar in this meditative form, with four hands symbolizing divine power and grace. The image quickly became a treasured addition to my sacred space, inspiring a renewed sense of connection and devotion. I continue to revere it deeply, sensing that through this extraordinary representation, the timeless presence of Shri Mahavatar reaches out to guide and illuminate my own spiritual path, weaving a silent yet potent thread between the eternal and the everyday.

During this pivotal period in my spiritual journey, an unexpected encounter with Shri Subhash Patri Ji (who is no longer in his physical form now), the revered spiritual leader and founder of the Pyramid Spiritual Societies Movement, left an indelible impression on me. Just a few months after immersing myself in the profound teachings of Yogananda's journey, I found myself attending a spiritual session in Lucknow where Shri Patri Ji was conducting a program designed for corporate leaders. Though my initial participation was driven more by obligation than genuine curiosity, the experience quickly took a transformative turn. During a casual lunch gathering, while seated at some distance, I was taken by surprise when Shri Patri Ji beckoned me over. Approaching him, I felt the warmth of his gentle hand resting on my shoulder as he inquired about my meditation practice. When I confessed my lack of experience, explaining that I had never meditated simply because I didn't know how, he leaned in and whispered words that resonated deeply within me: "*You know everything, but it's veiled. Simply sit quietly, and you will rediscover your true self.*" His message, delivered with quiet authority and compassion, pierced through the fog of my uncertainty, awakening a powerful urge to explore meditation as a path toward self-discovery and inner awakening. That moment became a catalyst, gently urging me to embark on a deeper exploration of my spiritual self, guided by the wisdom and encouragement of a truly enlightened teacher.

As I returned to the office, Patriji's words continued to reverberate within me, their gentle wisdom stirring a profound impact that seemed to touch every fibre of my being and linger long after our encounter had ended. It was as if his message had awakened a dormant yearning, compelling me to look inward and embark on a journey of self-exploration that I had long postponed. Motivated by this newfound desire, I began to set aside time each evening after work to meditate, seeking the quiet space within where, as Patriji had assured me, my true self awaited rediscovery. Yet, despite my sincere efforts, I found myself grappling with a persistent contradiction: my habitual consumption of alcohol, a familiar comfort that often undermined my resolve and clouded the clarity that meditation was beginning to reveal. This internal struggle was not without its frustrations, but even as I faltered, I could sense a subtle yet unmistakable transformation unfolding within me. It was as though a window, long shuttered, had been opened to the fresh air of possibility, and a gentle light was beginning to illuminate the landscape of my consciousness. The changes I experienced were not always dramatic, but they were undeniably real-a quiet shift in perspective, a growing sense of presence, and an emerging awareness that my lifelong quest for meaning and fulfilment had finally found a true and promising direction. Despite the shadows of old habits, I felt a deepened commitment to this path, trusting that each small step in meditation was bringing me closer to the essence of who I truly was and to the spiritual awakening that now seemed not only possible but inevitable.

I count myself truly fortunate to have been blessed with three consecutive meetings with Patriji within just a single quarter, each encounter leaving an indelible mark on my life and deepening my sense of awe for his spiritual presence. Among these, one meeting stands out with particular vividness in my memory, for it was during this time that Patriji revealed something astonishing about my past-a revelation that continues to echo in my consciousness. Our third meeting took place in the warm, inviting atmosphere of a friend's home in Lucknow, where Patriji was playing his flute that evening, the gentle, haunting melodies weaving an air of tranquility and reverence throughout the room. As I sat quietly among the gathering, I was filled with a restless curiosity, an inner longing to receive some insight from him about my own being, for I was convinced that he possessed a profound understanding not only of my present existence but of the life that came before. When he finally set aside his flute, the room seemed to fall into a hush, and he turned to me with a gaze both grave and mystical, addressing me affectionately as *"Swamiji"* and inquiring after my well-being. I replied that I was doing well, but my curiosity got the better of me, and I asked if he might share any insights about my true nature and the mystery of human existence. For a moment, he remained silent, his face illuminated by an intensity that seemed to transcend the ordinary, as if he were peering into the depths of my soul and the vast continuum of lives that lay behind it. In that charged silence, I felt a sense of anticipation and reverence, aware that I stood on the threshold of a revelation-one that would not only shape my understanding of myself but also deepen my journey along the spiritual path.

(Shri Yogi Subhash Patri ji, the man who first watered the seed inside me)

With a gentle yet penetrating gaze, Patriji began to reveal a truth so mysterious and profound that it seemed to momentarily suspend the very flow of time in the room. *'Look!'* he said, his voice carrying both compassion and certainty, *"You are a Walk-in-Soul. The soul you were born with has departed, and in its place, a new, spiritually evolved soul has assumed your body."* His words sent a shiver through me as he continued, *"I am sure you remember having met with a major accident in your life-that was the pivotal moment when the soul transition occurred. Now, the soul residing within you is of a much higher spiritual order, one that has come from a higher realm, and this exchange was predestined to guide you toward new and extraordinary experiences in your life."* As I absorbed the gravity of his message, Patriji elaborated further, his tone both subtle and authoritative: *"That accident must have been fatal; you must have died, at least in the sense that your original soul departed. For soul exchanges, such accidents are not mere coincidences-they are cosmically orchestrated events. While most people perceive these occurrences as random misfortunes, their true purpose is rarely understood. I am certain that after that event, your life underwent a rapid and dramatic transformation, for, from that point onward, the new soul began to fulfil its own predestined karma through your body. And I know, without a doubt, that this soul is highly evolved and divinely spirited."* As his words settled over me, I felt a strange sense of clarity and awe, as if the hidden architecture of my life had suddenly been illuminated. The inexplicable shifts I had experienced, the sudden changes in my outlook and aspirations, now seemed to fit within a larger, cosmic narrative-a narrative in which my own existence was but a vessel for a higher purpose, guided by forces far beyond ordinary human understanding. In that moment, the mystical and the real merged, leaving me with a deep sense of wonder and a renewed commitment to honour the extraordinary journey that was unfolding within and through me.

That extraordinary revelation left me in a state of profound vibration, as if an invisible current was coursing through my entire being, awakening layers of awareness I had never touched before. In the hours that followed, I found myself compulsively revisiting the memory of the electrocution incident, a moment I had always regarded as a mere physical accident-an unfortunate but ultimately survivable brush with mortality. Yet now, with Patriji's words echoing in my mind, the event took on an entirely new dimension, its significance expanding far beyond the boundaries of the material world. I pondered how easily we had all dismissed that day as a random twist of fate, never suspecting that it might have been a cosmic turning point, a gateway through which something far greater had entered my life. My thoughts oscillated endlessly between the most minute details of that harrowing experience-the sudden jolt, the confusion, the razor-thin divide between life and death-and the almost miraculous return to normalcy that followed, a transition I had never fully questioned until now. The notion of a 'walk-in-soul' was utterly foreign to me, a concept I had never encountered in any spiritual text or conversation, and yet, as I absorbed this newfound understanding, I was overcome by a complex blend of awe, humility, and deep introspection. It felt as though the fabric of my identity had been subtly rewoven, and I was being invited to contemplate the mysterious, unseen forces that shape our destinies. In that moment, I realized that my life, which I had always thought of as a linear journey, might actually be part of a far more intricate and wondrous cosmic play-one in which every experience, even those shrouded in pain or confusion, holds the potential for profound spiritual transformation.

As time rolled on, I found myself increasingly drawn to the quiet embrace of meditation, setting aside nearly an hour each evening to sit in stillness and explore the shifting contours of my inner world, even as my longstanding habit of consuming a few glasses of alcohol before bed continued to cast its familiar shadow over my nightly routine. Despite this persistent contradiction, my meditative practice began to open doors to realms I had never consciously visited before; during these sessions, I was transported into vivid visions that felt both hauntingly real and otherworldly. I would see myself wandering through dense, mysterious jungles, the air thick with the scent of earth and ancient foliage, or standing in silent awe before the towering, snow-capped peaks of the Himalayas, their grandeur evoking a sense of both insignificance and transcendence. These experiences seemed to dissolve the boundaries between the physical and the spiritual, leaving me with a sense of wonder and a growing conviction that something profound was unfolding within me. On February 19, 2006, compelled to make sense of these transformative experiences, I turned to my diary and carefully recorded my thoughts, hoping to capture the fleeting essence of this journey and to better understand the subtle yet powerful changes that were gradually reshaping my consciousness. In those written reflections, I sought not only to document the extraordinary visions that meditation had awakened, but also to trace the delicate interplay between my struggles and my aspirations, my old habits and my emerging sense of spiritual purpose.

"I yearn to keep my evenings sacred and undisturbed, embracing the profound tranquility that gently unfolds as the world transitions from the radiant glow of daylight into the deep, enveloping darkness of night. This silent moment, suspended between day and night, holds a unique and profound significance for me-a time I cherish deeply, when the vibrant hues of the dusk sky slowly fade into muted shadows and the first stars timidly emerge to adorn the heavens. In this delicate interlude, I find myself naturally withdrawing from the external world, seeking refuge in solitude where I can be fully present with myself. Being alone in these quiet hours is not merely a retreat but a transcendental experience, a sacred communion with my inner self that feels like basking in the eternal light that exists beyond time and space, even as darkness gathers around me. The stillness that envelops these moments nourishes my soul, allowing me to listen deeply to the subtle whispers of my heart and to savour the rare and precious beauty of simply being. In these solitary evenings, I discover a timeless sanctuary where the boundaries between the self and the infinite blur, and I am reminded that within the quiet embrace of solitude lies the essence of peace, presence, and profound spiritual awakening."

As I reflect deeply on the unfolding journey of my spiritual awakening, I come to understand that Patriji's words were far more than abstract theories or philosophical musings; they were living, experiential truths that resonated profoundly within the core of my being. His teachings, conveyed with a quiet yet compelling authority, gradually permeated the layers of my consciousness, sparking subtle but powerful shifts in how I perceived myself and the world around me. These were not fleeting moments of insight, but enduring transformations that gently reoriented the trajectory of my inner life, guiding me toward a deeper awareness and a more expansive sense of presence. This profound impact is vividly captured in a diary entry I penned on July 3, 2006, a heartfelt record that encapsulates the essence of the awakening Patriji's guidance inspired within me. In that entry, I sought to articulate the profound shift in perspective that had begun to take root-the embrace of silence as a sacred teacher, the recognition of the sacredness embedded in every moment, and the courage to journey inward despite the uncertainties that lay ahead. Revisiting those words now, I am filled with gratitude and awe for the transformative power of his teachings, which continue to illuminate my path, nurturing a steady unfolding of self-discovery, inner peace, and spiritual depth that shapes every step I take.

As I settled into the gentle rhythm of my breath, I could sense a subtle unfolding within, each inhalation and exhalation drawing me closer to a state of profound stillness that was paradoxically alive with blissful energy. In this tranquil expanse, a remarkable vision began to take shape: I witnessed the radiant emergence of the Sun in the lower centre of my forehead, its golden brilliance illuminating the inner landscape of my consciousness and casting away any lingering shadows of doubt or distraction. The Sun's presence was both grounding and uplifting, filling me with a sense of luminous clarity and warmth that seemed to permeate every fibre of my being. As I gazed deeper into this inner radiance, the silvery Moon gracefully entered the Sun's orbit, and together they performed a harmonious celestial dance, their movements perfectly synchronized in a delicate balance of light and serenity. Amidst this cosmic interplay, a tiny, bright star appeared, its gentle flicker weaving in and out around the Sun and Moon, as if tracing the invisible threads that connect all things in the universe. The star's subtle, fluctuating movement was a silent testament to the dynamic equilibrium at the heart of existence, a reminder that even in stillness, there is perpetual motion and infinite possibility. Immersed in this inner constellation, I felt a profound sense of unity and awe, as if the mysteries of the cosmos were being revealed not in some distant sky, but within the sacred sanctuary of my own being, inviting me to embrace the boundless wonder and interconnectedness of all life".

The vision of the Sun, accompanied by a tiny, radiant star, persisted within my inner landscape for days, unfolding with mesmerizing transformations in colour that seemed to carry profound spiritual significance beyond mere imagery. As I recorded in my diary on July 8, 2006, *"these luminous phenomena were not simply fleeting visions but potent symbols marking pivotal shifts along my spiritual path. The multiple-coloured Suns, each radiating distinct hues-from golden brilliance to deep crimson, serene indigo, and vibrant emerald-felt like reflections of the evolving states of my consciousness, each shade embodying a unique energy and lesson that beckoned me to delve deeper into the mysteries of my inner world. The tiny star, ever-present and gently orbiting alongside the Sun, served as a quiet yet steadfast companion, a beacon of guidance and balance amidst the dynamic dance of light and colour. Together, they wove a celestial narrative of awakening and transformation, reminding me that spiritual growth is not a static destination but a fluid, ever-changing journey marked by moments of illumination, challenge, and grace. These visions became a sacred language through which the universe communicated with me, urging me to trust the unfolding process, embrace the unknown, and remain open to the infinite possibilities that arise when one surrenders to the profound depths of inner awakening."*

Immersed in deep meditation, I gradually transcended the boundaries of ordinary awareness, slipping into a state of absolute blankness where the world's noise faded into a distant memory and only the subtle pulse of my own consciousness remained. In this profound silence, I suddenly found myself transported to a realm that felt unmistakably like Gyan-Ganj, the legendary ashram veiled in Himalayan mystique and revered in spiritual tradition as a sanctuary for enlightened souls. Before me stood a modest clay structure, its exterior shrouded in a gentle dusk yet radiating a soft, inner luminescence that seemed to beckon me forward. The surrounding landscape, though rugged and rocky, was suffused with just enough ethereal light for me to walk with confidence, each step grounding me deeper in the reality of this other worldly vision. As I circled the structure, searching for an entrance, I discovered a hidden pathway that led to a beautifully carved wooden gate, its intricate patterns hinting at ancient wisdom and secret initiations. Passing through, I entered a rectangular courtyard, dominated by a tall central pole crowned with a living flame, its light flickering upward and casting shifting shadows across the veranda and the arches that lined the courtyard's edges. Within each arch, Yogis sat in deep, unwavering meditation, their figures bathed in a serene glow that seemed to emanate from within. The air was thick with a sense of timelessness and reverence, as if every stone and beam had absorbed centuries of silent contemplation. Suddenly, a swift-moving Yogi approached and, without a word, guided me toward one of the arches where Shri Lahiri Mahasaya sat in tranquil majesty, his presence radiating an aura of profound peace and spiritual authority. Overwhelmed by the gravity of the moment, I mustered the courage to ask, "*Who am I?*" To which he replied, his voice both gentle and absolute, "*You are a form of my own being.*" The simplicity and depth of his answer reverberated through me, dissolving the boundaries between self and other, teacher and seeker. As my meditation drew to a close, I returned to ordinary awareness suffused with a deep sense of spiritual connection, clarity, and awe, carrying with me the indelible imprint of this sacred encounter and a renewed understanding of my place within the infinite interplay of existence".

On the 18th of July, I wrote and I quote from the notes of my diary below:

"*During this morning's meditation, I was drawn into an extraordinary inner journey, one that unfolded with such vividness and depth that it seemed to transcend the ordinary boundaries of perception. The experience began with a striking vision of my own body walking outside my house, as if I were witnessing myself from a higher vantage point, both observer and participant in a scene that gently unsettled my sense of identity and presence. As the day gave way to evening, the fabric of my inner world became even more intricate: I beheld a radiant cluster of stars, their collective brilliance illuminating the darkness and evoking a powerful sense of connection to the vast, mysterious cosmos. In the midst of this celestial vision, an eye appeared at the centre of my forehead, its clarity and intensity impossible to ignore. Within this eye, a luminous orb took shape-alternately reminiscent of the Sun or the Moon, its true nature eluding precise definition, as if it embodied the very essence of duality and the eternal dance of light and shadow. The eye's unwavering presence seemed to anchor me in a space of profound self-awareness, while simultaneously opening a gateway to deeper mysteries. Then, as if summoned by the energy of the moment, a figure with flowing, open hair materialized before me, bearing the unmistakable likeness of Shri Mahavatar Babaji, his serene and compassionate gaze radiating an aura of divine guidance and reassurance. In the final moments of this visionary sequence, I saw myself once more, completing a symbolic cycle of self-recognition and spiritual integration. These layered and deeply symbolic visions left an indelible mark on my consciousness, marking a significant milestone in my spiritual journey-one that spoke of expanding self-awareness, cosmic unity, and the gentle, ever-present guidance of higher wisdom, filling me with a sense of awe, gratitude, and renewed purpose as I continue along the unfolding path of inner discovery."*

I could distinctly feel that a dormant seed, long nestled in the quiet depths of my physical being, was at last being gently awakened, as if some unseen force was carefully nurturing and nourishing it with the same devotion that a gardener bestows upon a fragile sapling. This sensation was both subtle and profound, reminiscent of the way a plant instinctively responds to the life-giving presence of water and sunlight, slowly stirring to life, unfurling its delicate shoots, and reaching upward with quiet determination. With each passing day, I became more attuned to this inner unfolding-a sense of growth and renewal that seemed to suffuse my entire body and spirit with new vitality and possibility. Yet, even as I marvelled at the miracle taking place within me, I remained utterly unaware of the greater purpose or meaning behind this mysterious phenomenon. It was as if I had been granted a rare glimpse into the sacred mechanics of transformation, allowed to witness the emergence of something beautiful and unknown, while still being kept in the dark about its ultimate significance. Despite this uncertainty, I found myself filled with a deep sense of wonder and humility, content to simply observe and honour the process, trusting that in time, the meaning of this awakening would reveal itself and illuminate the path I was meant to follow.

Chapter - 2

Dancing with Death: A Journey Beyond Dying

When I recount on the preceding years, in early 1993, a harrowing electrocution triggered a profound transformation within me-one that remained invisible and incomprehensible to those around me, at the time. While to others it appeared as a mere unfortunate accident, for me it marked the inception of a metamorphosis that transcended physical injury. Astonishingly, my vitality surged to heights previously unknown, a phenomenon I shared with my physician, who could offer no rational explanation. Alongside this remarkable renewal of energy came a heightened sense of elevation, as if I had been lifted into a loftier realm of existence. My confidence, once modest and restrained, blossomed into a formidable force, empowering me to confront life's challenges with a strength that seemed to emanate from beyond the corporeal. Though my body bore the visible scars of the ordeal—cuts and stitches—I felt no pain or suffering; instead, I was enveloped in an extraordinary aura of vigour and flamboyance. Where once I had been shy and reserved, I now possessed a commanding presence and an inner assurance that, to some, might have seemed arrogant, yet was truly the natural outgrowth of a deep and lasting personal awakening. Though the finer details of that experience have faded with time, its essence remains vivid, allowing me to frame it within the larger narrative of growth, resilience, and a profound reawakening of my perception of self and the world around me.

In 1993, while still immersed in the carefree spirit of youth as a student at Delhi University, I moved into Jubilee Hall, a men's hostel that stood as a vibrant hub of diversity and ambition on the university's Mall Road campus. This transition was made possible by my batchmate from Assam, Chandan Sharma, who had been assigned room number 36 for his M.Phil. studies and generously offered me accommodation there. Unlike Chandan, who was continuing his academic pursuits, I had resolved to step away from formal education to focus on preparing for administrative service examinations, marking a pivotal shift in my life's direction. Jubilee Hall was significantly larger than my previous hostel, housing nearly two hundred students from varied educational disciplines and regions across India, creating a rich tapestry of cultures, languages, and ideas. In the 1990s, the hostel was renowned for nurturing a remarkable number of future bureaucrats who would go on to serve the nation with distinction, making it a crucible of aspiration and determination. Living there not only exposed me to a broader spectrum of perspectives but also instilled a profound sense of camaraderie and purpose, as I witnessed firsthand the drive and resilience of my peers striving toward their goals. This environment, alive with youthful energy and intellectual fervour, played a crucial role in shaping my outlook and fuelling my ambition during those formative years.

In June 1993, I received the usual money-order from my father, a small but significant gesture that ensured my monthly expenses were taken care of during my time as a student. Around that period, a friend from Muzaffarpur, who was heading home, suggested I join him on his journey. After a moment's hesitation, I decided to accept his invitation, setting off for home on a whim. My arrival was completely unannounced, so my family was caught off guard and there were no special preparations or fanfare to mark my return. As I settled back into the familiar surroundings, I soon found myself grappling with an all-too-familiar allergic reaction-a recurring affliction in those years-which manifested as rashes erupting across my body, accompanied by relentless itching and a deep sense of restlessness that made it difficult to relax or find comfort. That evening, as the symptoms intensified, my discomfort became increasingly apparent to my father, who, concerned for my well-being, suggested that I visit the nearby doctor to seek relief. However, I asked him to hold off for a while, hoping that a soothing bath might calm my irritated skin and offer a brief respite from the persistent itching before I resorted to medical intervention. The episode, though routine in its discomfort, remains etched in my memory as a reminder of those unpredictable, formative days when even a simple trip home could unfold into an unexpected ordeal.

Back then, my house was a far cry from the modern homes of today, devoid of conveniences like piped tap water in the kitchen and washrooms, which meant that every drop of water for bathing or household chores had to be fetched from the hand pump standing resolutely outside. It was common for us to carry heavy buckets of water inside or, when the weather allowed, to bathe right there at the pump, under the open sky. On that particular evening, as dusk began to settle and the oppressive heat of the day gave way to a cooler breeze, I decided to take a bath at the hand pump, hoping the cold water would soothe my irritated skin. The atmosphere was tinged with the lingering effects of a violent storm that had struck just a day before my arrival, plunging our neighbourhood into darkness and silence by knocking out both electricity and telephone lines for nearly a full day-an inconvenience that we had come to accept as part of life. Our family occupied the ground floor of the house, which opened onto a generous expanse of yard where the hand pump stood, surrounded by the familiar sights and sounds of home. Above the pump, an iron wire stretched taut, serving as a makeshift clothesline, its ends fastened to an iron pole that also supported the exposed electric supply wire. In those days, the electric wire was neither plastic-coated nor properly insulated, its bare metal left exposed to the elements-a silent but ever-present hazard that we hardly gave a second thought to in the rhythm of our daily lives. The scene was a vivid blend of simplicity and latent danger, a testament to the resilience with which we navigated the challenges of a less technologically advanced era, and a poignant reminder of how such ordinary moments were woven into the fabric of my youth.

As I began bathing at the hand pump that evening, fate took a sudden and perilous turn when, without warning, the electricity-absent for nearly a day due to the storm-suddenly resumed. My towel, which I had casually hung on the iron wire stretched above the pump and connected to the electric pole, became the unwitting conduit for disaster. Unaware of the danger, I reached for the towel after finishing my bath, and in that instant, a powerful electric current surged through my body. My palms clamped involuntarily around the live wire, and within seconds, I lost consciousness, my body left hanging limply, still gripping the wire in a deathly embrace. From a nearby room, my parents witnessed the horrifying scene unfold and rushed outside in a desperate attempt to pull me free, only to be violently repelled by the relentless current. My father, thinking quickly, raced to cut the master switch in the hope of breaking the circuit, but to his horror, it had no effect-the electricity was flowing directly from the service line into the iron pole, bypassing the safety of the switch entirely. Helpless and frantic, my parents could do nothing but watch in agony for several long minutes, teetering on the edge of collapse as they faced the terrifying possibility of losing me right before their eyes, powerless against the invisible force that held me captive.

Just as my parents teetered on the brink of despair, powerless to intervene as the electric current continued its relentless assault, a visitor from the house across the street happened to notice the chaos unfolding in our yard. Sensing the urgency and understanding the peril, he acted with remarkable clarity and quick thinking. His eyes fell upon a sturdy, dry bamboo stick lying nearby-a simple object that would become the instrument of my rescue. Without hesitation, he seized the bamboo stick and, keeping himself safely insulated, struck the iron wire to which my hands were still desperately fused. With that decisive blow, the deadly circuit was finally broken, and the current that had gripped my body so mercilessly was instantly interrupted. Released at last from the wire's unforgiving hold, I collapsed onto the bricked ground below, my body limp and motionless but finally freed from the invisible force that had threatened to claim my life. In those few harrowing moments, the presence of mind and courage of a neighbour transformed what could have been a tragedy into a narrow escape, leaving an indelible mark on all who witnessed it and forever altering the course of my life.

In the aftermath of my collapse, a chilling stillness settled over the scene as it became painfully clear that there were no signs of life left in me. My parents, overwhelmed by shock and terror, desperately tried to revive me, calling my name and shaking me, but I remained utterly unresponsive, my body limp and motionless on the bricked ground. Neighbours, drawn by the commotion and the gravity of the moment, gathered in a silent, anxious circle around me, their faces a mixture of disbelief and dread. A local doctor arrived swiftly, his examination grim and hurried; he found no pulse, no heartbeat, only the blood trickling from my mouth and a deep gash on my chin as evidence of the trauma I had suffered. With a heavy heart, he pronounced me dead, a verdict that shattered the fragile hope still clinging to those present. The news was too much for my mother, who fainted from the shock, while my father, refusing to accept the finality of the moment, raced from person to person, frantically seeking any possible help or intervention. The neighbours, moved by compassion and helplessness, gently lifted my body and placed it on a wooden couch on our veranda, where I continued to show no response to any attempts at revival. In a desperate act of hope, an elderly woman tried to bring me back by rolling a wooden implement over my body, her hands trembling with urgency, but to no avail. Soon after, another doctor from the neighbourhood arrived and re-examined me, his assessment no different from the first- he too confirmed that I was dead. The air grew heavy with grief and disbelief, as my family and neighbours confronted the devastating reality of my apparent passing, their hearts weighed down by a sorrow that seemed both sudden and insurmountable.

Then, in a moment that seemed to suspend time itself, I suddenly began to stir, sending a shockwave of disbelief and awe through everyone gathered around me. The neighbours and my family, who had just moments earlier mourned my passing and resigned themselves to the unbearable weight of loss, now watched in stunned silence as my body arched abruptly on the wooden couch. I drew in a long, ragged gasp of air, the sound shattering the heavy stillness that had settled over the veranda. My eyes fluttered open, wide with confusion, and for a few disorienting seconds, I struggled to make sense of the anxious faces crowding around me, their expressions a mixture of fear, hope, and utter astonishment. My mind, slow to bridge the chasm between oblivion and consciousness, grappled with the chaos and urgency that enveloped me. The world felt unfamiliar, as if I were awakening from a dream into a reality that no longer fit the contours of my memory. As clarity gradually returned, I realized with a strange certainty that my first memory was not of the physical world I had re-entered, but of another realm entirely-a place beyond the reach of ordinary senses, vivid and profound, that lingered in my awareness even as I struggled to reconnect with the reality before me. The relief and amazement that swept through the crowd was palpable, their tears of grief transforming almost instantly into tears of joy and disbelief, while for me, the moment was marked by a lingering sense of wonder and mystery, as if I had brushed against the edge of something extraordinary before being pulled back into the embrace of life.

In that suspended state between life and awakening, I was enveloped by a vision of breathtaking clarity and tranquility-a scene that remains etched in my memory with a vividness that surpasses even the sharpest moments of ordinary existence. I found myself gently descending from a luminous, universal plain, bathed in a soft, radiant light that seemed to carry an unspoken promise of peace and belonging. At the crest of a gentle hillock stood two men, their figures draped in flowing white robes that shimmered with the same ethereal glow. Their faces were serene and wise, their eyes reflecting a deep, compassionate understanding as they smiled at me, bidding me a silent but heartfelt farewell. Behind them, a dense wall of lush, perfectly manicured forest rose up, its vibrant greenery forming a majestic backdrop that framed the entire landscape in a sense of otherworldly harmony. The ground beneath my feet sloped downward toward an open, sunlit expanse where the grass was impossibly green and alive, stretching out in rolling pastures that seemed to invite a sense of boundless freedom. As I walked away from the two figures, I was filled with a profound sense of serene joy and acceptance, as if we all shared an unspoken understanding of transition and purpose. There was no fear or regret-only a gentle, uplifting certainty that this passage was both natural and necessary, a moment of perfect unity with the universe and a reminder of the mysterious beauty that lies just beyond the threshold of ordinary life.

As consciousness slowly returned, the entire harrowing sequence of events surged back into my mind with a force that left me breathless-the simple act of bathing, the sudden, violent surge of electricity, the blinding, searing pain that consumed me, and the echo of my final, desperate cry that my parents had heard as I collapsed. Blinking in disbelief, I took in the scene around me: the veranda crowded with neighbours and family, their faces frozen in shock and awe, unable to comprehend the impossible turn of events. The silence was broken by a ripple of astonished whispers- *"Jee gaya!" ("He's alive!")*-as the reality of my revival spread through the gathering like a spark. Someone rushed to revive my mother, who had fainted from the trauma, and she awoke to the unimaginable sight of me, battered but upright, alive when all hope had been lost. Though physically weakened and shaken, I was overwhelmed by an inexplicable surge of energy, a raw and restless vitality that made me feel as though my body had been rebooted, charged with a force that was both foreign and exhilarating. The urge to slam my fists into the walls, to test the boundaries of this miraculous second chance, was almost irresistible-as if I needed to prove to myself that I was truly alive, that this borrowed life was real. Yet the pain and injuries were a sobering counterpoint to my inner vigour: blood still oozed from the deep gash on my chin, my tongue bore the sting of deep cuts from where my teeth had clenched down, and the impact of my fall had fractured both my upper and lower left molars. A persistent ache radiated from the base of my neck, a stark and painful reminder of how close I had come to the edge of permanent silence. In that moment, surrounded by bewildered loved ones and bearing the scars of my ordeal, I was acutely aware of the fragile boundary I had crossed-a boundary between life and death, pain and possibility, despair and the extraordinary gift of another chance.

"The soul is born and unfolds in a body, with dreams and desires and the food of life. And then it is reborn in new

bodies in accordance with its former works. The quality of the soul determines its future body--earthly or airy, heavy or light.

Shvetashvatara Upanishad, 5.11-12

My sudden return to life was a moment of pure astonishment and joy for everyone present, a dramatic reversal that transformed an atmosphere heavy with grief into one of incredulous celebration. For those who had just witnessed what seemed like the finality of my death, the experience was a powerful reminder of the astonishing fragility and unpredictability that underpins our existence. In that singular moment, the boundaries between life and death-so often regarded as absolute and unyielding-were revealed to be far more delicate and illusory than we typically allow ourselves to believe. It became clear to me, and perhaps to all who stood witness, that life and death are not the fixed states we imagine, but rather fleeting phenomena, as transient as bubbles gliding across the surface of water. Some bubbles burst quietly and are gone in an instant, while others emerge anew, shimmering briefly in the sunlight before vanishing, each giving the impression of substance and permanence, yet ultimately revealing the truth of their impermanence. My own experience had become a living metaphor for this dance of existence-an ephemeral crossing over and return that shattered the illusion of permanence and left me with a profound sense of humility and wonder at the delicate, ever-changing nature of life itself.

Once the initial shock and relief of my improbable return had settled, my father and his doctor friend, still grappling with the enormity of what had transpired, took me to a nearby surgeon for a thorough consultation. To everyone's amazement, I was able to walk comfortably to the nursing home, my steps steady despite the ordeal my body had just endured-a testament to the strange surge of vitality that seemed to linger within me. At the clinic, I lay down on a crisp white bed, the sterile scent of antiseptic in the air, while the consulting doctor listened in disbelief as my father recounted the events: the fatal electrocution, the absence of pulse or heartbeat, the pronouncement of death, and my sudden, inexplicable revival. The doctor, a seasoned professional not easily surprised, shook his head and remarked with genuine awe, *"In medical science, this is a case of a miracle."* With meticulous care, he examined me from head to toe, probing for hidden injuries and assessing the visible wounds, his hands gentle yet thorough as he checked my vital signs and tested my reflexes. While a nurse applied dressings to my cuts and abrasions, the doctor prescribed a regimen of medications to aid my recovery, his demeanour a blend of clinical precision and quiet reverence for the mystery he had just witnessed. The entire experience-from the astonishment in the doctor's eyes to the careful ministrations of the medical staff-left me with a profound sense of gratitude and wonder, reinforcing the extraordinary nature of my survival and deepening my appreciation for the fragile, unpredictable gift of life I had been granted anew.

In the days that unfolded after the accident, my improbable survival became the subject of widespread fascination, quickly turning into the talk of the town. Word of my ordeal and miraculous return from the brink spread far and wide, drawing a steady stream of relatives, friends, and even curious acquaintances to our doorstep, each eager to witness for themselves the young man who had, against all odds, come back from death's threshold. Local journalists arrived as well, their notepads ready, intent on capturing every detail of my story for the wider community. Yet, despite the growing crowd and the flurry of questions, I found myself largely silent, my ability to speak hampered by the multiple deep cuts that crisscrossed my tongue-wounds that, left to heal naturally, made every attempt at conversation a painful struggle. My parents became my voice, patiently and repeatedly recounting the sequence of events to each new visitor, their words carrying the weight of both trauma and relief. Meanwhile, my body began the slow and steady process of healing. The stitches on my chin, though tender, seemed to knit together with surprising speed, while my tongue's recovery lagged behind, making even the simple act of eating a daily challenge. Meals became careful, deliberate rituals, each bite a small victory over discomfort. Despite these difficulties, I managed to cope, buoyed by the unwavering support of my family and the collective amazement of the community. The constant presence of loved ones and the palpable sense of wonder that filled our home transformed those days into a time of both physical recovery and profound emotional affirmation-a reminder of the preciousness of life and the extraordinary resilience of the human spirit.

I remained in Muzaffarpur for nearly ten days after the accident, a period marked by slow but steady healing as my wounds closed and my strength returned, each day bringing a renewed sense of vitality that felt almost miraculous after all I had endured. Despite my parents' understandable reluctance to see me leave so soon, I was buoyed by a surge of energy and an unshakeable conviction that our physical bodies are little more than vessels-temporary vehicles steered by the spirit, each following its own mysterious, predestined course. Trusting in this deeper rhythm, I waited for the right moment and then set out for Delhi, eager to reengage with the life I had momentarily left behind. At that time, I was fresh from completing my Master's degree and wholly immersed in preparations for the civil services examination, a goal that had shaped much of my recent past. I had already appeared for the preliminary exam in May 1993, and the electrocution that nearly cost me my life had struck on June 20th of that same year, abruptly interrupting my plans but not my sense of purpose. Soon after returning to Delhi, the preliminary results were announced, and I learned that I had not qualified. Yet, to my own surprise, this disappointment barely registered; it felt almost insignificant in the wake of all I had experienced. Perhaps, I thought, my journey was meant to take a different turn, one that was still hidden from view. I found myself accepting, even welcoming, the uncertainty, sensing that the true trajectory of my life was being guided by forces and dimensions far beyond the reach of ordinary intellect or willpower. What lay ahead was still shrouded in mystery, but I was beginning to understand that some paths are revealed only as we walk them-and that this unfolding was something I was destined to experience once again.

Following that life-changing incident, my personal life began to shift dramatically. My younger brother Sudhakar also moved to Delhi to pursue his bachelor's degree, living in a rented accommodation as he chased his own dreams. Though I still aspired to join the civil services, financial realities soon set in. My father, burdened by the challenge of supporting both of us in an expensive city, voiced his concerns about our family's limited resources. Accepting the need to contribute, I turned my focus toward securing employment. With a Master's degree from a respected institution, I was well-qualified for promising entry-level roles and began attending interviews across the city. One interview, in particular, stood out-it was chaired by an IAS officer, a moment that filled me with both hope and nervous anticipation. Yet, at the time, I had no idea how I had performed, and I found myself anxiously waiting for the results. This period marked a pivotal turning point, where my dreams, responsibilities, and the uncertainties of life intertwined, setting the stage for the next chapter of my journey.

One afternoon, while enjoying tea with friends in the hostel's backyard canteen, I was unexpectedly informed that a policeman was looking for me. Curious, I stepped outside to meet him, and he handed me a handwritten letter on official letterhead from Mrs. C P Sujaya, IAS, the Resident Commissioner of the Government of Himachal Pradesh in Delhi. The letter was brief and to the point: *"You may like to talk with me at the telephone number given above."*

In those days, communication was far less convenient than today; mobile phones did not exist, and most calls had to be made from public telephone booths. Government offices had official lines, but for ordinary people, making a call meant waiting in long lines and having the exact coins to use the booth. Our hostel had a public phone booth, but it was often unreliable and prone to malfunction, making outgoing calls difficult and frustrating. Holding that letter, I felt a mix of curiosity and anticipation, aware that this simple message might lead to an important opportunity, even as the challenges of communication added an unexpected layer of suspense to the moment.

Fortunately, the public phone in my hostel was working that afternoon, a rare stroke of luck given its usual unreliability. While offering the policeman-a figure who would soon reveal himself as Mrs. Sujaya's bodyguard-a cup of tea in the canteen, I decided to call the number on the letter. A soft-spoken woman answered, and upon introducing myself, she immediately recognized me and identified herself as Mrs. C P Sujaya. Her tone was humble yet purposeful as she expressed a desire to have an important conversation and invited me to visit her official residence. We agreed to meet the following day at 3 p.m. at her home in Moti Bagh, New Delhi. After bidding farewell to the policeman, my mind buzzed with curiosity and anticipation. I wondered what the discussion might entail, especially since I had no memory of ever meeting Mrs. Sujaya before, leaving me both uncertain and intrigued about the purpose of this unexpected invitation.

The next day, I arrived punctually at the address in Moti Bagh, standing before one of the characteristic yellow government flats. When Mrs. Sujaya herself opened the door, recognition struck immediately-she was the very chairperson of the interview committee I had appeared before just days earlier. She welcomed me warmly and led me into a beautifully decorated living room, where multiple sofa sets were arranged thoughtfully around a central table, creating an inviting and elegant atmosphere. Mrs. Sujaya, likely in her fifties, spoke softly and humbly, her demeanour radiating both grace and quiet authority. As a senior bureaucrat from the Himachal Pradesh cadre serving as the state's Resident Commissioner in Delhi, she carried herself with effortless poise. Excusing herself to fetch tea from the kitchen, she left me a moment to absorb the room's exquisite decor-shelves adorned with cutlery and artifacts from diverse regions, each piece rich with history and culture. The space was unlike anything I had ever seen, blending warmth and sophistication in a way that left a deep impression, heightening my curiosity about the purpose of this unexpected meeting.

As we sipped our tea, Mrs. Sujaya gently inquired about my current situation and future aspirations, probing into my domicile and family background with genuine interest. I shared openly about my ambition to join the civil services and mentioned my recent unsuccessful attempt at the preliminary exam. Rather than offering the expected words of encouragement, she spoke with candid honesty about her own three decades in the bureaucracy, revealing a deep-seated disillusionment. She described the relentless cycle of transfers and postings, the political scapegoating, and the stifling constraints that often left her feeling trapped within the system. *"If you wish to be ensnared in this bureaucratic web, by all means, pursue it,"* she said with a mix of warning and realism. *"But if you seek a more creative, challenging path- one enriched by diverse sociocultural experiences-I can guide you."* She explained that the position I was interviewed for required proficiency in Malayalam and was based in Kerala, which explained my non-selection. Then, she presented an alternative opportunity: a research project focused on rural sanitation in Himachal Pradesh, in collaboration with NGOs. As the Resident Commissioner, she emphasized that this role would offer a far broader and more impactful understanding of India's developmental challenges, beyond the confines of conventional bureaucracy. She encouraged me to consider this path carefully and respond at my earliest convenience, opening a door to a new and unexpected direction in my journey.

After Mrs. Sujaya concluded our discussion, I expressed my gratitude and left her residence, returning to the hostel with a mind heavy with contemplation. It felt as if I stood at a pivotal crossroads, caught between two vastly different futures. As I made my way back to the university campus, her words replayed in my mind-the offer of an immediate opportunity that promised financial stability, something I desperately needed, contrasted sharply with my long-held dream of a career in the civil services. The choice was agonizing; accepting the offer meant sacrificing my aspirations, while holding on to my dream carried uncertainty and risk. Unsure of how to proceed, I sought the counsel of my roommate, Chandan Sharma, who was deeply engrossed in academic pursuits and had no ambitions for the civil services. Understanding my financial constraints, he advised me to embrace the opportunity Mrs. Sujaya had presented, highlighting the unpredictable nature and fierce competition of the civil services exam. We spent hours discussing and deliberating, carefully weighing the merits and drawbacks of each path. In that moment, I realized that this decision was not merely about a job or a career, but about defining the course of my life and the values I wished to uphold.

In the end, I came to accept that it is not merely our minds or intellectual abilities that chart the course of our lives, but something deeper and more mysterious-what I can only describe as predestination. Despite all the deliberation, advice, and weighing of pros and cons, I felt a quiet certainty growing within me, a sense that my journey was being guided by invisible hands toward a place and purpose I had yet to fully understand. The idea of finding myself in the sacred realm of the Himalayas began to feel less like a choice and more like a calling, as if the mountains themselves were summoning me to a new chapter. Embracing this sense of a preordained journey, I chose to accept Mrs. Sujaya's offer, feeling a profound confidence that this opportunity was not a detour, but rather a step in perfect harmony with the path that had been laid out for me long before I was aware of it. There was a certain peace in surrendering to this flow, in trusting that life's unfolding was guided by forces beyond my comprehension. With this acceptance, I moved forward not just with anticipation for the work ahead, but with a deep sense of alignment and readiness to embrace whatever the Himalayas-and destiny had in store for me.

Chapter - 3

The Sacred Himalayas: A First Encounter

My predestined path had quietly begun to unfold its intricate layers, though at the time, I was blind to the subtle signs guiding me forward. I clung tightly to the dream of joining the civil services, a goal that seemed both noble and attainable, shaping my every effort and thought. Yet, destiny had woven a different design for my life—one far removed from the conventional ambitions of my peers. While many of my fellow students remained within the familiar confines of the university hostel, immersed in their own pursuits and aspirations, I was on the cusp of embarking on a journey that would transcend ordinary experience. This journey promised to open windows into otherworldly dimensions, revealing realms of existence and understanding that few dare to explore. It was a path that would challenge my perceptions, expand my consciousness, and ultimately transform the very essence of who I was. Though I could not see it then, the universe was gently steering me toward a destiny far richer and more profound than I had ever imagined.

In February 1994, I found myself boarding a Haryana Roadways bus bound for Himachal Pradesh, embarking on a journey that would become a defining chapter in my life's story. Until that moment, my world had been relatively sheltered, my travels confined to the familiar contours of home and routine, with little exposure to the vastness that lay beyond. The mere thought of venturing into the Himalayas-a realm I had only encountered in books, photographs, and distant dreams-filled me with a heady mix of excitement and nervous anticipation. As the bus journeyed its way through the plains and began its ascent into the foothills, the landscape gradually transformed, and so did something within me. The air grew crisper, the horizon stretched wider, and soon the first glimpses of towering, snow-capped peaks emerged, standing like silent sentinels against the sky. I was awestruck by their sheer scale and majesty, a feeling unlike anything I had ever known. That initial encounter with the Himalayas was more than just a physical journey; it was a spiritual awakening, a passage into a world where nature's grandeur dwarfed human concerns and invited a deeper contemplation of life's mysteries. With every mile, I felt the boundaries of my own existence expanding, as if the mountains themselves were calling me to explore not just their rugged slopes and hidden valleys, but also the uncharted territories within my own soul. That trip marked the beginning of an unending exploration, a lifelong love affair with these magnificent landscapes that would go on to inspire, challenge, and transform me in ways I could never have imagined on that first, unforgettable journey.

As I stepped off the bus at Dharampur, Solan, the scene left me incredulously enchanted. Snowflakes gently fell around me, blanketing the surroundings in a serene silence. The air was filled with the fragrance of smoke, reminiscent of divine incense. The snowflakes seemed to find their own designated places, some settling on teak trees while others covered the forest, creating a breathtaking canvas. Despite the biting cold, my joy was unbridled, and I shivered more from pleasure than chill.

Dharampur was a small stopover for vehicles heading to Shimla and other mountain regions. It had a brewery that produced alcoholic beverages, and below the highways, there was a tiny station for the toy train that ran between

Kalka and Shimla, covering about ninety-six kilometres. The famous hill destination Kasauli was connected via a link road from Dharampur. The mountains were largely covered in pine trees and other forests. Solan, in earlier times, was a dynastic principality ruled by a king. As my first workstation was in the Solan district, I began my work in the Dharampur area and its periphery. Visiting the serene Kasauli was always a joy, and it was part of my work area. These regions were sparsely populated, where nature appeared untouched and wild due to limited human presence. Villages were scattered along the mountain curves, and after sunset, life would come to a standstill, especially during cold weather. Nocturnal animals, including leopards, posed threats to humans and livestock. Despite these challenges, the villagers were welcoming and hospitable.

My job involved selecting a randomized sample of blocks and villages across districts to conduct physical verifications of household-based sanitation units. The state government provided financial assistance to individual households for sanitary facilities. The best part of my role was the constant travel from one block to another, covering multiple villages each week. Block officials would accompany me on these verifications. Sometimes, our sample villages were up to ten kilometres from the roadhead, requiring us to park our vehicles and walk. We'd either ascend or descend, and in both cases, I felt equally thrilled and passionate. The varied topography, with its barren cuts and curves, was fascinating to explore.

From Solan, I began visiting numerous other districts. Himachal Pradesh, then and even now, had twelve districts. Districts like Kullu, Lahaul and Spiti and Kinnaur were particularly remote, with villages that were more difficult to access compared to others. The Sirmaur district, headquartered in Nahan, also presented challenges due to its distant location. The main roads connecting to

Sirmaur's blocks were often made of slate stones, making travel arduous. Adverse weather conditions sometimes hindered our progress. Despite these challenges, I remained committed to visiting all the designated sample villages, no matter how remote they were.

I was always accompanied by a driver and a local assistant who doubled as a guide to the designated locations. Before this, I had never seen snow-capped mountains, but in the upper regions, numerous high and widespread snow peaks were clearly visible from the roadheads. These sights mesmerized me, and I would often stop the vehicle to gaze at the milky lines, which seemed so close. At block headquarters, we would stay in guesthouses managed by the Public Works Department (PWD) or the forest department. These were old inspection bungalows built during the British era, strategically located to offer breathtaking views of the mountains, rivers, waterfalls, and expansive landscapes. The natural beauty I experienced daily was beyond anything I could have imagined.

One memorable experience was our visit to Silaai, a block about a hundred kilometres northwest of Nahan. To reach Silaai, there was a direct road going upward through Kafota. The mountain trail on this side was largely rocky and barren, with little vegetation and no villages for miles. The road to Silaai wasn't paved with tar; instead, it was made of slate stone plates covering a long distance. Despite the challenging terrain, we were determined to travel. Silaai was a small marketplace with a few shops, government buildings, and private houses on the lower part. A high land rose upward through a wide-open space, featuring a statue of Mahatma Gandhi. Next to it was the PWD inspection bungalow where we stayed.

In the early morning, without curtains on my windows, I woke up to a breathtaking sight—a golden-brown mountain resembling the top of Kailash. I stared at it for a while before rushing out to see it more clearly. Locals referred to it as Chhota Kailash (mini-Kailash). Having seen images of Kailash before, I was familiar with its shape, and what I saw was identical. In the morning sunlight, its eastern face appeared gold-plated, while the other sides looked dark brown. The combination of gold and brown was stunning. I asked someone to place a chair outside so I could fully enjoy the view. My two companions joined me, and together we savoured our morning tea amidst the gentle cold of Silaai.

On another occasion, I had a memorable experience in Lahaul and Spiti, the largest and most remote district in Himachal Pradesh. My task was to verify samples in villages like Khibber, which required traveling to Keylong and beyond. The district's population was just 15,000, and reaching Khibber wasn't easy, even in late March, due to thick snow cover on the roads beyond Solang Valley in Manali. The roads were non-motorable, and I had to complete the site visit within a stipulated time frame.

I discussed my plans with district officials from Kullu, who appreciated my determination to reach the most inaccessible parts of the state. They arranged for me to fly via a paramilitary chopper from Bhuntar in Kullu. Upon arrival, I found the region around Keylong fully snow-covered, with locals conducting business on snowy platforms. Rubber boots were essential for navigating the area. I had to walk long distances amidst huge snow blocks to reach my sample locations. Local block officials were supportive throughout the effort.

The weather changed almost hourly, and yaks were ubiquitous, domesticated by the locals. The intense cold at night was mitigated by blankets made from yak fur. The area had limited vegetation, with seasonal crops like fruits, potatoes, and tomatoes. Locals wore thick, colourful woollen attire, and their residential units were stacked one over the other, possibly as part of deliberate planning. Narrow lanes passed through rows of houses, reflecting a harmonious social structure despite the harsh living conditions. The government's sanitation program was better implemented here compared to other districts. For me, experiencing this Himalayan terrain felt like a divine gift.

For the first time in my present existence, I experienced a deep sense of blissfulness. In retrospect, I realize that sensing this bliss was crucial, as it forms the foundation of spiritual realization. Achieving this state often requires practicing various techniques to align with cosmic consciousness. Our minds struggle to comprehend the events and purposes in our lives until we reach a level of consciousness that synchronizes with the universe. We interpret life through our material mental programming, influenced by cultural collectives and accumulated knowledge. However, we operate under a cosmic karmic design, guided by forces from a parallel world. Whether this is scientifically tangible is not the point; everything visible has an equal degree of the invisible. Our thoughts, part of the unseen dimensions, arise from consciousness, which is constantly evolving. Our Karma influences the nature of this consciousness. This is why most traditions emphasize peace, cohesion, mutual respect, and harmony to maintain elevated consciousness. In the Sanatan tradition, we are taught to establish coherence with all elements, human and non-human, including plants.

During my travels in Himachal Pradesh, I was constantly on the move, meeting a diverse array of people across different regions. I traversed varied topographies, witnessing the vibrant energy of the Himalayas through its numerous fountains and rivers, both narrow and wide. In the early 1990s, the population in hilly states like Himachal Pradesh was sparse. As I travelled, I would often come across villages located off the main roadheads. Narrow link roads would lead to small hamlets or townships that weren't very large. By 7 pm, most shops would start closing, and their owners would return to their villages, some trekking uphill and others descending. Buses connecting destinations were scarce, and missing the morning bus meant waiting for the next one, which could be challenging. People often relied on lifts from passersby, and offering a ride would bring smiles and heartfelt thanks. Despite the hardships, life seemed simple and spontaneous.

My journey through the Himalayas felt like a recast of a life or lives spent in the region before. Everything seemed familiar—people and places alike. I often felt as though I was revisiting where I had left off before. From February 1994 to the end of 1995, I travelled extensively in Himachal Pradesh, discovering places beyond my wildest imagination. One of the most memorable experiences was accidentally catching a glimpse of Kailash from close quarters. This was quite an interesting encounter to recount.

Chapter - 4

A Journey of Shared Destiny

My marriage was solemnized amidst a whirlwind of unnecessary societal drama, largely fuelled by those closest to us. There were voices raised in concern over the disparity in our economic statuses, and many fretted about how the community would judge this perceived mismatch. Egos were bruised, and deeply ingrained prejudices and preconceived notions came to the surface, casting shadows over what should have been a joyous union. Yet, despite the noise and resistance, I remained steadfast and clear in my decision, anchored by a commitment that transcended material considerations and societal expectations. In hindsight, I recognize that this event was far more than a mere ceremony; it marked a profound dimensional shift in my life, a subtle yet powerful transformation that often goes unnoticed by the casual observer. Such shifts are like the quiet unfolding of a flower's bloom-gradual, delicate, and beyond the comprehension of ordinary minds. They arrive in disguise, hidden beneath the surface of everyday events, yet their impact resonates deeply, altering the course of one's existence in ways that only time and reflection can fully reveal. This experience taught me that true change often emerges not in grand gestures or loud proclamations, but in the silent, steady evolution of the heart and spirit, quietly reshaping our understanding of ourselves and the world around us.

On May 24, 1995, I married Purnima, a mathematics student at the University of Delhi. Our families belonged to the same community and region, and we had known each other well before deciding to unite our lives. However, despite this familiarity, our path to marriage was fraught with societal resistance. The economic disparity between our families became a focal point for objections and fuelled concerns about how the community would perceive our union. Egos and entrenched prejudices created significant obstacles, yet I remained resolute and unwavering in my commitment to Purnima. In hindsight, I see this union not merely as a social contract but as a predestined event-a profound dimensional shift that transcended societal drama and brought us together in a bond that has shaped and enriched my life in countless ways.

Shortly after my marriage, I embarked on a new professional journey by accepting a position at a public health institution in Jaipur, famously known as the Pink City and the historic capital of Rajasthan, one of India's grand princely states. Before my interview, we stayed at an ashram rooted in the lineage of Kriya Yoga-a connection that resonated deeply with me on a personal level. This was especially meaningful because my father-in-law had been initiated into Kriya Yoga by Shri Pahari Baba (Hariharanand Giri), a revered Yogi and spiritual guide within this tradition. This spiritual heritage added a profound dimension to my transition, weaving together my professional aspirations with a legacy of inner discipline and awakening.

Pahari Baba, originally from undivided Bengal, experienced a profound personal transformation-shifting from his role as a police officer to becoming a devoted follower of Subhash Chandra Bose, before ultimately embracing the ascetic life. His spiritual journey led him to be initiated into Kriya Yoga by Shri Satyanand Giri, a direct disciple of Shri Yukteshwar Giri. This esteemed lineage traces back to Mahavatar Babaji, the legendary Yogi credited with reviving Kriya Yoga in the modern era. The great masters of this tradition-Shri Yukteshwar Giri, Lahiri Mahasaya, and Paramhansa Yogananda-are revered as the foundational pillars of the Sanatan Yogic tradition and celebrated as enlightened ambassadors of the eternal wisdom contained in the Shrimad Bhagavad Gita and the Patanjali Yoga Sutras.

After spending two days at the ashram in Jaipur, I attended my job interview at a public health institution located in the southern part of the city. Fortune favoured me, and I was selected for the position, with the institute requesting that I join as soon as possible. Following this, we returned to Delhi, gathered our belongings, and relocated to Jaipur to begin this exciting new chapter. The institute provided us with an apartment, where we set up our first home as a married couple-a humble yet meaningful space that marked the start of our shared journey together.

During my time in Jaipur, a subtle yet profound process of divine awakening began to take root within me. On festive occasions and some Sundays, my wife and I would visit the Kriya Yoga ashram, often settling quietly in a corner, simply observing the ebb and flow of visitors. The ashram attracted a diverse community-regular devotees alongside occasional guests who travelled from distant states, all drawn by the spiritual energy of the place. Many had a deep connection to the ashram dating back to the days when Pahari Baba (Shri Hariharanand Giri) was present in his physical form. Today, the ashram continues to thrive under the devoted guidance of Swami Bhuvaneswaranand Giri, who upholds the sacred traditions and reverence instilled by his honourable Guru with unwavering dedication.

Shri Pahari Baba was widely known for his candid demeanour and his unmistakably powerful spiritual presence. His ability to make startling prophecies often left those around him in awe. One particularly memorable incident involved Hardev Joshi, who would later rise to become the Chief Minister of Rajasthan. During a visit to the ashram, Baba famously uttered, *"Hardev ko Kurshi do"* (Give Hardev a chair). At the time, this cryptic statement baffled everyone, especially since the ashram traditionally did not use chairs. Yet, in a remarkable turn of events, Baba's prophecy came true, cementing his reputation as a mystic whose insights transcended ordinary understanding and deepening the reverence his followers held for him.

Swami Bhuvaneswaranand Giri, lovingly called Gurudev, has been a silent Yogi who lived the essence of simplicity and truth-in every gesture and moment. During my visits to the Jaipur ashram, I never witnessed him preach; instead, his quiet presence conveyed a profound spiritual depth that needed no words. The ashram itself was a sanctuary of silence, where conversations were held only when absolutely necessary, preserving an atmosphere of calm and introspection. Visitors were offered prasad, a simple yet nourishing mix of fruits and nuts, while those staying longer were served wholesome meals that reflected the purity and simplicity cherished by the community. What touched me deeply was seeing Gurudev himself occasionally walk to the kitchen, quietly ensuring that everyone was well cared for-a humble act that spoke volumes about his compassion, accessibility, and unwavering dedication to the well-being of all who came seeking solace and guidance.

Gurudev adhered to a consistent and disciplined daily routine, adjusting only subtly with the changing seasons. His presence was quietly powerful-serene yet deeply penetrating-as if he could see into the very core of a person without uttering a single word. Though I often felt a shy reserve in his presence and rarely found the courage to speak directly with him, my wife Purnima would sometimes gently speak on my behalf, bridging the silence and fostering a quiet but meaningful connection.

One of the most extraordinary episodes in Gurudev's spiritual journey is his profound darshan-a divine vision- of Shri Mahavatar Babaji at the Jaipur ashram between 1972 and 1974. This remarkable encounter is recounted in vivid and heartfelt detail in Gurudev's recently published journey, where he shares intimate reflections on his personal interactions with the legendary Yogi. Although Pahari Baba (Hariharanand Giri), Gurudev's revered Guru, was not physically present at the ashram during this time, he later confirmed the authenticity of the experience through his own deep spiritual insights. Babaji's visit stands as a defining moment in the ashram's history, deeply enriching its spiritual heritage and solidifying its sacred legacy for generations to come.

While working in Jaipur, my professional responsibilities often took me to distant corners of India, turning each journey into more than just a work assignment-it became a spiritual quest. Wherever my travels led, I made it a point to visit places of religious significance, seeking moments of divine connection amidst the demands of duty. Among these sacred destinations, Jagannath Puri in Odisha held a uniquely special place in my heart. I returned to its temple time and again, irresistibly drawn to the sanctum sanctorum, the Garbha Griha. Standing before the two profound eyes of Lord Jagannath, I felt my entire being dissolve into his divine gaze, as if time and space ceased to exist. The yearning for darshan was so powerful that each visit to Odisha felt preordained-a sacred pilgrimage that continually nourished and transformed my soul.

The Jagannath Temple, a masterpiece of Kalinga architecture built in the 12th century, is not just a religious site but a living embodiment of devotion and spirituality.

Dedicated to Lord Jagannath (a form of Vishnu), along with his siblings Balabhadra and Subhadra, the temple is steeped in legends and rituals that transcend time. The annual Rath Yatra and the daily offerings of *Mahaprasad* add to its divine aura. For me, these visits felt like reconnecting with something left incomplete in another lifetime.

During this period, I also had the opportunity to visit other sacred places like Nathdwara in Rajasthan, dedicated to Shri Krishna, and Balaji (Tirupati). Each visit deepened my spiritual journey, sowing seeds of introspection and devotion. Whether it was the serene darshan at Nathdwara or the vibrant energy at Balaji, these experiences seemed to align with a cosmic design beyond my understanding.

Looking back, these travels were more than professional assignments—they were milestones in a journey that blended physical exploration with spiritual awakening. Life appeared so intricately articulated, weaving together work and devotion in ways that only divine orchestration could explain.

My stay in Jaipur was not for long. I was hardly there for a period of two years or so. In 1998, I transitioned from Jaipur to Patna, the capital of Bihar, to serve in a public health program focusing on family planning and reproductive health for women. Bihar, my home state, was then undivided (Jharkhand had not yet been carved out). This new role allowed me to travel extensively across the state, exploring its high-energy magnetic plains and connecting deeply with its historical and spiritual legacy.

Bihar has long been a cradle of spirituality, where vibrant souls like the Buddha and Shri Mahavira lived, taught, and journeyed. The state is home to profound historical landmarks such as Nalanda and Vikramshila Universities—institutions that were unparalleled centres of learning during their time. Scholars from around the world, including the

Far East and Northern regions, flocked to these universities. The creators and patrons of these institutions deserve eternal reverence for their contributions to global knowledge.

However, the tragic destruction of Nalanda University by Bakhtiyar Khilji in the 12th century remains a dark chapter in history. The library burned for six months, and countless teachers and students were brutally killed. Despite this devastation, Bihar continues to stand as a testament to resilience and spiritual richness.

As my professional journey progressed, I found myself immersed in a mundane temporal lifestyle, enjoying physical pleasures and comforts. With dozens of individuals reporting to me, my mind was often swayed by delusions of grandeur and a false sense of self-importance. I was captivated by a consciousness that was temporary and illusory. The modern facilities provided for my travel, stay, and dining further contributed to this lifestyle. I had a preference for non-vegetarian food, even on auspicious days, which went against the cultural and customary practices of the Sanatan tradition. My family found my behaviour perplexing and struggled to align me with the prescriptions of traditional Sanatan Dharma. My senses were fully engaged with the glitter of material life, which, though appealing, was not truly valuable.

Before delving deeper into the story of my life, I feel it is essential to take a step back and paint the backdrop of my early years—the foundational period that shaped my very being in this physical incarnation. Without a clear understanding of these formative experiences, the larger narrative of my life's journey would remain incomplete and difficult to fully grasp. These early moments, with their joys, struggles, influences, and lessons, laid the groundwork for the person I would become. They provide crucial context for the choices I made, the challenges I faced, and the path destiny carved out for me. To truly appreciate the unfolding of my life's tale, one must first appreciate the roots from which it grew—the environment, the relationships, and the inner stirrings that quietly moulded my character and spirit long before the more visible chapters began to take shape.

Chapter - 5

Insights into the Early Years

I was born into a traditionally oriented Brahmin farmer's family in a village called Mani Fulkahan, located about ten kilometres from the city of Muzaffarpur in North Bihar. Our ancestral home remained in this village until the present day. Despite its proximity to urban areas, the village retained its rural character with minimal influence from modernity during my childhood. There was no electricity, and the darkness after sunset could be intimidating. Our joint family lived in a large house with a spacious courtyard that seemed to stretch up to the sky. Outside, a big open area accommodated our cows and buffaloes, and harvested crops were manually processed and stored. A well outside the house used to serve as our sole source of drinking water, and we also used it for bathing. I fondly remember taking baths at the well, with someone from our domestic help fetching water and giving me a refreshing wash. Those moments were truly enjoyable.

The geo-topographic setting of my village was such that it would experience relentless rains for weeks during the four months from June to September. Every patch of low land would fill with water, and the excess would drain into ponds or flow out of the village. For me, the sight of clouds bursting in the open skies, especially in the north, was always exhilarating. Witnessing days of rain was a constant delight. As an inquisitive child, I would often play with the drops and droplets dripping from the tiled roof of our traditional home. On rainy days, our domestic cattle, usually kept outside, would be sheltered in makeshift arrangements. I still cherish the memories of catching small fish with my friends. We would find plenty of them swimming in the rainwater, and it was a thrilling adventure.

Nights in those times were incredibly dark, but during the bright moon phase, the moon would shine gloriously, casting milky white rays that illuminated everything, including the green grass outside my house. There was a long veranda where I would stand and watch the full moon, captivated by its beauty. Even as a child, my eyes would be drawn to the full moon, though I couldn't explain why it fascinated me so much. Nature in that setting seemed to embody its own absolute consciousness, and people lived in harmony with it. Looking back, it's no surprise that my ancestors coexisted with dangerous cobras and other venomous snakes in that wild environment. Encounters with snakes were a regular part of their lives. I vividly remember one occasion when I saw a big cobra eating curd from an earthen pot. My mother and I had gone to fetch fresh curd from the same pot. As an inquisitive child, it was one of the most amazing moments of my early life to see a big black snake uncover the pot and eat the curd in its own way. My mother screamed, but I wanted to stay in the moment and witness it without fear. I held onto her sari, yet I was mesmerized by the scene.

The village where I grew up was still quite rural, with customs and practices deeply rooted in traditional mindsets that influenced every aspect of family life. My mother, if I recall correctly, faced challenges in my father's home due to varying levels of consciousness among family members. She came from a family that had experienced cultural advancements by the standards of India in the 1960s and 1970s. However, social restrictions limited women's mobility, and they were rarely allowed to leave the residential boundaries. Occasionally, I would see my mother accompany my father on outings. The covered bullock cart was a primary mode of transport between our village and the small town of Muzaffarpur, although limited bus services had also begun. My mother, who developed heart problems early in life, often needed to be taken to the town or even to Patna, eighty kilometres away, for medical treatment. Some of my sharpest memories include crossing the mighty Ganga using the huge steamers of the time. In those days, there were no bridges connecting north Bihar with its southern counterpart, so people from the north had to travel to the state capital by steamer.

As a child, I was quiet yet inquisitive, sensitive to the happenings in our closed village setting. I was fortunate to have enjoyed a full and joyful childhood, growing up surrounded by people who loved me as a companion. I would often be taken from one house to another, sharing meals from different kitchens. The village was nearly self-sufficient, with villagers venturing into the local town only occasionally for items like clothing or new farming products. I lived in a social setting where some people had never seen an urban marketplace, despite living close to the town. For them, the village was the totality of their universe.

Our village had a large tank known locally as "Rani Pokhari," surrounded by a high mud embankment covered in a thick forest. This forest was home to creatures like porcupines, snakes, and jackals, which would often appear in the early evenings. Without electricity, locals were cautious about passing through the forest, especially at night. When necessary, men would use battery-operated torches to navigate the non-concrete pathways, occasionally encountering nocturnal animals in the torchlight. The village was a hub for social gatherings, and my family held significant social influence as one of the zamindars of the time. Although the zamindari system began to decline in the early 1960s following India's independence from British rule, remnants of it persisted for years.

Although the zamindari system was phasing out, its remnants still prevailed, and I witnessed part of it. Our traditional housing landscape was spread out, with dozens of livestock in front. There were classified service providers and helpers who managed various domestic and occupational duties. My father's elder brother was the main 'malik,' the head of the estate. We had many big bulls for agricultural activities and cart transportation, as well as cows and buffaloes for milk production. I remember the abundance of milk and a room dedicated to storing milk and curd. The house was old and large, with a big rectangular courtyard surrounded by verandas leading to different rooms. Due to its age and muddy walls, it was a habitat for snakes, which were commonly seen creeping around. There was an extended veranda facing east and north, connected to the main house, where adult males and domestic help would often stay. Females typically stayed indoors. A well on the northern side provided drinking water for the household and travellers. Strangers passing by would often stay at our place, receiving food, water, and shelter. It was a life vastly different from today. Occasionally, sarangi players—ascetic musicians who had renounced worldly life—would stop by, sing, and play. As a child, I was fascinated by their performances. My mother would give me a bowl of grains to offer them, which I did happily. Seeing them was a joy for me. My black kitten, Moti, would often bark at them from a distance.

In the centre of one of our large land patches stood a majestic banyan tree, thick and widely spread, providing shelter to generations of birds and other creatures. Its main trunk had a hollow space where we would hide during rains, playing as children. Outside, there were acres of open grazing land for our cattle and those of other villagers. I still cherish memories of that banyan tree, especially the hole inside it, which I found fascinating. I would often pass by the tree with my little pet dog, Moti, who was very dear to me. His untimely and unnatural death left me deeply saddened. My mother consoled me for days, saying that Moti had returned to God's kingdom.

    I preferred being alone, lost in my own realms of imagination. I didn't enjoy the company of my cousins, as they were more rustic, while I was drawn to simplicity and sophistication. One of my elder cousins was often harsh with me, so I kept my distance. The house was large, making it easy to find a secluded corner. We children received tuition from a local government school teacher who lived and ate with us. Every evening, we would have a two-hour class under the light of kerosene lanterns. Everyone, mostly women and older children, would prepare the lanterns daily, cleaning and filling them with kerosene. Some lanterns would stay lit all night, while others would be dimmed. Light was scarce, which is why villagers would retire early and rise with the sun. My family would go to bed by seven every evening.

    As I mentioned earlier, my mother struggled to cope within the family ecosystem. Constant disputes between my uncle and aunt created a tense atmosphere, filled with unnecessary noise. There was little harmony among family members, and this affected the children as well. They would frequently fight and trouble each other, and I wasn't spared either. The situation added to my mother's emotional distress, especially after losing two of my elder siblings under unclear circumstances. When I was born, the entire extended family was apprehensive, and many prayers and rituals were performed to ensure my safe birth and health. In those times, as is still common today, rural Indians believed in witchcraft and black magic. The untimely deaths of my two brothers were sometimes attributed to these beliefs. Combining all the emotional setbacks and hardships, my mother yearned to move to a peaceful place, away from the negativity caused by regular domestic conflicts.

(My mother with my younger brother)

Soon after my birth, the family landscape began to change as my father realized it was challenging to continue living amidst the inharmonious quarrels. He may have received some divine guidance that led him to purchase a patch of land in the local town, about ten kilometres east of my village. During this time, my right eye developed a disorder that caused vision loss. I was around ten years old when this problem surfaced, prompting my father to take me to a city-based ophthalmologist for treatment. The process was long and arduous. I stayed in a rented accommodation near our new land with my father and regularly visited the doctor, who administered painful injections around my right eye. These shots were agonizing, and I endured them for about six months. In retrospect, I now contemplate that the vision loss and the purchase of city land were cosmically orchestrated to bring about immediate transformations in my life.

Just before my ophthalmic problem surfaced, my elder cousin and I were taken on a short pilgrimage to Gaya, Rajgir, Pawapuri, and Nalanda. This was my first exposure to the outer world and places of historically spiritual significance. Our local school teacher, Shri Ratnesh Chaturvedi, who was also my first formal teacher, accompanied one of his teachers on this journey. Gaya, as it is still revered, serves as a physical destination where subtle bodies embark on their journey to their respective destinations. For those who follow Sanatana Dharma, Gaya is a sacred site where they visit to free their ancestors' subtle bodies from the earth's orbit through rituals like Pind-Daan. In Pind-Daan, "Pind" refers to the subtle body, and "Daan" means to offer or give away. I vividly remember the Falgu River, which appears dry on the surface but yields water when dug just a few centimetres deep. All Pind-Daan rituals are performed on its banks. Gautami, one of the greatest Yogis in Sanatan cultural history, is believed to have spent significant time practicing various forms of yoga. He was an exponent of Sanatan yogic science and a master of Ashtanga Yoga. Sujatha, who lived across the Falgu River, shared some common practices of Dhyan and meditation with Gautami. Interestingly, my spirit seemed to guide my body to visit Gaya in the early stages of its present physical form.

On my maternal side, my grandfather, Shri Devendra Narayan Mishra, was a devoted follower of Shri Hanuman. He was an exceptional singer, classical Indian instrument player, and performer of Hindu rituals. I remember him singing and completing the entire Ram-Charit-Manas in twenty-four hours. As a child, I would observe him chanting mantras early in the morning, and reciting Ram-Charit-Manas was part of his daily routine. I was always in awe of his rhythmic singing, which would start late in the evening and continue through the night. A small group of people would gather to listen, while a few others would accompany him on instruments like the Dholak, Harmonium, and Kartals. Occasionally, my mother would join him, singing verses of the epic in perfect harmony. I still recall how my body would resonate with the rhythms, connecting my present existence with past lives.

My mother hailed from the Mithila region of Bihar, specifically from Darbhanga district. Although Muzaffarpur and Darbhanga are geographically close, they differ culturally and linguistically. Mithila is renowned for its intellectual traditions, rich literary history, art, crafts, and classical music. It has been a foundational base for several cultural and linguistic traditions, including Bengali and Assamese. The theory of civilizational evolution suggests that migrations occurred from the north down to all three directions, which is reflected in Darbhanga's name, derived from *"Dwar-Bang"* or *"Gateway to Bengal."* Both regions share cultural similarities, from language to culinary traditions like fish consumption. Historically, the Mithila region was ruled by the Maharaja of Darbhanga, whose wealth rivalled that of other prominent princely states like Jaipur, Jodhpur, or Gwalior, and even Nepal on the northern side.

One of the key differences between my father's and mother's sides was the nature of conversations. On my father's side, people often engaged in subjective gossip, whereas in my mother's village, discussions were more objective. Even in remote areas of Bihar, one could hear people discussing international politics. On spiritual fronts, the Darbhanga district was quite elevated. Lakshmi Nath Gosain, whom I will mention later, hailed from a sub-region of Mithila's Darbhanga. During India's freedom struggle, prominent leaders from Pator village, such as Shri Janki Raman Mishra and Pandit Ram Nandan Mishra, played significant roles. Pandit Ram Nandan Mishra was an elevated Yogi and disciple of Shri Totapuri. My maternal grandfather would often speak of him as a distant relative. One of his sons, Shri Vijay Raghav Mishra, is also known to be a notable figure who ran a publishing house, Nav Bharat Prakashan, in Darbhanga. This publishing house published works like "Bharat ke Mahan Sadhak" (Great Yogis of India).

Even today, the Mithila region remains somewhat outside the mainstream, yet its rich cultural heritage continues to shine through its religious, spiritual, and musical traditions. These aspects have allowed Mithila to align with other advanced cultural contexts in India. I still recall how the elders in Pator, my mother's village, would tune into All India Radio to listen to instrumental classical music, which would play for almost an hour. There are memories of men holding overnight kirtans, leading to a state of transcendental frenzy for both the singers and the listeners. It was an ecstatic experience. Families on my mother's side were largely non-vegetarians, consuming a variety of fish and mutton, though not chicken. This is where I was introduced to non-vegetarian food. In contrast, my father's side followed a stricter diet, avoiding even onions and garlic. My father's family belonged to a tradition that had struggled for power and wealth, known for being assertive and resilient.

Back home, new developments unfolded one after another. My father decided to construct a house on the newly purchased land, which took about a year and a half to complete. Meanwhile, my mother was desperate to escape the toxic family environment. So, our nuclear family moved to the town and started a new life. I was enrolled in a new private school, marking the beginning of a new process in 1975. This period took me on a journey of exploration, witnessing the continuity of the cosmic frame. In retrospect, 1975 and the first five years of the seventies were the start of one of the most vibrant phases of my life. Many monumental changes occurred, breaking away from age-old family establishments.

Chapter - 6

Adolescence: The Transformative Years

My school days were not particularly bright, mainly because I struggled with studies. My inner motivation was lacking, which worried both my parents. As a result, I changed schools several times during my early years. I was influenced by one of my cousin elder brothers, who would often distract me from focusing on my studies. The ninth and tenth standards were crucial, as they set the stage for future academic success. However, I frequently bunked classes and went to movie shows instead. This led to disappointing results in the ninth standard, though my tenth standard results were satisfactory, if not outstanding.

It was during the rainy seasons of 1982 that a new trait began to emerge in me. I started seeking seclusion, often sitting quietly in a darkened room during sunset. My mother would search for me and find me in this state, which was both surprising and disturbing to her. As an adolescent, I had previously enjoyed mingling with peers and engaging in outdoor activities. However, I began to withdraw inwardly, and the outdoors no longer held the same appeal. Despite this change, I passed my matriculation with a first division. At the time, there was a strong trend for students to pursue science subjects for higher studies, and those who didn't were often perceived as less intelligent. I still don't fully understand the reasons behind this perception.

My college life began with a transformative shift in how I approached my personal growth and academic responsibilities. The first year was marked by a renewed enthusiasm for acquiring knowledge, leading me down two parallel paths: intensifying my interest in studies and forming meaningful friendships with peers who shared my academic values. I developed a passion for studying Hindi and English literature, and I started composing serious poetry in Hindi. I actively participated in seminars, symposiums, and poetry recitation sessions. Muzaffarpur, where I grew up, has a rich tradition in art and literature, and my college, Langat Singh College (L S College), was highly regarded. It was a source of pride to study at an institution where Dr. Rajendra Prasad, the first President of India, had taught. Being part of this prestigious college undoubtedly added value and inspired me to pursue my studies more seriously. I transformed from a casual student to one who studied late into the night and attended classes regularly. This dedication was reflected in my college results, culminating in distinction marks in American history during my final year. Alongside history, I also studied Economics and English literature.

During the first five years of my college life, I was fortunate to have the company of good friends, many of whom were older than me. Those of my age were not as intellectually evolved, but the elder generation possessed unique traits that were uncommon. I firmly believe that the company you keep shapes who you become. Several individuals from that time remain significant to me today. One such influential personality was Lt. Rajendra Prasad Singh, a highly acclaimed poet who lived in the town. I would often visit him to discuss various topics, including history and literature. He was equally proficient in Hindi and English and was an extempore orator who could mesmerize audiences. He would commute using a paddle rickshaw operated by a man named Vidhuri. I vividly remember how he would join a literary group every evening at Banaras

Bank Chowk, which I also attended frequently. This period was incredibly enriching, offering knowledge that even universities couldn't provide, which eventually translated into wisdom. The person I became later in life was heavily influenced by those formative years. They taught me social conduct, personal manners, and oratory skills, particularly how to choose words effectively. Gradually, I shed my shyness and hesitation, blossoming like the petals of a flower. I still believe that companionship is crucial, and I continue to follow this principle today.

I was living in a small town with my parents, my younger sibling, and a cousin. Over time, more cousins joined us, and we all shared a large room set up like a dormitory. I had a bed assigned to me and was pursuing higher secondary studies in social sciences and languages, which genuinely interested me. I never had an inclination towards science subjects, and as a result, I was often perceived as a mediocre student. During this period, my mother's heart problems would flare up occasionally, and as the eldest sibling, I quickly took on daily chores. I would cook, clean, wash clothes, attend college, and study simultaneously, while also caring for my mother's health. I also recall finding a small, vibrant Hanuman idol, which I placed between my bookshelves. I would worship him every morning and felt drawn to him. Although I couldn't fully explain why I was performing these daily tasks, they had become an integral part of my life.

In my younger years, I maintained a sophisticated demeanour in how I dressed, spoke, and presented myself socially. Over time, I began to realize that I was becoming a straightforward, no-nonsense person. I would tolerate nonsense but react when necessary. I had a lot of anger, minimal greed, some hatred, but no jealousy. Desire, or Kama, started to play a significant role in my life. Around this time, I befriended a Bengali girl, who was studying chemistry at my college. She was impressed by my oratory skills and my physical appearance, which I had been gifted with good skin tone and sharp features. This was my first friendship with someone of the opposite gender, but the friendship lasted only for about a few months. Eventually, predestination decided I pursued higher studies in Delhi at a prestigious institution.

During my bachelor's course, I was actively engaged in writing poetry and participating in literary circles. I frequently took part in poetry recitation sessions and was recognized among emerging writers from Muzaffarpur. Some of my poems were published in literary magazines, which helped shape my written and verbal communication skills. In July 1988, I attended a national poetry recitation conference in Kolkata. This trip also gave me the opportunity to visit Dakshineshwar, the revered site associated with Shri Ram Krishna, the spiritual guru of Swami Vivekananda. I had the privilege of seeing the Kali idol that Ram Krishna worshipped, believed to have conversed with him. His room still radiates powerful vibrations that envelop one's mind and quiet all thoughts. The holy Ganga flows parallel to the temple compound. Although I was initially unaware of the significance of my visit, I remember sitting in his room for a while before leaving the temple grounds.

My father was opposed to the idea of me moving to Delhi for higher studies. He had landed property, but it was controlled by his elder brother, and he struggled with a regular monthly income. This financial insecurity likely influenced his reluctance. However, I was determined, or perhaps my destiny was guiding me. My mother, on the other hand, supported my decision, despite her poor health due to cardiac complications. She had undergone surgery at AIIMS in New Delhi a few years prior, but her condition would fluctuate with seasonal changes and emotional stress. Our family faced economic hardships, which worried my mother. My father wasn't diligent about securing a steady income, and as I grew up with my younger sibling, material scarcity was a concern. My mother's health issues added to my responsibilities. She would cook for six to seven people, and when she fell ill, her duties became mine. At that time, cooking was done on firewood ovens or kerosene stoves. Using a firewood stove was challenging but provided valuable learning experiences. Being around the "chulha" was like becoming fire itself, filled with raw smoke. I witnessed my mother embody this daily, and I experienced it myself on several occasions. Despite the challenges, food cooked on firewood was delicious and fulfilling.

In 1989, as my bachelor's degree results were anticipated, I embarked on a new journey to Delhi, the capital city, on December 31st. I arrived amidst the extreme foggy winters and settled in Nirankari Colony, an emerging urban centre in northern Delhi that still had the feel of an urban village. I moved into a rented accommodation shared with some of my seniors from Muzaffarpur College, each with their own aspirations. One was pursuing journalism, another a master's degree, and a third preparing for competitive examinations. I often wonder why someone would travel 1000 kilometres to prepare for examinations in a rented-room, when it could be done just as easily at home.

I managed to stay in Nirankari Colony for a few months before my seniors decided to move our accommodation to Parmanand Colony, a nearby location. The three of us lived together, with two of them being my seniors. I was responsible for kitchen duties, but they often assigned me unnecessary tasks and would sometimes fight with me. Pandey, who is no longer with us, would trouble me the most. One afternoon, we had a heated argument, and I responded with equal vigour. This led me to decide to leave immediately. However, finding an equally affordable place was a challenge, and I was stuck for the moment. After packing my belongings, I left them in a corner and went out to search for a new place. It was around three in the afternoon when I sat at an open tea stack and ordered a cup of tea. Many thoughts were racing through my mind, and some of them worried me. I was facing uncertainties in Delhi, a city where I didn't know many people. I had relatives, but they lived with their families in different parts of the city.

As I sat sipping tea, lost in thought and tension, Manoj suddenly appeared and sat down beside me. We exchanged surprised glances, and I shared my immediate problems with him. He revealed that he lived nearby and offered me a place to stay without delays. I was amazed! It was as if solutions were unfolding alongside my problems. We often underestimate our own capacity for finding answers. Shortly after, we walked back to my previous accommodation, gathered my belongings, and returned to Manoj's tiny room, barely ten feet by ten feet. Initially, I was apprehensive about managing comfortably, but circumstances have a way of teaching us the best coping strategies.

Manoj would often walk almost a kilometre to eat at an outside joint, despite having all the necessary utensils and a kerosene stove for cooking. Initially, I joined him for meals outside, but soon I convinced him to start cooking in our room. He agreed reluctantly, stating he wouldn't assist as he didn't know how to cook. We rearranged our room's setup and began cooking there. The home-cooked food was incredibly delicious. At that time, Delhi was less crowded, and living there was comfortable. Pollution was minimal, and our room, located next to the main road, wasn't too noisy. The marketplace was not yet overwhelmed by cars and motorbikes, which were limited in both brand and number.

Manoj wouldn't study at all, and I couldn't understand why he was there without a future plan. He would stay in the room but not pursue any academic goals. As for me, my next step was to enrol in a Master's course. I had started taking entrance exams for various programs. One afternoon, I was returning from Jawaharlal Nehru University (JNU), where I had checked the results of an entrance test, I had taken earlier. Unfortunately, my name was on the waitlist, and I wasn't happy about it. On the bus ride back, I met Mukesh Nemani, a close friend from Muzaffarpur. I shared my disappointment with him, and as we passed through the Delhi University campus, he suggested applying for the Sociology course at the Delhi School of Economics, which I knew nothing about. As he finished speaking, our bus stopped at the Hindu College bus stop, and we got off. I walked to the Department of Sociology and met the clerk, regarding applying for the entrance examination scheduled for mid-June 1990.

"The effulgent Self, who is beyond thought, shines in the greatest, shines in the smallest, shines in the farthest, shines in the nearest, shines in the secret chamber of the heart."

- *The Mundaka Upanishad*

India's education system has historically been unequal across states, with significant qualitative differences between urban and rural institutions, as well as between private and public schools. Additionally, there is a perceived superiority of students educated in English over those from vernacular backgrounds. I faced this bias during my time, which affected my confidence in public appearances involving English communication. Despite being proficient in English, I lacked the sharpness of tongue that was expected. After receiving my JNU entrance results, my confidence was shaken, and I was hesitant to take the written entrance test. However, Manoj proved to be a great motivator, encouraging me to take the test. I went ahead and wrote extensively, answering in descriptive long notes. It seems that destiny played a role, as it often does. Upon returning to our room, Manoj reassured me, *'you will get through'.*

Before I delve into my Master's program admission and other stories, I must share an intriguing paranormal experience that occurred while I lived with Manoj in his room. I would often study late into the night. One evening, Manoj was away visiting relatives, leaving me alone in the room. It was around 1:30 am, and I was studying using a table lamp. The window had an iron net, allowing me to see outside if there was any activity in the lane. Suddenly, a human face caught my attention. As I looked closer, I was convinced that it was a girl wearing a pink frock standing outside. I immediately stood up, opened the door and saw a girl standing there in pink top and frock. My legs didn't move any further and I fainted, falling onto the mattresses on the floor. I lost consciousness for about two hours, lying there profusely sweating and feeling as if I had been beaten up. I was scared and alone. Summoning some courage, I left the room and went to another boy's room, explaining what had happened. I asked him to lock my room from the outside, and I stayed with him until morning. The image of the girl in pink kept recurring in my thoughts, and I tried to figure out if I knew her. In the back of my mind, I felt she might be someone I knew before, but I couldn't recall or identify her.

Although I had experienced a couple of paranormal incidents in my early life, they were distant and didn't leave me as frightened as this encounter did. I was convinced that I was being visited by a spirit, and she stood just a few feet away from me. At that time, mobile phones didn't exist, and connecting with family members wasn't easy. We had to use public telephone booths to make calls. I didn't feel it was right to call my mother and share the incident that had shaken me for several days. When Manoj returned to the room, I shared the experience with him. Over time, the emotional setbacks I suffered as a young boy began to heal.

The entrance test results for Delhi School of Economics were announced in the first week of July 1990. To my surprise, I ranked third in the merit list. It was astonishing how life can turn events around before one fully understands them. Securing the third position was hard to believe, especially considering the numerous competitors from more affluent backgrounds than mine. The written test had been highly competitive. I informed my parents about the news and decided to secure an early admission. At that time, the admission fees charged by the University were relatively low and affordable, making it manageable for me.

As soon as I became a Bonafide student at the University of Delhi, I decided to visit my parents and spend some time with them before returning to Delhi for classes. Upon arriving home, my mother offered me some food and shared news about a neighbourhood girl who had been considered for a marriage proposal with me. Unfortunately, she had passed away from blood cancer just a few days prior, and my mother had witnessed her death. I was awestruck and couldn't help but stare at my mother. In response, I shared with her my own experience of seeing the girl in a paranormal encounter back in Delhi, which had left me terrified. My mother was shocked by my story. My maternal grandfather, a deeply religious and evolved person, was informed about what had happened. He rushed to see me and advised, *"Stay firm, confident, and fearless"*. He explained that the spirit had wanted to be close to me in its physical life but, having failed, reappeared to visit me. He suggested that it might appear again or not at all, but I should remain steadfast and recite the Hanuman Chalisa. My grandfather's advice was instrumental in helping me build confidence.

Although I was preoccupied with past experiences, time helped me return to my normal self. As my Master's classes resumed, I became accustomed to the teaching patterns and approaches at Delhi University, particularly at the Delhi School of Economics, which everyone referred to as the "D'School." The environment was vastly different from what

I was used to in Muzaffarpur. English became my primary language on campus, which helped refine and sharpen my tongue and vocabulary. Some of my professors, like Andre Beteille and A M Shah, were renowned sociologists. Initially, understanding their lectures was challenging, but I worked hard to catch up and learn as much as possible. Given the setbacks in my primary education, it took time to overcome the academic challenges at Delhi University. One of the biggest hurdles was comprehending chapters from a book and presenting them to the entire tutorial group—a skill my college education system had not prepared me for.

Following my entrance test results and merit list placement, I was allotted a single room at the P.G. Men's Hostel, which was a significant advantage given the challenges I faced living outside. Manoj bid me farewell, and I shifted to the hostel within a month of my Master's admission. Hostel life was well-organized and smooth, with meals provided by the hostel kitchen, for which I was appointed as a Secretary. As time passed, life gained momentum in this new community setting. I successfully completed my Master's course in 1992. During my stay, Chandan Sharma from Assam, who hadn't been allotted a room, became my room-mate. We lived harmoniously, and I learned much about Assamese culture and traditions from him. We remain well-connected and share a strong bond. Currently, he teaches Sociology at Tezpur Central University.

Chapter - 7

When Alcoholism Tore Family Apart

Between 2008 and 2010, my life navigated a particularly tumultuous period. My alcohol consumption had spiralled out of control, with no limits to my daily intake. Each morning began with at least three to four glasses of raw alcohol, followed by an endless stream of drinking throughout the day and late into the night. This habit had developed over years of regular drinking, gradually eroding any self-control I once had. I had become so deeply dependent on alcohol that I couldn't function without it, nor could I sleep without consuming substantial amounts. This vicious cycle had taken hold, leaving me trapped in a state of constant intoxication.

My struggle with alcoholism had severe repercussions on both professional and social fronts. I found it impossible to attend public events without consuming alcohol, and my professional reputation suffered significantly due to the perception of being a drunkard. The final blow came in 2007 when I lost my job and was forced to return home, a major emotional setback. Despite the urging of those close to me to quit, I couldn't shake off the dependency. Alcohol had become an integral part of my life, making it unimaginable to live without it. The grip of addiction was so strong that I felt trapped, unable to envision a future without its influence.

As my alcohol consumption reached alarming levels, my wife, witnessing the devastating impact on our family, made the heart-wrenching decision to leave with our two children, seeking refuge with her parents. This departure left me isolated in Lucknow, devoid of any physical support or emotional solace. In this desolate state, alcohol became my sole companion, fuelling a vicious cycle of dependency that eclipsed all other aspects of life. My intake increased exponentially, while my food consumption dwindled, leaving me a shadow of my former self. The emotional numbness was so profound that I felt an inner "demon" driving my self-destructive path, rendering me indifferent to the absence of my loved ones and the darkness that had enveloped my existence.

As my Lucknow neighbour informed my father about my rapidly deteriorating physical and mental state, he swiftly intervened by sending my younger brother, Sudhakar, to Lucknow to assist me in relocating to our parental home in Muzaffarpur. Within a week, I was moved along with all my belongings, marking a significant change in my environment. However, this shift did little to alleviate my struggles with alcoholism. My wife, having taken up a teaching position at a local college, continued to live with her parents and ceased visiting me, further exacerbating the emotional isolation I felt. Despite my father's unwavering support and efforts to help me reduce my alcohol intake, my addiction only intensified, spiralling out of control at an alarming rate.

The emotional isolation I faced within my family was profound. Despite living just a kilometre away, my wife refused to see me, and my children were barred from visiting. Even my pleas to my in-laws to allow my children to spend time with me were met with indifference. Occasionally, my brother-in-law would bring them for brief, fleeting moments before whisking them away again. The alienation and callousness I experienced were almost unbearable.

The emotional detachment from my closest family members reached its peak. My wife acted on her parents' advice to sever all contact. She wouldn't call me, nor would she receive my calls, leading to repeated emotional setbacks. Under these circumstances, alcohol continued to serve as my only perceived solace, a means to momentarily escape the mental and emotional turmoil. Often, I felt an overwhelming urge to end my life, a temptation that intensified when I was intoxicated. Yet, somehow, I lacked the resolve to act on it, as if the universe itself was withholding the courage and power to carry out such an act.

Despite my deteriorating health, numerous relatives attempted to intervene and persuade my in-laws to reconcile with me. However, their efforts were met with indifference. Even my father-in-law, a medical doctor himself, failed to offer substantial support. He, along with others, mistakenly believed that my alcohol consumption was a matter of personal choice rather than a symptom of addiction. They were unconvinced that I was struggling with alcoholism as a disease. My father, however, continued to seek help, taking me to doctors based on advice from others. By then, my alcoholism had become a subject of local gossip, attracting visitors with various recommendations. While my father considered some of these suggestions, they ultimately offered little respite from my addiction.

Occasionally, representatives from my in-laws' side would visit me, not to offer support, but to witness my deteriorating physical condition and heap scorn upon my suffering. I was repeatedly humiliated in my own home, subjected to cruel sarcasm and ridicule. My brother-in-law was the one of the frequent visitors from their side, but his visits were far from comforting. He would loudly berate me, ensuring that my neighbours were aware of my supposed transgressions. His public accusations were designed to justify why my wife was not allowed to visit or care for me. The humiliation I endured during this period still haunts me today, contributing to the strained relationship I have with my in-laws and their associates. A particularly painful memory from that time is being excluded from the last rites and related events when my wife's grandmother passed away. Neither I nor any member of my immediate family was invited, a stark example of the discrimination I faced during my darkest hour.

During a particularly poignant moment, I encountered my wife's sister's husband (brother-in-law) at a railway platform in my hometown while I waited to catch a train to Lucknow. Despite my respectful greeting with folded hands, he astonishingly ignored me, pretending not to recognize me. This encounter was especially jarring given our age difference, as he was significantly older than me. Meanwhile, my wife, who passed by our house daily on her way to the college, chose not to visit or even call to check on my well-being. Her deliberate avoidance and refusal to communicate further underscored the deep rift in our relationship and the emotional isolation I faced during that challenging period.

I share this narrative for several reasons. Firstly, I aim to be candid about the trials my life has faced, offering a genuine account of my experiences. Secondly, I hope to convey that life is merely a series of fleeting moments and reflections, often misunderstood as permanent realities. Thirdly, I believe that relationships in this life are continuations of past connections, bound by emotional threads that draw us to some and distance us from others. These karmic echoes influence our daily lives, shaping our paths forward.

In today's world, where material desires often overshadow spiritual connections, I've witnessed how people prioritize wealth over the well-being of loved ones. In my case, many focused on what I couldn't provide materially for my family, while I found humour in their remarks. Though uncertain about the future of my relationships at the time, I was struck by how others valued financial success over saving a family member's life. This experience underscored the importance of recognizing and nurturing the deeper, spiritual bonds that truly enrich our lives.

My alcohol consumption had reached its peak, and I was determined to quit and restore balance to my life. However, alcohol seemed reluctant to let go of its grip on me. I was admitted to rehabilitation centres, where doctors and therapists emphasized the importance of family support, particularly from my wife. Unfortunately, she was unwilling to provide it, and her father consistently turned down such requests on her behalf. It seemed as though I was destined to experience a phase of life that would teach me detachment from human relationships, especially with my wife. Throughout my struggles, she never reached out to inquire about my well-being, leaving me to face my challenges alone.

Despite these hardships, I began to confront the negativity that had accumulated in my life. With each passing day, I grew more resolute in my determination to emerge victorious. The thought of giving up or succumbing to my circumstances never crossed my mind, even when others around me would suggest that I might not survive. I remained convinced that I would overcome this catastrophic period, no matter the obstacles. This unwavering optimism became my strength, driving me forward even in the darkest of times.

As I struggled with my personal demons, I found myself losing faith in those around me, especially those closest to me—my immediate and distant relatives. The layers of illusions surrounding relationships were slowly peeling away, revealing the harsh reality of how inhumanly demeaning and demotivating people close to me could be. In a state of suffering and poor health, I desperately needed emotional support and the backing of my immediate family during those critical times. Instead, I was met with fabricated stories, gossips, and a blame game where I was unfairly labelled as the main culprit.

Living in a small city where everyone knew each other and close families resided in proximity, it was heartbreaking that no one would visit to offer empathy or support. My children, still in primary and secondary schools, were deliberately kept away from me, and I wouldn't see them for months. They lived with their mother at their maternal grandfather's home, just a kilometre away from me. This painful state of affairs was truly heart-wrenching, leading to a realization of the false consciousness of emotional paradigms I had been living under.

By then, I had reached a profound realization that I was trapped in a vicious cycle of alcoholism and was desperate to break free. My struggles to liberate my mind and body were intense, often culminating in hours of solitary tears in my lonely room. Yet, there was no one to share my anguish with, leaving me feeling utterly isolated. I vividly recall those three years spent confined to the ground floor of my ancestral home in Muzaffarpur, where my only solace was the unwavering care and support of my father. He selflessly cooked for me, fed me, and tended to my health with a compassion that was both comforting and humbling. During my occasional outbursts of frustration, he was the sole witness and source of calm. While others around me remained silent spectators, my father's presence was a beacon of hope. Even in my broken mental state, I couldn't help but reflect on the stark reality of our modern society—how inhumanly we often treat each other, especially within the fabric of close relationships. The brutal circumstances I faced were, in many ways, a reflection of the broader societal flaws that prioritize materialism over emotional connection and spiritual well-being.

Despite being emotionally shattered and socially isolated, my devotion to Shri Mahavatar Babaji remained unwavering. I deeply believed that he would not abandon me, and this faith provided a beacon of hope during my darkest moments. The melancholy solitude I endured, devoid of festive celebrations or meaningful human connections, became a transformative crucible. As I battled the dual challenges of alcohol addiction and emotional devastation, I struggled to understand why I was suffering so profoundly. The desertion by loved ones and gossip from acquaintances only intensified my pain. To me, they appeared as human in form but lacked the consciousness that truly defines humanity. The societal humiliation I faced, including being called a "beggar" by my brother-in-law, marked one of the most painful moments in my life.

I saw them all in their own different forms (my mind would relatively term them as 'cruel'). To me, they only appeared in their human forms but did not carry the consciousness of being human. However, amidst these trials, I began to sense a deeper transformation unfolding within me. I saw my suffering not merely as misfortune but as a transformative fire, burning away karmic debts from past lives. While the events around me seemed harsh and unpleasant, they carried profound karmic significance. This perspective allowed me to view my experiences as part of a larger spiritual journey, one that would ultimately lead to liberation and higher awareness.

As I had mentioned earlier, there were times when I felt an overwhelming urge to end my life, with thoughts of hanging myself from a fan frequently crossing my mind. However, my spirit seemed to resist these impulses, as the desire to live often overpowered the urge to die. It was as if the universe wanted me to continue living, using my body to manifest various illusions or "Mayas" that shape our perception of the world. Despite consuming large amounts of alcohol, I miraculously avoided contracting any major illnesses, which would have likely been fatal. People around me, including my father, had begun to anticipate my demise. He, being the closest witness to my decline, was in a state of utmost desperation. Yet, he stood by me unwaveringly, fighting my battles on all fronts—emotionally, economically, and socially.

I vividly remember how he would coax me to eat, much like a mother tends to her child. The absence of my children was a constant source of emotional pain, their thoughts lingering in my mind and refusing to fade. Amidst this turmoil, I was uncertain if I would ever regain normalcy, feeling trapped in an unrelenting whirlpool of despair. However, my prayers to Shri Mahavatar Babaji remained my last bastion of hope. I offered all my pain and suffering to him, surrendering my burdens to his divine care. Was I being guided toward a state of absolute surrender, where I would let go of all resistance and allow the universe to guide me toward healing and redemption?

As I navigated through multiple setbacks and relapses, I began to slowly and steadily rebuild myself. While I still struggled with alcohol, I managed to maintain periods of sobriety. However, my family situation remained unchanged, with my nuclear family continuing to distance itself from me. I was deliberately isolated, forced to endure emotional setbacks without any support or acknowledgment from those closest to me. My in-laws seemed indifferent to the possibility of reuniting my family, leaving me to witness firsthand the insensitivity that humans can display. It was a stark reminder that many people fail to understand the concept of karma, unaware that their actions can have repercussions that ultimately return to them.

Amidst the cracks and chaos that had enveloped my life, I continued to endure one of its most painful chapters. However, as time unfolded, transformation began to take root. Determined to rebuild myself, I started applying for new jobs. To my fortune, I was invited to interview with one of India's leading corporations. Traveling to Mumbai for the interview, I discovered that none other than Mrs. Godrej herself, the Chairwoman, was conducting it. More than the content of our discussion, I felt a resonance in our vibrations—a connection that seemed almost divine. Shortly thereafter, I received an appointment letter to serve as the National Advocacy Director for their HIV program, based in Delhi.

This opportunity felt like a divine gift, pulling me back into the mainstream of worldly consciousness. Overnight, my life began to turn around, as if propelled by a karmic force that still had unfinished business for me to undertake. Moving to Delhi, I began living alone and continued my battle with alcohol. While occasional relapses occurred, I sensed that alcohol was gradually losing its grip on me. It felt as though this chapter of my physical existence was nearing its end.

This new phase marked not only a professional revival but also a deeper spiritual realization. It reminded me that even in the darkest moments, life can pivot in unexpected ways, offering a chance to heal and grow. The journey ahead would still hold challenges, but with each step forward, I felt closer to reclaiming my life and purpose.

The year 2010 marked a turning point in my life, setting the stage for profound changes that began to manifest physically in 2011. Settling into Delhi brought new opportunities and challenges, but it also ignited a period of self-awakening. For the first time, I began to reflect deeply on my life, realizing how shallow and unaware of myself I had been. This newfound consciousness restored my confidence and self-esteem, motivating me to fight back and rebuild my life.

Amid this transformation, my anger boiled over as I resolved to reunite with my family. In September 2010, while still organizing an interfaith international conference with the Art of Living headquarters in Bengaluru, I called my father-in-law. With firm resolve, I gave him a deadline to send my family back to my home. I made it clear that upon my return, I would take them back by any means necessary, signalling the end of his manipulative attempts to break my family apart. This was a pivotal moment where I chose to confront the situation head-on, adopting a resilient and determined stance to reclaim what was mine. The necessary courage and strength were graciously granted by the divine.

This period was not just about external battles but also internal growth. It marked the beginning of a journey toward healing, self-realization, and reclaiming control over my life. The challenges I faced became catalysts for transformation, pushing me toward a stronger and more conscious version of myself.

As anticipated, my strong message from Bengaluru sent ripples of nervousness through my in-laws' household. In response, my father-in-law began reaching out to mutual friends and relatives to mediate the situation. One elderly lawyer, a respected family friend and relative, stepped forward to facilitate a meeting at my in-laws' home. Despite the complexities and absurdities that had developed over time, I chose to remain calm, focusing solely on reuniting with my family. On the evening of Dussehra in 2010, after nearly three years of separation, I was finally able to bring my children back home. Initially, this reunion brought a sense of relief and seemed to mark the beginning of the end of a painful period. However, as time passed, this respite proved to be short-lived, revealing itself to be a fleeting mirage rather than a lasting resolution.

Upon my wife's return, I was met with a stark change in her demeanour. She had become more demanding, aggressive, and argumentative, often reflecting the influence of her family's status and wealth, which she used to assert superiority over my middle-income background. Her actions were frequently controlled by her parents, and she would regularly visit them, reinforcing their influence in our domestic affairs. Trivial issues would escalate into heated arguments between us, and with my father as well. She often compared our material possessions unfavourably with those of other close families, fostering a sense of discontent.

These frequent conflicts took a toll on our children, who began to view me as the source of all problems. As is often the case, children tend to side with their mother, leaving me feeling like the family's scapegoat. Despite my demanding national travel schedule for work, I made it a point to visit home regularly to fulfil my household responsibilities. Bihar was one of my official destinations, allowing me to travel there frequently. However, despite these positive developments, my wife's attitude and arrogance remained significant barriers to restoring peace and harmony in our family.

At times, I wondered if she was intentionally creating these conflicts to keep our family psychologically occupied. Alternatively, I sometimes suspected that she might be struggling with a mental imbalance, which seemed consistent with her behaviour. This uncertainty only added to the complexity of our situation, making it challenging to navigate our relationship effectively.

I had a multitude of responsibilities to manage simultaneously. My primary quest was to fully recover from the alcoholism that had consumed three years of my life. Maintaining my official duties to ensure a steady income was my second priority. Thirdly, I was committed to attending to my family's needs and demands. To fulfil this, I would travel to my hometown almost every weekend. Additionally, I began to focus on the upkeep of our ancestral village property, a responsibility I had previously neglected.

In this period, my life became a complex tapestry of overlapping tasks and responsibilities. Yet, despite the challenges, life was transforming at an incredible pace, drawing energy from an unseen source. It felt as though an invisible companion was walking alongside me, guiding me through the most difficult times. Solutions would emerge in sequence, often miraculously, providing exits from seemingly insurmountable situations. This journey was not just about managing multiple responsibilities but also about navigating a profound transformation that was unfolding in my life.

Throughout my journey, I was tested on every front, compelled to witness, realize, and move forward despite the challenges. No circumstance could deter my path, as I was driven by a profound sense of resilience. Though deeply hurt by people and situations, I consistently found the strength to rise again and take action. I felt a strong conviction that a powerful, supreme force was operating alongside me, urging me not to succumb to the physical trials orchestrated by those around me. These individuals were enacting their own Karmas, which I was destined to witness for reasons beyond my understanding.

(My nuclear family today)

To me, life has become a manifestation of Karmic forces—bundles of energies that we either live through ourselves or observe in others. Emotions, feelings, attachments, detachments, sorrow, suffering, pain, and pleasure are all offshoots of the Karmic bundle we carry within us. It's akin to a process of de-accumulation, where we gradually burn away these Karmic debts. In my case, as with others, living out these Karmic accounts was a necessary step toward liberation, a process of burning them to ashes and moving forward unencumbered.

Chapter - 8

Celestial Control from the Sacred Himalayas

In the summer of 2011, I relocated to Wazirabad, an urban village in North Delhi, situated beyond the University of Delhi. The decision to move there was influenced by the proximity of one of my first cousins, who lived nearby. I settled on the ground floor of a double-story building in an area that, while part of Delhi's urban sprawl, retained its village-like charm. The locality was characterized by its quietness, contrasting with the city's usual hustle and bustle. Outside my house stood a majestic Neem tree, which added a serene touch to the surroundings and became a source of quiet delight.

Wazirabad, like many urban villages in Delhi, offered a unique blend of rural and urban elements. Despite being engulfed by the city's expansion, it preserved certain traditional features while adapting to modern urban life. The area remained relatively calm and unassuming, making it an ideal place for someone like me who preferred to maintain a low profile. This shift marked a new chapter in my life, providing both a physical and emotional space for reflection and renewal amidst the challenges I was navigating.

During this period, my official assignment allowed me the flexibility to work from home most of the time. Although I was provided an office space on the first floor of the Delite Cinema building in central Delhi, near Asif Ali

Road, I would only visit it once or twice a week. The rest of my work was handled from home, enabling me to focus on my responsibilities while maintaining a low profile. My role also required frequent travel, with trips to Mumbai almost twice a month and visits to South Indian states like Andhra Pradesh, Karnataka and Tamil Nadu.

In June 2011, amidst the scorching summer heat, I found myself feeling extraordinarily restless. An internal wave seemed to sweep through me day and night, leaving me sleepless and unsettled. I often stood outside at night, gazing at the majestic Neem tree and the open sky, trying to make sense of the turmoil within. While everything appeared normal outwardly, I could sense something profoundly abnormal happening inside me. It felt as though an unseen force was communicating with my mind, repeatedly urging me with the words, *"Pithoragarh jao"* (go to Pithoragarh).

This message was so vivid and persistent that I felt like a direct recipient of a cosmic calling. For three days, I waited for this feeling to subside, but it remained unchanged. Pithoragarh, known for its Himalayan beauty and spiritual significance, seemed to hold some unknown purpose for me. This mysterious pull marked the beginning of what felt like a transformative phase in my life—one driven by forces beyond my comprehension.

Feeling an unshakeable urge to visit Pithoragarh, I sought guidance from my cousin, Bibhuti, who kindly explained the route. Early one morning, around 7 am, I reconfirmed the directions with him before heading to the bus depot. Upon arrival, I spotted an Almora-bound AC bus, with the conductor calling out for passengers, 'Almora, Almora.' It felt as though his call was directed specifically at me, prompting me to board the bus. To my surprise, one of the front seats was vacant, as if reserved for me. As I settled in, the bus began moving slowly, and outside, a gentle drizzle started to fall, creating a serene backdrop to what felt like the beginning of a transformative journey. The synchronicity of events—boarding the bus just as it was departing and finding a seat waiting for me—felt almost divine, as if the universe was guiding me toward Pithoragarh with a purpose.

As I arrived in Almora around 8 pm, the initial urge to continue to Pithoragarh mysteriously dissipated, as if it had never existed. Settling into a hotel in the heart of Almora, I felt a sense of peace with this unexpected change of plans. However, by the next morning, a new and unexplained desire emerged—to visit Dwarahat. Without fully understanding why, I felt compelled to act on this impulse. I promptly booked a cab at the hotel reception and soon found myself on the winding Himalayan roads, heading toward Dwarahat. The scenic drive through the mountains only added to the sense of mystery and anticipation that accompanied this unplanned detour. It felt as though the universe was subtly guiding my journey, redirecting me toward a purpose yet to be revealed.

For those unfamiliar with Dwarahat's significance in the Indian spiritual landscape, it's essential to highlight its profound importance. Located in the Almora district of Uttarakhand, Dwarahat serves as a gateway to the majestic Dunagiri mountain range, home to the revered Dunagiri Mata temple. This region is deeply intertwined with the spiritual journeys of Shri Lahiri Mahashaya and Shri Mahavatar Babaji. In 1861, Lahiri Mahashaya is believed to have had his first physical encounter with Babaji in the Dunagiri region, including his initiation into Kriya Yoga atop the Dunagiri mountains. This pivotal event occurred during Lahiri Mahashaya's brief transfer to the area by his British employers.

Shri Mahavatar Babaji is said to have orchestrated these events, explaining to Lahiri Mahashaya, *"I am the one who caused your transfers. And this is for a purpose. Once that is completed, you will be sent back to where you have come from. And then, for the rest of your life, you will live out of Varanasi."* This divine intervention underscores the area's role as a spiritual link, where profound mystical experiences and initiations have taken place.

(Shri Lahiri Mahashaya had lived in and around Dunagiri, Dwarahat and Ranikhet for about a month or even more before returning to Danapur, Bihar).

As I embarked on my journey to Dwarahat in the last week of June 2011, I was driven by an inexplicable urge, unaware of the purpose or destination of my travel. Approaching Dwarahat via Ranikhet around 10 am, I felt a sense of uncertainty about what lay ahead—whether it was a person, a place, or an experience that awaited me. However, as the Taxi journeyed beyond Ranikhet, I began to lose consciousness, and my memories of the subsequent events were shrouded in mystery. Subsequently, I became fully unconscious.

When I regained consciousness nearly twenty-four hours later, I found myself in a government hospital bed in Almora district. Disoriented and struggling to recall the events that had led to my hospitalization, I inquired with the guard-like-person seated beside my bed about who had brought me there. His response was enigmatic, repeating *'tum jao, tum jao'* ("you go, you go") with an air of mystery. Still hallucinating but physically stable, I left the hospital compound into the gentle drizzle of the Himalayas, surrounded by an aura of the unknown.

In retrospect, the man seated beside my hospital bed seemed out of place among the hospital staff. His age and appearance—old, unattractive, and thinly-bodied—made him stand out. When I first noticed him, he was intently observing me, as if waiting for something. It's unclear whether he was specifically assigned to watch over me or simply present to ensure I regained my composure. His response to my inquiry about who had brought me to the hospital was mysterious: *'tum jao'* (you go). This simple yet profound phrase, often associated with spiritual guidance or divine intervention, has remained vivid in my memory. The secret surrounding this man and his role in my recovery continues to intrigue me, leaving me with more questions than answers about his identity and purpose.

As I walked uphill, I became acutely aware of my mind's disarray. Strange, fragmented thoughts swirled relentlessly, pulling me into a haze of confusion. My body bore inexplicable dark scars, and my hair had grown unnaturally coarse and thick—physical anomalies that mirrored the turmoil within. My consciousness seemed untethered from reality, drifting toward vague, half-formed memories and events I couldn't grasp. The stillness I once relied on had vanished, replaced by a relentless mental storm.

Exhaustion weighed heavily on me; my legs ached as though I'd trekked for miles, yet I couldn't recall moving at all. Sleep clawed at my senses as I staggered toward the cab station. Amid this chaos, a single word pulsed obsessively in my mind: *Gwaldom*. The name felt foreign yet eerily familiar, as if etched into my soul. It repeated like a mantra—*Gwaldom, Gwaldom, Gwaldom*—each iteration amplifying my distress. My psyche fractured further, torn between the tangible world and this haunting, unseen fixation.

With every step, certainty grew: whatever had happened during those lost hours had left me irrevocably changed. The scars, the fatigue, the spectral whispers of *Gwaldom*—none of it felt ordinary. I was adrift in a waking dream, grappling with forces beyond reason, yet undeniably real.

I experienced a peculiar phenomenon in which, upon closing my eyes, my forehead would transform into a cinematic screen. Initially, it would appear in an ash-like hue, followed by a rapid succession of scenes from different eras—none from my current life. These visions featured people from pre-modern times, often set in rural landscapes with ponds and riverbanks. The characters would appear and disappear swiftly, making it challenging to recall all the details now. This recurring phenomenon significantly disrupted my sleep, as closing my eyes would activate this 'forehead cinema screen', plunging me into a dream-like state while remaining fully conscious. I could remember some of these visions later, while others faded away. Whether day or night, the mere act of closing my eyes was enough to trigger this experience, leading to restlessness and a struggle to maintain normal sleep patterns.

During that period, I found myself overcome with intense emotional vulnerability, often crying uncontrollably like a child. My physical senses seemed dulled, and I spent most of my days lying down, disconnected from the world around me. This behaviour led to mental disorientation, making me wonder if I was succumbing to a psychological or neurological condition. However, I couldn't fully convince myself of this, which is why seeking medical help never seemed like an option.

To my family, I appeared normal, no longer indulging in alcohol and staying at home. My drinking had been a significant part of my daily life until I returned to Delhi and then Muzaffarpur, where my family resided. During this time, I felt an intense longing for my family and wanted to return home sooner. I vividly recall this period as being between the last week of June and the first week of July. Nights were spent staring at the ceiling of my room while my wife slept beside me. I avoided engaging in conversations with family members, preferring silence instead.

This period marked a significant departure from my usual self, both emotionally and behaviourally. The absence of alcohol and the lack of engagement with family members highlighted a profound shift within me, one that was both puzzling and unsettling. Despite the outward appearance of normalcy, I was grappling with internal turmoil, unsure of what was happening or how to navigate these changes.

During this transformative period, I continued to eat the same home-cooked meals as my family members. However, a significant change occurred: my desire for alcohol, which had been a staple of my evenings until then, began to wane. This marked a crucial step in my detoxification process. As the days passed, my appetite increased, and I found myself moving toward a state of detoxed normalcy. The absence of alcohol and the shift in my dietary habits were contributing to a profound cleansing of both body and mind.

As I struggled through those sleepless days, I felt both physically restless and mentally lost. The constant barrage of visuals that appeared whenever I closed my eyes only added to my distress. In this state, I began to lose hope about returning to a normal life, convinced that some unknown ailment had taken hold of me. My family remained unaware of the turmoil I was experiencing, and I found myself uncertain about how to share my struggles with them. As a result, I faced this challenge alone, grappling with the uncertainty and fear that accompanied it.

This period was marked by a sense of isolation, as I navigated the uncharted territory of my own mind and body without external support. The lack of sleep and the persistent visions made it difficult to distinguish reality from illusion, further exacerbating my feelings of despair and confusion. Despite the challenges, this solitary journey became a catalyst for introspection and self-discovery, ultimately leading to a deeper understanding of myself and the world around me.

Chapter - 9

A Mysterious Guru from Gyan-Ganj

On the night of July 6, 2011, I lay awake in the stillness of midnight, my gaze fixed on the ceiling. My wife slept soundly beside me, while outside, the sky unleashed a torrent of rain. Suddenly, a wave of intense heat swept through my room, and I began to sweat profusely, feeling increasingly restless. The urge to rise from bed and take a walk was overwhelming, yet I remained frozen in place. With my eyes closed, I found myself witnessing episodes from a realm I couldn't quite grasp. My body and mind seemed to synchronize, as if anticipating something profound. Suddenly, in the centre of my lower forehead, between the eyebrows, a brilliant flash of yellow light appeared, radiant like a shell bursting with unimaginable brightness.

The shell-like light remained for a few seconds before transforming into a milky white hue, maintaining its shape and radiating an unimaginable illumination. Both the yellow and milky white lights shared the same shell-like form and centred on the middle of my forehead. Internally, I felt a profound sense of blankness, as if my mind had transcended its normal functioning. Something extraordinary was unfolding, and I was acutely aware of it. The atmosphere within and outside my room had shifted, imbued with a new aura that was both serene and powerful.

I sensed the presence of a high-spirited being outside my room, a feeling that was both calming and awe-inspiring.

Simultaneously, a gentle voice whispered in the background, *"pahchano swayam ko, ye ho tum"* *(recognize yourself, this is who you are)*. I was fully cognizant of this presence, enveloped by a sense of divine intervention that controlled my entire being. A profound feeling of bodilessness enveloped me, as if I were lifted into the air. My consciousness ascended, rising above the material realm, transcending the boundaries of the physical world.

After the voice delivered its message, the background sound faded into silence. I lay flat on my back with my eyes closed for a while, feeling the stillness that had settled over my forehead, which had previously been turbulent. The heavy rain outside had ceased, and an absolute peace enveloped me, both internally and externally. My body felt light, as if floating in the air, though I was physically weak and feeble. Yet, I felt fully empowered.

I rose to my feet and began walking around the room and outside, my movements guided by an unseen force. My wife, still fast asleep, was unaware of the profound transformation I had undergone. I gently but firmly woke her and asked for a new yellow Dhoti, a request that initially puzzled her. I repeated my request more clearly, and she understood. She brought me a new yellow Dhoti, which I then tore into two pieces. I took a shower, covering my lower body with one piece and my upper body with the other. Returning to my bed, I sat down with my head slightly tilted backward, ready to embark on a new journey, both physically and spiritually.

As I sat with my eyes closed, my gaze turned upward, much like the serene posture often depicted in images of Shri Mahavatar Babaji. My forehead was calm, yet I felt a deep, pulsating sensation at my Agyan Chakra. I remained in this state for some time, until the voice spoke to me once more. This time, the tone was shorter and more concise, like a gentle teacher offering guidance. *"Tum ek shuddhatma ho. Shri Guru ne mujhe tumse sampark karne ka aadesh diya hai.*

Tum aise hee dhyan karte raho" (You are purest of souls. The great Master has ordered me to be in touch with you. You are advised to keep meditating). The voice was clear and distinct, as if I were listening to a conversation on a phone-call. Though I couldn't see the speaker, I felt a deep connection to his words.

As I listened, my mind and body synchronized, lifting me into a state beyond earthly dimensions. My breathing became irregular, and I experienced an upward flow of energy from my navel through my Sahasrara, the crown chakra. My body felt ablaze, generating intense heat that made me sweat profusely. Yet, in this meditative state, I transcended my physical form, witnessing my spirit soar through the majestic Himalayan terrains. Layer by layer, the higher Himalayas unfolded before me, and I could see the galaxy glittering as I traversed cosmic space. This journey was both exhilarating and profound, a testament to the boundless potential of the human spirit.

My initial conversation with the Himalayan Guru, who had introduced himself as being in touch with me from Gyan-Ganj, lasted for a few minutes. Convinced that I was genuinely interacting with someone and not experiencing a mere hallucination, I began to engage in a dialogue with him. For the sake of clarity, I will present our conversation in English, though it originally took place in Hindi. I recall posing several worldly questions to him, which I will outline below:

Me: Who are you?

Answer: I am .... (but you are requested not to reveal my name to any one). I am in touch with you following an order from Shri Guru (the great Master), who asked me to be your mentor. And therefore, I am going to be in touch with you.

Me: Where are you speaking with me from?

Answer: I am located at Gyan-Ganj in the uppermost Himalayan region.

Me: Why are you in touch with me? Any specific reasons? I happen to be a worldly person who has been involved in drinking and eating non-vegetarian food. I considered myself to be impure to enter into any spiritual discourses.

Answer: As I told you before, following an order of Shri Guru, I am in touch with you to provide some mentoring support. I have been told that you were a Shuddhatma (a pure soul). All of the elementals you have referred to me just now will be washed away in due course. You keep on meditating. I will revisit you tomorrow at the same time, between 8-9 pm.

I was awestruck by the two unimaginable experiences that had unfolded before me. My meditative state had reached an unprecedented level of depth and diversity, leaving me incredulous about the profound sensations coursing through my body. The cosmic intervention that accompanied these experiences was equally astonishing, as if the universe itself was orchestrating this transformation.

The first night's experience was both fascinating and unsettling, plunging me into deep contemplation. Yet, the meditative experiences that followed filled me with an overwhelming sense of bliss and extraordinary fulfilment. My entire being was enveloped in absolute pleasure, as if every fibre of my existence was saturated with joy and contentment. This dichotomy—between the initial bewilderment and the subsequent bliss—marked the beginning of a profound spiritual journey, one that would continue to unfold with each passing day.

The first night of spontaneous and intense meditation lasted about an hour, after which I finally succumbed to a deep sleep—a welcome respite after ten sleepless nights. The next morning, I woke up feeling refreshed and light, both in mind and body, still wearing the yellow Dhoti from my meditation the previous night. I descended to the living room on the ground floor and gathered my family, including my two school-going children. With a sense of conviction, I made a vow before them: *"From today onward, I will abstain from consuming non-vegetarian food and alcohol."* Although they listened attentively, they were sceptical, having heard similar promises from me before. Yet, this time felt different, as if a profound shift had occurred within me.

Following the profound experience on July 6, my body felt incredibly light, as if floating in the air. The hangovers that had plagued me for so long had vanished, and my mind remained mostly blank throughout the day. My forehead, once a site of turmoil, was now at peace. Whenever I closed my eyes, even during mundane tasks, I would vividly see Shri Kailash and its surroundings, as if standing right before the sacred mountain. The descending plains around it were equally clear, and I would often gaze at these visions with my eyes shut. Sometimes, when my eyes remained closed for longer periods, my breathing would slow, and I would experience a transcendental shift, moving beyond physical dimensions into a realm of cosmic solitude where tranquility and peace reigned supreme.

My family noticed that I was often quiet with my eyes closed, lost in contemplation. My wife, a teacher at a management college, was frequently away, and my children were in school, leaving me ample time for personal reflection. This solitude allowed me to focus on my spiritual endeavours without distraction. Interestingly, my office in Mumbai, where I worked as a Senior Director of a Public Health communication program, barely contacted me during this period. It was as if the universe had collaborated to give me the space I needed for this profound transformation. This was the year 2011, a time of significant spiritual awakening for me.

The next day unfolded peacefully, with no urge for alcohol surfacing. I spent most of my time in quiet contemplation, occasionally closing my eyes to experience higher dimensions. I interacted minimally with family members and outsiders, preferring to stay within my own introspective space. I eagerly anticipated my meditation time at 8 pm, having earlier purchased a new meditation carpet to enhance my sessions. As the appointed hour arrived, I sat in meditation at the same spot as the previous night.

With my eyes closed, my physical breathing gradually suspended, and I felt the activation of a cosmic breath. I was uplifted, and just then, the familiar voice reappeared, saying, "*Tum aa gaye, main tumhari hee pratiksha me tha. Dhyan karte raho, main tumhare saath bana rahunga*" (*Good, that you have returned. I was waiting for you. Keep meditating. I will continue to stay in touch with you*). As I meditated, I transcended into realms beyond comprehension. I soared across hills and high-rise mountains, sometimes venturing into higher domains where galaxies and star clusters unfolded before me.

Occasionally, I would settle at my Agyan Chakra, witnessing differently coloured suns that would appear and then fade away. These visions were so vivid that they seemed to be viewed through open eyes. At times, a bright star would emerge and slowly disappear. Throughout my meditation on the second day, my Guru was present, watching over me from an unseen dimension. His narrative began to unfold, guiding me through the mystical journey.

He: '*Tum Shri Guru ke atyant priye ho, unhi ke aadesh se main tumhare sampark me noon. Aur abhi se main tumhare saath bana rahunga.*'

(The message I received was both reassuring and profound: "*You are dear to Shri Guru, the Great Master. Following his own orders, I am with you. I have been asked to continue being in close association with you and that I will stay on.)"* This guidance underscored the sacred bond between a Guru and a disciple, where the Guru serves as a divine channel, offering wisdom and mentorship to aid the disciple's spiritual growth. The assurance of continued guidance reflected the Guru's commitment to my spiritual journey, emphasizing the importance of sustained meditation and receptivity to divine wisdom. This connection was not merely a physical presence but an inner link that transcended boundaries, operating through subtle dimensions of consciousness to awaken my dormant spiritual potential.

Myself: aap kiss Shri Guru kee baat kar rahe hain?

(Which Shri Guru are you talking about?

He: Shri Guru Mahavatar Babaji!

Myself: kya mujhe unke darshan prapt honge?

(Will I be able to get to see him?)

He: unki jaisi kripa

(It is at his will)

Myself: kya main aapko dekh sakta hoon?

(Can I see you?)

He: haan, uchit samay par aisa sambhav hai.

(Yes, it is possible at the right time).

Myself: mere liye aur kya aadesh hain.

(What else am I supposed to be doing?)

He: Abhi tum bus dhyan kiya karo. Jo aage hona hai, wo Shri Guru ke aadesh se main karta rahunga.

(For now, you just concentrate on your meditation. Rest of everything will be guided by me following the gracious guidance of Shri Mahavatar Babaji).

As the Guru's words concluded that evening, I slipped into a profound transcendental state, where my consciousness transcended the boundaries of mind and body. The next few minutes remain a blur, lost in the depths of my inner journey. Upon returning to normalcy, I felt my body light and my mind almost empty, with a gentle heat emanating from my being. My physical breathing had become thin, replaced by a subtle beam of energy rising from my navel through my crown chakra. The cosmic spectacle I witnessed was beyond words—a divine play that left me speechless and my senses dormant.

My family, unaware of this inner transformation, saw only my quiet demeanour. I shared fragments of my experience with my wife, who, having been initiated into Kriya Yoga by a revered Guru, could grasp some aspects of this spiritual metamorphosis. However, the full depth of my journey remained unspoken, not because I chose to conceal it, but because such experiences defy verbal expression. How could I convey the sensation of breath becoming light or the dissolution of mountains into stardust?

As I had previously mentioned, I transitioned to a vegetarian diet and completely abstained from alcohol, feeling no inclination toward these habits anymore. Throughout the day, I would remain at home with my eyes closed, navigating the realms of the fourth dimension. My days unfolded in blissful tranquility, untroubled by any disturbances from the office. When my wife inquired about my office responsibilities and attendance, I would respond with conviction and clarity, *"Unless I choose to engage, my office won't bother me".*

On the third evening, at the appointed hour of 8 pm, I returned to meditation, having spent the day in blissful anticipation of the evening's spiritual intensity. As I sat, I sensed my Guru's presence nearby, though at a distance, yet feeling intimately close. He spoke once more, *"Achha hai, tum aa gaye, chalo, dhyan me doob jao"* (Good that you have returned, now dive deep into meditation). As my physical breathing began to suspend, I felt myself ascending to a higher plane, guided by an unseen force. In an instant,

I found myself standing before the majestic Holy Kailash. I saw my own form standing in front of the divine dome, where a long vertical crack was visible. Under the serene moonlight, I watched my body walking around the rocky surfaces, descending down the dome. I was alone, with no other human presence in sight, standing tall before the brightly shining holy mountain.

As I continued my spiritual journey, I found myself standing beside the serene waters of Lake Manasarovar. The tranquility of the lake, revered for its spiritual potency in multiple traditions, enveloped me. I sat down, and suddenly, I sensed a presence behind me. It was my Guru, appearing in a subtle yet fully formed shape, though his face remained unseen. He guided me to take some water from the lake and anoint my body with it, which I did as instructed. His next words were both profound and mysterious: *"Abhi se tumhara adhyatmik naam .... hoga"* ("From now on, you will bear the spiritual name of ...."). As advised, I am not to reveal this name publicly. With these words, he continued to impart more wisdom that evening:

'*Bhavishya me tum aadhyatmik sthano ka bhraman karoge. Aur dheere dheere tumhara adhyatmik utthaan hoga*'.

(In years to follow, you will visit places of spiritual significance. And you will spiritually uplift yourself in due course).

'*Shri Guru ke aadesh ke anusaar, main sukshma roop me tumhare saath har samay bana rahunga. Tum jahan bhi rahoge, tum mujhe apne paas hee paaoge*'.

(As per the orders of Shri Guru, I will always be with you in subtle form. Wherever you will be, you will find me there with you all the time).

'*Aaane wale samay me tum adhyatmik prakriti ke logo se miloge aur unka saanidhya prapt karoge*'. *Un sabhi ki vilakshan urja se tum anupranit hote rahoge*'.

(In time to unfold, you will get to meet people of spiritual traits and qualifications. Their energy will continue to guide your own spiritual journey forward).

'Main nirdisht samay par phir tumhare seedhe sampark me aunga. Ab tum apne dhyan me kendrit ho jao'.

(I will return to you per the designated schedule. You may continue to concentrate on your meditation now).

As the discourse unfolded, I found myself in a transcendental state, partially disconnected from the physical realm. My entire being was enveloped by an energy field that transcended the dimensions I knew. With my Guru's narrative concluding, my consciousness turned inward, and a surge of cosmic energy began flowing in and out of my body. Interestingly, the meditation mat I sat on started becoming wet from beneath its surface. I continued meditating for nearly another hour, deeply immersed in the spiritual dimensions surrounding Holy Kailash and Lake Manasarovar.

That evening, my consciousness was centred around this mystical realm, often filled with visions of Kailash, the holy lake, and the rugged terrains. Alongside these visions, I encountered beings who did not belong to our physical world but seemed to inhabit another territory. They would appear and disappear in flashes, sometimes lingering for a brief moment. Although I couldn't identify most of them, a few would occasionally draw close, causing me a momentary sense of discomfort. Yet, I remained undeterred by their presence and felt no fear whatsoever.

The vision of my previous life: On one of those evenings, I was in the deepest contemplative state of being, submerged in the totality of myself. A few black and white images started to appear. In the middle of that, I began to find myself wearing a police uniform surrounded by a few other policemen. The individual I had become was tall, fair and handsome. I saw myself standing in front of a police station that bore its name in Bengali. People around me also spoke that language. Someone else I saw emerged from somewhere (probably my senior) calling my name 'Vishwajeet'. I received some instructions from him. And then, next I found myself trying to diffuse an explosive article at an unidentifiable location. And suddenly, the article I was trying to manage was busted. Next was an absolute blackout. I continued with my meditation but later in the same session I was absorbed in breathless tranquility with a load of energy emanating out of the naval flowing out of my crown chakra. Towards the end of the session, I received a cosmic message *"tumne Vishwajeet Chakravarti ke roop me bhi ek janma dharan kiya tha kuchh samay ke liye Bangal me"* (you had lived briefly as Vishwajeet Chakravarti in your previous lives in Bengal).

Post that evening meditation, I became more thoughtful than maintaining the normal state of bliss. I often found myself preoccupied with memories and thoughts of the profound experiences I had undergone in recent days and nights. These recollections would frequently resurface, enveloping my thoughts and making me feel somewhat encapsulated. I had a persistent sense of being accompanied by a presence, which became increasingly evident to me. It reached a point where I felt that my Guru's presence was actively involved in my life, handling many tasks with minimal effort from me. Whenever I encountered a problem, it would somehow resolve itself with less of my direct involvement. My body seemed to act merely as a medium, while the presence guided and facilitated the resolution of challenges.

I found myself in a state of dilemma, yearning to share the extraordinary experiences unfolding within me, yet uncertain about who to confide in. The fear of being met with scepticism or dismissal by those with a worldly mindset held me back. Months later, I travelled to Jaipur and sought out reverend Gurudev Swami Bhuvneshwaranand ji, whom I trusted could provide insight. Upon meeting him, I recounted the events that had transpired, and he listened attentively. After a moment of contemplative silence, he shared his thoughts: *"Jo tumhare saath hua, wo do hee awastha me hota hai. Ya to vyakti ki mansik sthiti theek nahi ho, ya vyakti par vishesh daiviye kripa huyi ho. Mansik star par to tum mujhe swasth dikhai padate ho"* (*Whatever you have narrated to me happens only in two situations. One in which a person is suffering from a mental disorder and the second that the person has received a special divine grace. In your case, to me you don't appear to be suffering from a mental imbalance*). His brief yet profound words were enough to address many of the questions that had been troubling my mind for months.

Chapter - 10

Astral Travel to Gyan-Ganj

My Guru communicated with clarity and precision, engaging in a month-long discourse that transcended conventional dialogue. During this period, all my questions seemed to resonate with him intuitively, and he would respond without needing me to articulate them. His guidance was both eloquent and direct, offering profound insights into my present life and future, some of which have been shared in previous chapters. This experience embodies the essence of spiritual mentorship, where the mentor not only provides wisdom but also serves as a catalyst for inner growth, helping the individual navigate their spiritual path with clarity and purpose.

Under the direct supervision of my Guru, my meditation deepened significantly. On certain evenings, I would sense his presence around me, though we would not exchange words. During these periods, I experienced profound dimensional shifts within my body. It became common for me to perceive my astral form outside my physical body, witnessing my own self with clarity. Occasionally, I would see my consciousness concentrate at my Agya Chakra, transforming my being into a Shiva Lingam—sometimes small, sometimes larger than the normal. A blue star would often play hide and seek on my forehead, occasionally focusing between my eyebrows for a few seconds, shining with a soothing intensity. Sometimes,

I would see the star concentrate in between my eyebrows for a few seconds.

The appearance of milky white light above my forehead became a routine phenomenon, as did the sun shining precisely in the centre of my forehead. This sun was brighter than the physical one we see outside, and its colours would change—yellow and deep red being the most common. Each time I experienced these visions, I remembered Shri Lahiri Mahashaya, who documented similar patterns in his meditation diaries. His expression, *"Hum uuhe surooj"* (Me, the same Sun), resonated deeply with me, symbolizing the unity of the self with the divine light.

One evening, as I sat in meditation, I witnessed a breathtaking phenomenon: my spinal cord transformed into a beam of light, pulsing with an intense yellow energy that flowed upward into an expansive space of light. The sheer volume of energy boiling within this beam left me awestruck. These extraordinary experiences, though challenging to contain, were becoming more manageable with divine grace, allowing me to keep them within myself.

On another evening, I felt a profound sensation: my own nectar began to drip from above my tongue, spreading throughout my oral cavity with a sweetness that defied comparison. This taste, unlike anything I had ever known, would linger for hours after each meditation session. As multiple drops continued to fall, the sweetness intensified, leaving me in a state of wonder.

As these experiences deepened, my body began to feel incredibly light, as if it were dissolving into nothingness. I felt as light as air, and whenever I closed my eyes, I would ascend into space. This sensation of weightlessness and transcendence was both exhilarating and humbling, reflecting a profound shift in my consciousness and connection to the divine.

Occasionally, my Guru would interject with insightful statements during my meditative sessions. These moments of guidance were pivotal, as his words, though brief, carried profound wisdom and served to deepen my understanding and spiritual growth. The timing of his interventions seemed almost intuitive, as if he were attuned to the precise moments when his guidance would resonate most deeply within me. This subtle yet powerful communication underscored the transformative role of a spiritual mentor, who not only imparts knowledge but also fosters inner awakening and connection to higher states of consciousness.

'Tumhare dhyan kee gati achhi hai, ise poori pratibaddhata se dharan kiye raho. Main tumhare saath bana hua hoon'.

(You are maintaining a good pitch of meditation. Stay committed to it. I am continuing to be in close contacts with you).

During my leisure time on ordinary days, I would often remain at home, maintaining silence and reflecting on the extraordinary experiences I had been having. These recollections left me in awe, yet I managed to contain my emotions. I was acutely aware of my Guru's presence around me at all times. Moreover, I felt that my physical being, mind, and intelligence were under the direct influence of celestial powers beyond Earth's orbit.

One evening, as my Guru appeared to me, I found myself walking with him across the rocky plains at the foothills of Holy Kailash. He moved behind me like a shadow, invisible yet palpable. Occasionally, I sensed his presence beside me. I had requested him to reveal his full form, and he graciously granted my wish. For a brief moment, I saw him as a tall, serene figure with a long beard, clad in a dhoti, radiating light from his being. His appearance reminded me of Shri Rabindranath Thakur—dressed in a kurta and wrapped in a shawl, with his dhoti reaching just above his knees.

Following this encounter, my meditative practice gained momentum. The outflow of nectar intensified that evening, and for the first time, I began to hear the cosmic sound—a continuous hum, like "huuuuuuuuuum" or the reverberation of 'Oem Oem and Oem'. This experience marked a significant milestone in my spiritual journey, deepening my connection with higher consciousness and the divine.

Following my evening meditation sessions, I would often find myself in a state of profound silence, unable to speak even when my wife asked me questions. Despite this, I maintained a disciplined routine, adhering to regular times for eating and sleeping. Occasionally, during the morning hours, I would share fragments of my experiences with my wife, guided by the understanding that she, having been initiated into the Kriya tradition by the revered Shri Bhuvneshwaranand, could grasp the transformative shifts I was undergoing. Her background in Kriya Yoga made her a trusted companion in this spiritual journey, allowing me to confide in her about the profound changes unfolding within me.

As my spiritual journey deepened, my daily life became increasingly organized, transitioning from an erratic lifestyle to one marked by discipline and routine. The metaphysical shifts I was experiencing had both direct and indirect impacts on my physical life, noticeable not just to me but also to those around me. However, during this period, I had largely disengaged from my professional duties. Despite this, I was convinced that I was being guided away from these responsibilities for a reason. My wife expressed concern about my absence from work, but I would reassure her firmly, *"By divine grace, I will regain my professional momentum once this period unfolds. No one from the office will contact me unless I desire it."* It was remarkable how I found the courage to make such statements with conviction.

And remarkably, events unfolded exactly as I had declared: I remained disconnected from office affairs for a month without receiving a single call from colleagues or supervisors.

As my meditation continued daily, the universe unfolded itself in profound ways. One evening, I transcended my physical breathing and found myself walking past Mount Kailash through rugged terrain, illuminated by the soft glow of moonlight. I was ascending to a higher plane, moving north-westward around the holy mountain, surrounded by a desolate yet majestic landscape devoid of trees and human presence. The ground beneath my feet was scattered with rocky chips and thorny grasses. In the distance, a house-like structure began to emerge, radiating a warm yellow light that seemed to emanate from within. As I drew closer, I realized that this structure was infused with a cosmic light, which reflected from every corner without the need for artificial illumination. The presence of need-based yellow lights everywhere underscored the mystical nature of this place, where divine energy seemed to permeate every aspect.

As I continued my journey, I found myself drawn toward the structure, which was marked by a large open gate. The complex spanned at least an acre, with concrete pagodas standing sentinel at each corner. The two front pagodas, clearly visible to me, resembled the crowning features of a temple. I approached the gate as if being gently pulled into this serene realm, my footsteps the only sound in the stillness. There were no other human beings in sight, just my own presence amidst this tranquil setting.

Upon reaching the entrance, I passed through a long wall that served as a divider, guiding me toward further openings on both sides. I turned left, entering a spacious courtyard surrounded by long verandas on three sides. This vast open area was bathed in a soft, ethereal light, creating an atmosphere of profound peace and tranquility.

As I paused in the courtyard, I was mesmerized by the breathtaking view before me. The veranda, lined with several arches set deep within thick clay walls, seemed to radiate a serene elegance. The walls, polished to a subtle sheen, reflected light from an unseen source, imbuing the space with an ethereal glow. Within each arch, I saw Yogis seated in profound meditation, their bodies aglow with an intensely powerful cosmic light. Most of them appeared to be elderly, with an elderly lady seated in the first arch on the left. The aura surrounding them was unimaginably soothing, filling the air with a sense of deep tranquility.

I continued walking, bowing in reverence before each arch and the Yogi, my movements a testament to the profound respect I felt for this sacred space. As I moved through the courtyard, I noticed a few young men clad in short white loincloths and long shirts, quietly attending to their duties. The atmosphere was marked by complete silence, with no one speaking to another. This experience encapsulated the essence of a mystical realm, where spiritual seekers encounter profound energies and enlightenment.

As I moved past the three sides of the veranda, I felt as though I was levitating rather than walking, my movement seemingly guided by an unseen force. The entire scene appeared to be predestined, unfolding with a sense of inevitability. My Guru was nowhere to be seen, and I didn't feel the need to search for him. From within the courtyard, I discovered a connecting entrance leading to a larger, second courtyard. Here, I encountered about ten-eleven Yogis seated in their respective arches, each with long matted hair and thick beards, radiating a similar intensity of light as those in the first courtyard. The atmosphere remained silent and reverent, with no one speaking to me or to each other.

In this second courtyard, I also noticed younger Yogis walking about, carrying various items in their hands. The seated Yogis seemed to embody immortality, their presence transcending the bounds of time. Even now, thirteen years later, as I reflect on these experiences, I can recall only a few of their faces. The revered Yogini bore a resemblance to Maa Anandmayi, though in a larger physical form. One of the male Yogis looked similar to Brahma Baba, the founder of the Brahma Kumaris, while another resembled Shri Lahiri Mahasaya in a larger human form. Most of the others, however, remain indistinct in my memory. I eventually made my exit through another gate situated between the second flank.

As I transitioned back to my physical level of consciousness during meditation, I found myself drenched in sweat, with my entire body radiating intense heat. The experiences of that evening were overwhelming, making it difficult to contain them. Although I had returned to my normal state, I struggled to speak and instead chose to remain silent, lost in contemplation of the profound journey I had just undergone. Despite sitting normally, my physical breathing was almost suspended, and my navel breathing was so subtle that I had to focus to perceive it—a true state of breathlessness.

In many ways, I witnessed the magical play of cosmic consciousness manifesting through my physical form. I had transcended earthly consciousness, and for that moment, I felt disconnected from my family members around me. They were present, yet I felt no emotional attachment to them. I maintained a state of neutrality, observing everything as a detached witness. It was as if I was the cause of this state, yet simultaneously, I was merely observing it unfold.

The repeated appearance of Mount Kailash had become a common sight for me, visible in both the broad daylight and under the celestial glow of the moon and stars. I could discern the intricate curves, turns, and twists of its topography, as well as the uneven spread of its plains. The mountain's colours would change frequently, sometimes appearing painted in golden hues and at other times displaying a kaleidoscope of colours. One evening, I had a vivid vision of a tall figure in golden light standing atop Kailash. The clarity of this vision was as if I were seeing it with my naked eyes, despite the distance. The figure was none other than Shri Mahavatar Babaji. As soon as I beheld him, I received the answer to my unspoken question about his identity, along with the message that Kailash was his abode. This revelation came from the same dimension as the other phenomena I had experienced. With these encounters, I was left in awe of how my human body had become a vessel for the magical manifestations of the cosmos.

'There is something beyond our mind which abides in silence within our mind. It is the supreme mystery beyond thought. Let one's mind and one's subtle body rest upon that and not rest on anything else' (Maitri Upanishad)

As these extraordinary events unfolded, I found myself drifting away from my routine mental state, feeling disconnected from my body, mind, family, and the collective world around me. It became increasingly difficult to relate to family and professional affairs, and I was being kept completely disconnected from my offices in Delhi and Mumbai. My being seemed to be under the total control of the cosmos, with the universe flowing out of my physical form in a way I had never imagined. This profound transition was nearing its second week, and my family, particularly my wife, was growing concerned about my inability to attend to my official duties. Despite her own busy schedule and our young children's needs, she remained supportive, while my father maintained a watchful neutrality, with minimal conversation between us. Amidst this backdrop, I continued my meditation sessions as scheduled, deeply immersed in the transformative journey that was unfolding within me.

As I sat in meditation each evening, new dimensions unfolded before me, revealing experiences that I have begun to share. While the Yogic tradition generally advises against disclosing such personal experiences, there have been notable exceptions where spiritual masters have chosen to share their journeys publicly. For instance, Shri Muktananda from Ganeshpuri Ashram documented his profound experiences in *The Play of Consciousness*, offering a glimpse into the mystical realms of Yoga. Similarly, Shri Shivom Teerth of the Shakti-Paat tradition courageously detailed his spiritual journey in his Hindi book *Hriday Manthan*, though it was not widely circulated. These accounts serve as a bridge between the esoteric and the accessible, helping seekers connect with the cosmic phenomena that govern all dimensions. Inspired by these examples, I too felt encouraged to document my experiences, so that future generations might relate to them and be inspired to explore various techniques of self-realization.

During an evening meditation session, as I transcended the physical realm with the gradual suspension of my breathing, I found myself ascending higher and higher into a distant realm, far removed from Earth's surface. The sun's presence faded, and I passed through an intensely powerful glaze of light. The next moment, everything dissolved, and I found myself walking on a surface illuminated by a soft, dusk-like light. The landscape was dotted with numerous high-rise temples, their sharp peaks reaching toward the sky. Some of these structures were so tall that their tops seemed to recline, defying comparison to any physical buildings I had seen. To aid understanding, I might liken some of these temples to the vertical construct of the Eiffel Tower, though they were painted in a maroon hue with grey undertones. There were no houses or human settlements in sight, only barren land with clusters of these majestic temples. The terrain was rocky, with varied elevations, similar to the region around Mount Kailash. My stay in this realm was brief, lasting perhaps a minute or two, before I returned to my physical consciousness, only to embark on another journey.

Meditational journeys are the same as physical journeys. One is never at one place but will keep travelling from one location to the other. Similarly, when one leaves the physical plain and transcends, the spirit wanders around per its own Prakriti. Dualities that we perceive are delusional to our minds but not real. Physical state is the manifestation of the larger subtleties of metaphysical realms. It is the social and environmental conditioning that prevents us from experiencing the state of non-duality. Oneness is all there is, and we are included. *'When you go beyond awareness, there is a state of non-duality, in which there is no cognition, only pure being. In that state of non-duality, all separations cease'*- Nisargadatta Maharaj.

"In the state of Pure Being, the distinction between the natural and the supernatural ceases to exist. When Consciousness is being revealed in its undivided Oneness, some find themselves in a pure Self-conscious Silence ('advaita'), while it presents itself to others as His Divine Play. He is Form ('vigraha'), and at the same time He is not. The word 'samagra' (whole, complete) denotes that 'sama' (equality) comes first and foremost ('agra'). If it is not realized that equality comes first of all, it means that one will still observe from the viewpoint of the world, which is not 'advaita'. Whereas, when 'advaita' has been attained, this signifies the recovery of one's original state."

~ Sri Anandamayi Maa

(From "Words of Sri Anandamayi Maa" Translated and Compiled by Atmananda, page 169)

In our physical making too, there is a gateway provided for, that allows us access to that oneness, the real 'I'. Remember, Jesus!

'The light of the body is the eye:

If therefore thine eye be single,

Thy whole body shall be full of light'.

Becoming 'full of light' is becoming one with the Supreme.

I consistently felt that my mind was being controlled and reconfigured, with my thoughts guided toward shifting my consciousness away from the earthly material plane that I was accustomed to. The upward fixation of my gaze would centre my mind around the Agya Chakra, which served as the primary gateway to the cosmos within. Once I reached this entrance, further upward movements would commence, though the direction was not something I consciously decided. Instead, it changed daily, taking me to different heights. During these experiences, my thoughts would arise and dissipate while my mind remained suspended, largely disconnected from the physical world. The mind would prevail, generating thoughts without attachment to earthly concerns. As the journey gained momentum, a beam of energy would begin flowing into space through the crown chakra. On most occasions, the crown chakra would heat up, signalling the intense flow of eternal energy.

During those extraordinary days, my body underwent experiences so profound that I was uncertain about who could truly understand them. Common individuals would struggle to relate to such phenomena, and I knew no spiritual guide other than Shri Bhuvneshwaranand Ji of Jaipur Ashram. Yet, it seemed that all the questions troubling my mind were being heard by my Guru. In my subsequent meditation sessions, he would return with precise answers to the critical queries my mind grappled with. Beyond addressing these questions with remarkable clarity, he also made predictions about my future and that of my family. He assured me that he would always remain by my side like a shadow and that I would eventually meet people of spiritual calibre as my journey unfolded. He shared insights into several aspects of my life, though for obvious reasons, I choose not to disclose them here.

Those evenings were typically filled with celestial visions and experiences of non-physical subjects, including encounters with non-earthly beings. The timing and duration of these appearances were unpredictable, with some establishing eye contact while others flashed by and faded. I frequently found myself wandering through Himalayan realms, witnessing the majestic peaks one after another. Post-meditation, I would recall these visions with vivid clarity, though some details would elude my memory. The oceanic regions also appeared in my meditations, albeit less frequently, where I would see my spirit soaring over vast expanses of water. Similarly, I would immerse myself in dense forests, walking miles to behold rich flora and fauna. Occasionally, I would pause in a valley of flowers, standing amidst its breathtaking beauty.

During meditation, the Mooladhar Chakra would consistently heat up, signalling the activation of the coiled energy at the base of my spine. As cosmic breathing commenced, this energy would undergo a powerful vibration, propelling me into an almost breathless state. As my meditation intensified, the energy would rise through my spinal cord, ascending toward the higher chakras. On multiple occasions, I envisioned a majestic brown snake—ancient in appearance—emerging from my spine and towering above my head at the crown chakra, its tongue darting in and out. One evening, this serpent took flight, soaring above my being into the high skies before circling back and re-entering my body. These recurring experiences left me enveloped in a profound silence, as if my physical form was being cleansed by cosmic rains. This state of blissful tranquility provided deep insights into the metaphysical systems governing existence—realities that often remain veiled from ordinary perception.

Throughout the first month of my spiritual journey with my Guru, I experienced a multitude of profound encounters. At times, he would appear directly to guide me, while on other occasions, he remained observant without manifesting his presence. It became increasingly clear that these transformative experiences were being orchestrated not only by him but also by other revered masters from a higher dimension. Many of these divine beings would appear to me, radiating an intense, ethereal glow, with long beards and thick hair that seemed to convey an ageless wisdom. Some lingered for a longer duration, while others appeared only for brief moments. Though I was often tempted to engage them in conversation or pose questions, something restrained me from doing so. Later, my Guru would reveal the identities of those I had encountered, providing clarity and insight into these mystical interactions. Out of reverence for his teachings and guidance, I choose not to disclose specific names.

As July 2011 drew to a close, the changes in my spiritual journey, as foretold by my Guru, began unfolding with remarkable clarity. His appearances became less frequent, and our communication gradually diminished, yet I always felt his presence around me, like a constant shadow guiding my path. It seemed as though my body was no longer under my own control; instead, it was being steered by an unseen force while I remained a mere witness to the unfolding events—a phenomenon that continues to this day. The sense of doer-ship had dissolved entirely, replaced by an effortless flow where tasks seemed to accomplish themselves through a higher energy. I often found myself brimming with vitality, completing in a single day what previously took me days or weeks to finish.

This natural flow of consciousness began reshaping my perspective on life. I started perceiving myself as an integral part of the whole, and the cosmos itself seemed to revolve within me. This shift was nothing short of magical, revealing the linkages between the self and the universe in ways that words can scarcely capture.

As time passed, my relationships began to feel increasingly mechanical and temporary, devoid of strong emotional attachment. I found myself naturally drawn to solitude and traveling to spiritually vibrant locations, as if guided by an unseen force. While I remained diligent in fulfilling my worldly responsibilities, especially those related to my family and children, I approached them with a sense of detachment, viewing them as a divine mandate entrusted to me. Every task I undertook seemed to be supported by a divine force operating in the background, allowing me to complete them effortlessly without struggle. On the physical plane, I experienced heightened energy and activity. Professionally, I became more innovatively creative, earning recognition and appreciation from my seniors and supervisors.

Following a month of spiritual sojourn and discourse with my Guru, I began to notice his physical appearances gradually phasing out, as if by divine design. Although his direct presence diminished, I continued to feel his guiding presence around me, like an unseen force that remained constant. His visions would occasionally manifest during meditation, offering reassurance and subtle guidance. Upon returning to Delhi, I faced family apprehensions about my past habits, but I felt an unwavering confidence that divine intervention had eradicated all tendencies toward alcohol and meat consumption. In practice, I found myself no longer drawn to these indulgences.

My personal conduct underwent a profound transformation. I naturally gravitated toward *Maun* (observing silence) and solitude, engaging with others only when necessary. Conversations became infused with spontaneous spiritual insights, as though an inner voice spoke through me. A newfound restlessness to travel and explore spiritually vibrant locations replaced any desire for stagnation. Amidst these changes, my meditation practice continued to unfold new experiences daily.

Among the recurring experiences during my spiritual journey, the vision of my own third eye stood out with striking clarity. It appeared with the vibrancy and intensity reminiscent of Shiva's third eye as depicted on his idols. The pulsating vibration and shifting colours of the third eye were mesmerizing, often lasting for extended periods. Unlike other visions that would swiftly fade, this one felt deeply immersive, inviting me to enter its realm and embark on journeys into celestial dimensions. Physically, I experienced palpitations and vibrations around the lower forehead, where the third eye is located. It felt as though a concentrated energy was accumulating between my eyebrows and gradually ascending into infinite space.

Some visions of the third eye took on unique forms, resembling shells with their heads positioned toward the open expanse above. During such moments, my head would heat up and feel heavy before gradually lightening over time. These experiences not only brought profound physical sensations but also offered glimpses into higher realms of consciousness.

Visions of Shiva Lingams were a recurring theme in my meditations, appearing in diverse forms, shapes, and sizes—sometimes towering at 6-7 feet tall, while other times they were small. Their colours varied from white to black, blue, purple, and red, each hue imbuing the experience with unique spiritual significance. Frequently, my being would be enveloped by these massive Shiva Lingams, and I would become one with them, transcending the boundaries of my physical body. This profound merging occurred often, symbolizing a deep union with the divine. The visions typically manifested in the middle of my forehead, lingering for a while before disappearing. At times, the lingams would rotate, while on other occasions they remained still.

Their visions mostly appeared in the middle of the forehead and would rest for some time. Beyond these experiences, what became increasingly important to me was embracing the candid divine expressions that arose during meditation. Each day brought a new set of experiences and realizations, which helped clear the mind's delusions. This process allowed me to reflect on the true nature of the self, contrasting sharply with how I previously perceived my existence. The journey was transformative, gradually revealing the essence of my being and fostering a deeper understanding of the universe.

A mysterious third eye, horizontal in shape, would frequently manifest at the centre of my forehead, just above the actual location of the third eye. It felt as though someone was gazing at me from a vast distance, yet their singular eye would suddenly come incredibly close, looking onto me with an intense, penetrating glance. The experience was vivid and lifelike, as if a real, living presence was observing me. Each time this vision appeared, it left me slightly shaken due to its sheer intensity and activity. The appearance of this third eye typically lasted for about ten seconds and never repeated within the same meditation session. Its occurrence was entirely beyond my control, manifesting only by divine will. Days or even weeks would pass without such visions, but then, without warning, it would flash during a meditation session. The enigmatic nature of this vision and the profound effect it had on me are beyond words to fully explain.

Another manifestation of the third eye that I witnessed was its vertical placement at the centre of my forehead. It would appear in a latent physical form, as if to remind me of its presence. This third eye remained perfectly still, devoid of any movement. Its size was notably larger than my physical eyes, and it displayed a warm, earthy colour—a blend of brown and yellow. The expression of this third eye was meditative, resembling the intense focus of *tratak*, a state of deep concentration. It would remain visible for about five to six seconds before disappearing from sight.

In Barwani, I felt an irresistible pull toward the sacred Narmada River. Every evening, I would drive to Rajghat, a place of rustic serenity where time seemed to stand still. The river bank retained its ancient charm, appearing unchanged from centuries past. Small hamlets of fisher families dotted both sides of the bank, predominantly on the northern side. A couple of old temples provided refuge for travellers undertaking the *Narmada Parikrama*, walking miles along the river's path. The northern bank often bustled with groups of pilgrims who cooked, feasted, and chanted together until late into the night.

As dusk fell, the riverbank grew strangely quiet and secluded, its solitude both intimidating and alluring. Drawn by its subtleties, I often meditated there once the crowds dispersed. Sitting near a tiny temple dedicated to Maa Narmada, my breath would naturally suspend, leading to a swift upward surge of energy that aligned me with transcendental fields. In those moments, I experienced profound states of non-duality— *'eko hum dwitiyio nasti'*—a realization of oneness and nothingness.

These evenings were transformative, akin to diving into lasting silence and shedding all sense of being. Physically, my body remained fixed, with my gaze transfixed on the infinite layers of sky above. Some meditation sessions extended longer than others; during one such session, I vividly saw my body walking through a smoky corridor—a wide yet narrowly long space enveloped in hazy formations. My body ascended within this corridor, an experience both surreal and deeply spiritual. On other occasions, I encountered non-physical beings in cosmic realms—entities that appeared briefly face-to-face before vanishing into the ether. Each evening at Rajghat was not merely a meditation but a journey into realms beyond physical existence—a sacred communion with the infinite.

Occasionally, my local Project Manager, would accompany me to Rajghat, where I would meditate. He would wait nearby, observing my meditative state with curiosity. Sometimes, he would comment on how my physical demeanour appeared to outsiders, noting that the inner transformation was visibly reflected in my outer being. He mentioned that his gaze would become transfixed while watching me meditate, and occasionally, passersby would approach him with questions about my state, which he would answer humbly.

After about an hour and a half of meditation, I would return to an ashram on the same banks to meet with a Swamiji who resided there in a small dwelling. He was a learned man from West Bengal, who had been living there since his youth. During my interactions with him from 2014 to 2016, I learned that he was around 65 years old and had a habit of smoking cigarettes. He lived a simple life, often surrounded by a few people in the evenings.

Adjacent to his living quarters was a unique, red, pumpkin-sized Shiv Lingam, which he would worship regularly. One evening, when I inquired about it, he shared an intriguing story about its origins and the devastating impact it had on a householder who once kept it. He emphasized that possessing such a Shiv Lingam was not advisable for householders, highlighting its special characteristics and the caution required in handling it.

At Swamiji's ashram, I often encountered Prof. Kapse, the Principal of Barwani's district college, who would arrive every evening after sunset on his motorcycle. He would bring a large, multi-layered lunch carrier from which he would offer home-cooked food to Maa Narmada, a ritual he had been performing for nearly two decades. His dedication was unwavering, only interrupted by his travels away from Barwani. I was intrigued by this daily act of devotion and decided to ask him about it. Prof. Kapse explained that he felt a deep connection with Maa Narmada, and this offering was his way of expressing gratitude and reverence to the sacred river.

One evening, as I sat on the Narmada's banks, Prof. Kapse arrived with his offerings for Maa Narmada. He invited me to join him at the water's edge, where he lit a floating lamp that danced on the river's waves. With a gentle smile, he asked if I would like to feed Maa Narmada with my own hands. I nodded, and as I placed the food items on the water, I felt an unusual sensation—my fingers seemed to vibrate, as if drawn by an unseen force. The experience filled me with a profound cosmic bliss that transcended words. We stood in silence for a moment before returning to the banks, with only a heartfelt gratitude for Prof. Kapse for sharing an experience that felt like a once-in-a-lifetime blessing.

(While preparing to feed Maa Narmada with Prof. Kapse in Barwani)

While my project in Barwani was ongoing, I learned from a colleague that Prof. Kapse was taking voluntary retirement. I decided to meet him during one of my visits, and our last encounter took place at a farewell dinner he had organized at Narmada Ghat at 9 pm. Although I hadn't received a formal invitation, I felt an inexplicable pull to attend. At 8:30 pm, I asked Rakesh to take me to the Narmada Ghat, which was usually our time to return to the city. Upon arrival, we saw a gathering with food being served, but from a distance, we couldn't identify the attendees. As we drew closer, we recognized Prof. Kapse and his colleagues and students. He was visibly surprised to see us, especially at that hour and on such an occasion. He explained it was his farewell party and expressed his unawareness of my presence in town. I reassured him that the physical invitation was needless; I had received his call in a different way. We shared smiles, enjoyed the delicious food, and bid each other farewell. As we parted ways, Prof. Kapse mentioned that he would soon embark on the sacred Narmada Parikrama, a journey of spiritual devotion and self-discovery. This marked our final meeting.

My time in Barwani district and my frequent proximity to the sacred Narmada River spanned two and a half years, concluding in mid-2016. Despite this prolonged engagement, I could never fully grasp the intrinsic divine purpose behind my visits to Barwani or my recurring encounters with the Narmada. However, I grew increasingly convinced that my predestined path was guiding me toward places resonating with high cosmic frequencies and subtle energies.

During my travels across project districts, I often visited different banks of the Narmada, each offering unique tranquility and spiritual depth. Among them, Maheshwar stood out as a place of profound transformation—a site where the sacred river seemed to dissolve subjectivities into objectivities, beings into non-beings, and static existence into dynamic flow. The serenity of Maheshwar's banks felt like stepping into a realm beyond ordinary perception, where the divine essence of the Narmada revealed itself in its purest form.

To truly experience the subtle expressions of divine consciousness, one needed to stay on Maheshwar Ghat post-sunset. The tranquil atmosphere of this sacred site often felt like a gateway to higher realms. Among the many places I was fortunate to visit, Omkareshwar Narmada stood out as another deeply spiritual location, which I had the privilege of exploring multiple times. As my Himalayan Guru had foretold in 2011, *'tum adhyatmik yatrayen karoge' (you will undertake spiritual travels)*, this period of my life was a manifestation of that prophecy, unfolding in profound ways.

The Barwani project office became my temporary residence during my visits, as the city lacked suitable hotels. I preferred staying in the office itself, which was more convenient than searching for alternative accommodations. A kind lady from the office support staff would cook meals for me during my stay. Most staff members would leave by 5 pm, and after preparing my dinner, she would depart as well, leaving me alone in the first-floor office accommodation.

My visits to Barwani typically lasted a week, after which I would return to Delhi, where my headquarters were located. This routine became a part of my life during that period, blending work with solitude in a small city surrounded by the serene beauty of the Narmada River.

The first night in the office was a necessity, as I couldn't find a suitable hotel in Barwani. The spacious office became my temporary residence, and despite the initial desolation, I didn't feel much discomfort as night fell. The day had been hectic, and I drifted off to sleep easily. However, at midnight, I was jolted awake by an inexplicable sensation. As I tried to make sense of what had happened, I felt a strange presence around me—it seemed as though someone was moving about. Before my nerves could settle, the apartment was startled by the clatter of a fallen vessel in the kitchen. I quickly turned on the light, and in the other room, I could have sworn I heard the sound of a hammer pounding a nail.

Fear gripped me, sending shivers down my spine, but I remained steadfast. I knew that ghosts were creations of the mind, and I tried to rationalize the experience. I moved to the next room, which overlooked the porch. As I glanced out onto the veranda, I thought I saw the shadowy figures of a woman and her child. I rubbed my eyes, wondering if I was hallucinating. The next moment, there was nothing—only an unsettling sense of panic lingering in the air. I brushed off the incident, choosing not to dwell on it.

During one of my subsequent visits to the office, we held a meeting for all our District Managers, who were all women. They preferred staying together in the office, and their meals were prepared by the same lady staff member who cooked for me. We would often share food, and after dinner, the District Managers would sleep together in a large hall, while I would retire to my room.

One early morning, Nirmala, one of the District Managers, approached me with a question that left me both perturbed and frightened. For the first time, I was receiving a second opinion about the strange impressions I had been experiencing in that office. She asked directly, *'Sir, aren't you scared while staying here?'* I replied, *'No, I am not. What happened?'* She shared her experience, saying, *'You know what, late last night, I saw a lady with a small child peering through the windows. I woke up and saw them both staring at me through the windows, which were right next to where I slept. I couldn't sleep after that. Haven't you been scared at all here? It was very scary for me".*

After Nirmala shared her chilling experience of seeing a woman and child peering through the window, I became deeply thoughtful, connecting her account with the vague impressions I had been experiencing over the past few months. While my encounters were limited to sensing strange activities in the house, Nirmala's experience was more direct—she had seen these beings face to face. Despite her strength and composure, she admitted that the incident had unsettled her and even suggested that we consider changing the office building.

Her suggestion prompted me to open up about paranormal activities to other colleagues, and to my surprise, everyone had similar stories to share. Deepmala, another staff member, recounted hearing the sound of nails being hammered from inside a cupboard. Santosh, our Director-Operations, confessed that he could never spend evenings in the office without feeling scared. He was convinced that the building was haunted.

As we exchanged our experiences, it became clear that these occurrences were not isolated events but part of a larger pattern. We collectively agreed that shifting the office space was necessary. Everyone was tasked with searching for alternative locations, marking the beginning of our efforts to leave behind a place steeped in unsettling mysteries.

Shortly after we began discussing the office relocation, Rakesh, my Project Manager, shared an extraordinary experience that left us all stunned. On a quiet Sunday afternoon, while resting in one of the corner rooms of the office, he had a vivid and peculiar dream. In the dream, a woman appeared alongside a young girl. The woman spoke to him politely, revealing that she had been buried there for a long time. She requested him to take both of them to the Narmada River. In his dream, Rakesh agreed and held their hands as they walked toward the Narmada banks. Upon reaching the river bank, he abruptly woke up, drenched in sweat and overwhelmed with fear.

Listening to Rakesh's account, I was deeply struck by how his experience seemed to align with the strange occurrences we had all been sensing in the office. It made me reflect on how intricately designed our existence is and how limited our understanding of the environment around us remains. This incident further reinforced our decision to relocate the office space, as it became increasingly clear that these experiences were not isolated but part of a larger pattern that demanded attention.

During my tenure, I was unexpectedly taken to Alandi, a sacred site near Pune, where Sant Gnyaneshwar's Samadhi is situated on the banks of the Indrayani River. Despite having limited time, I was guided to spend an hour in meditation there. As I sat in contemplation, I completely disconnected from my physical surroundings and was overcome with emotion, crying profusely for reasons I couldn't understand. The atmosphere was vibrant, with Varkari devotees singing Gnyaneshwari Bhajans and playing the Ektara nearby.

In the midst of this spiritual fervour, I was oblivious to the world around me. The Varkari must have noticed my state and, after I returned to normal consciousness, he approached me. With a gentle gesture, he touched my head three times with the Ektara, leaving me humbled. I touched his feet in reverence and offered him some money. He then guided me to enter the shrine and pay homage to the sacred spot of Sant Gnyaneshwar's Samadhi. The entry was narrow, and the Samadhi itself was located deep within, visible only from above.

I pondered why I was brought to this place without prior planning. It seemed as though predestination had led me there, as someone in Pune had simply mentioned it, and the next day, I found myself at Alandi. Years later, I drew parallels between my visit and Sri M's experience in *"Apprenticed to a Himalayan Master,"* where he was called to Alandi by his Guru, Shri Maheshwar Nath Babaji.

By mid-2016, it was time for me to bid farewell to the Barwani and Narmada regions, a tribal area that had deeply fascinated me and allowed me to immerse myself in the vibrant ethnicity of Nimar culture. Beyond the places I had previously mentioned, there were other cosmically charged locations that left lasting impressions on me, such as Mandu, Bagh Caves, Khandwa, and several lesser-known sites imbued with vibrations of seclusion and mystery. Among these, Bawangaja stood out as a particularly memorable experience.

(Seated in meditation at Bawangaja, Barwani in MP)

My journeys and stay in Madhya Pradesh concluded abruptly on July 26, 2016, with a harrowing accident on the Indore-Mumbai highway. It was late evening, around 9 pm, when a speeding truck collided with our brand-new car, which was being driven by Pradeep. I was traveling with colleagues Radha, Deepmala, and Rakesh from Bhopal to Barwani. The impact was massive, smashing the car's boot space, damaging the rear shield, and uprooting the seats. All of us lost consciousness, with Rakesh and Radha regaining it soon after. It took about ten minutes for me to return to a state of semi-normalcy, still in a hallucinatory haze.

The accident occurred amidst heavy rain and waterlogging on the highway, which likely contributed to the truck's loss of control. In the chaos, I searched for my spectacles and miraculously found them intact amidst the broken glass above the back seat. We rushed Deepmala, who was still unconscious, to a nearby primary health centre for first aid. Pradeep suffered severe pain in his right leg, which wasn't functioning properly.

Despite the dire situation, I took on the challenge of driving the severely damaged car, covering about 120 kilometres to Barwani. One of my colleagues had to hold the back-rest seat in place while I drove. What was astonishing was that not a single drop of rain entered the car, despite it being open on all sides. We finally reached our office location, where family members were anxiously waiting. The accident left me with severe spinal injuries, making it difficult to stand straight or lie on my back. It took us nearly a week to recover physically.

The incident left us all with a profound sense of gratitude and awe, feeling that while one force seemed intent on harming us, another spirit intervened to save us. This event marked a turning point for me, signalling the end of my frequent travels in Madhya Pradesh. Indeed, August 2016 became my last trip to the region.

Chapter - 12

Pashupatinath: A Gateway to the Divine

On April 25, 2015, a devastating earthquake struck Nepal with a magnitude of 7.8 on the Richter scale, its epicentre in the Gorkha/Sindhupalchowk districts. The quake ravaged the Himalayan region and its adjoining plains in Bihar and Uttar Pradesh, causing widespread destruction. Nepal bore the brunt of the disaster, with mountains crumbling, buildings collapsing, and roads and bridges being displaced. The earthquake severely damaged many monumentally significant sites within Kathmandu and beyond, leaving most heritage houses in ruins.

On April 25, 2015, as I worked from home in Muzaffarpur, the earth suddenly began to shake violently around 1 pm, lasting nearly a minute. Panic and fear gripped everyone, with people rushing out of their homes and onto the streets, some collapsing from shock. Fearing aftershocks, many chose to stay awake through the night or sleep outside their homes. The quake left its mark on Bihar and neighbouring regions, causing cracks in numerous houses. The following day, another tremor struck at a similar time, though its intensity was lower, yet it still reignited panic among the already shaken populace.

I received a call from my humanitarian program's international office in Los Angeles, requesting me to assume additional responsibility for Nepal operations. They asked me to visit Nepal to assess the relief and rehabilitation needs and to help establish a development cooperation program. My CEO urged me to act swiftly and permitted me to travel by road from my location in Bihar to Kathmandu. While my family panicked upon hearing my deployment plan, I remained resolute and fearless, embracing the challenge as an opportunity to fulfil my *dharma* of serving humanity. Anticipating market closures in Nepal, I hired a car and stocked it with essential medicines and food supplies for the journey.

Upon arriving in Kathmandu, I witnessed a city still gripped by panic and devastation. Markets remained largely closed, and debris from collapsed buildings littered the streets. Older structures, including princely estates, heritage buildings, and government properties, had suffered far greater damage than modern constructions. Many homes with severe cracks had become unsafe, forcing residents to vacate and seek refuge in temporary shelters provided by the government or nonprofit organizations. Open grounds across the city had been transformed into makeshift camps for displaced families. Ambulances moved victims between locations, while mortuaries were overwhelmed with grieving families lining up with the deceased. The recurrence of aftershocks at short intervals heightened fear and unpredictability, as Nepal grappled with one of the most catastrophic disasters in its history.

Upon arriving in Thamel, the heart of Kathmandu, I found the area surprisingly quiet, with most hotels nearly vacant due to the exodus of tourists following the earthquake. The usual influx of foreign visitors and Indian travellers had ceased, leaving behind only development professionals and relief workers dedicated to rehabilitation efforts. My role involved mapping affected sites and assessing health needs in the severely impacted regions of upper-northern Nepal. Areas such as Dhading, Sindhupalchowk, Gorkha, and parts of upper Kathmandu were among the worst affected, with extensive damage to infrastructure and roads. Helicopters became the primary means of accessing remote villages, where destruction was widespread and aid was desperately needed.

In Kathmandu, the unpredictable recurrence of tremors was both fierce and unsettling, often striking in the dead of night with high intensity for a few seconds. Each quake sent people rushing out onto the streets, where they would wait for hours before cautiously returning home. The cityscape was dotted with houses bearing severe cracks, their occupants too fearful to stay inside. My hotel, once bustling with guests, was now nearly empty, except for the family of the owner, Nabin Giri, who had fled their own damaged home. I occupied a room on the first floor, near the staircase, and kept my shoes on at all times, ready to evacuate quickly if needed. Yet, beyond the momentary fear, I found myself drawn to a deeper reflection—witnessing what seemed to be the play of cosmic consciousness. At midnight, I would often retreat to the outer courtyard of Pashupatinath Temple, where I spent substantial time in contemplation, pondering the fragility of human existence amidst such natural upheaval.

Sometimes, I would spend the night outside Pashupatinath Temple with my driver, as staying in the open felt much safer than being inside the hotel premises. The sight of countless dead bodies being collectively cremated on the banks of the Bagmati River was a stark reminder of life's fragility and impermanence. It was both heart-wrenching and surreal to witness the evening *aarti* at Pashupatinath Temple, where priests chanted the Shiv Tandav Stotram, while funeral pyres burned nearby. My heart broke countless times, and I often found myself crying profusely as I sat on the riverbanks, overwhelmed by the divine's lesson on the temporal nature of existence— what we term as *Maya*.

In those moments, my Guru's words, *'You will undertake spiritual travels,'* echoed in my mind, offering me a sense of purpose amidst the chaos. I frequently questioned why I was in Kathmandu during such a time of upheaval and human suffering. Yet, for hours, I would sit in the temple's backyard meditating, immersing myself in cosmic subtlety and heavenly consciousness before returning to my work desk at the hotel.

The challenges extended beyond emotional resilience. Getting good food during those crisis hours was difficult, but the hotel owner, Nabin Giri, treated me as part of his family, which helped immensely. Meanwhile, my U.S. office operated during Nepal's night time hours, keeping me engaged even as the city around me grappled with its profound loss.

My official stay in Kathmandu provided a unique opportunity to be in close proximity to sacred sites where Yogis of high spiritual elevation had once resided, leaving behind an undiluted energy that still resonates through the temples of Kathmandu, Patan, and Bhaktapur. Meditating in these temples, especially within their sanctum sanctorum, is a profoundly transformative experience that draws one's spiritual consciousness into unity with the divine, awakening dormant vibrations and infusing a deep sense of self-realization. The local community deserves immense credit for diligently preserving these monuments over the years. Despite the setbacks from the earthquake, most of these monumental structures survived, although a few were reduced to rubble. Among the most spiritually potent sites were Boudhanath Stupa and Swayambhunath Temple, both of which continue to radiate profound spiritual energy and enlightenment.

(With Dr. Ram Baran Yadav, the first President of Nepal)

My frequent visits to Kathmandu during 2015-16 were a blessing, allowing me to explore the city's sacred sites and deepen my spiritual connection with places like Pashupatinath Temple. With a local team in place, I enjoyed quality evening hours discovering these treasures. Barsha Dharel, a key team member, remains a close friend to this day. As my visits became less frequent, memories of Nepal continued to resonate within me. I often felt a deep longing for Pashupatinath, as though I had been spiritually wedded to it during my time there. The presence of Shri Mahavatar Babaji and my Guru provided constant comfort and protection, making me feel that my journey was not just part of this life but a continuation of past lives. Even now, the spiritual energy of those sites remains vivid, a testament to the profound experiences I had in Nepal.

Chapter - 13

Maa Anandamayi: A Sanctuary of Spiritual Bliss

(Shri Maa Anandamayi, the Supreme Manifestation of Bliss)

Before 2017, I viewed Vrindavan as a sacred religious destination, much like many followers of Sanatan Dharma. However, between July 2016 and July 2017, my life was enveloped in a period of intense personal and professional turmoil. My health began to deteriorate, and my career faced significant setbacks, casting a shadow of uncertainty over my future. Family relationships also experienced periodic strain, leaving me feeling tormented and lost. There were moments when I felt like surrendering to the darkness, but an unseen force seemed to be holding me back, urging me to persevere despite the overwhelming challenges. This mysterious support gave me the resilience to keep moving forward, even as I struggled to find my footing amidst the chaos.

Rajesh Pandey, a former colleague and a Saadhak, residing in Vrindavan, had been inviting me to visit the holy city for some time. However, it wasn't until just before Janmashtami that the name 'Vrindavan' began to recur in my mind, as if beckoning me to make the journey. On the morning of Janmashtami, I felt an unmistakable call to visit, prompting me to reach out to Rajesh to confirm his availability and willingness to host me. He graciously agreed, expressing his pleasure at the prospect of my visit.

(With Rajesh Pandey in the middle and Devis Saha on the right)

Rajesh Pandey is a remarkable individual, deeply connected to the divine and cosmically aware. He has been blessed to live and work in Vrindavan, a city steeped in spiritual significance as the site of Lord Krishna's divine past times. For years, Rajesh has recognized my spiritual growth as a Yogi, a realization I had not yet acknowledged within myself. His profound insights into my advancement were accompanied by gestures of deep respect, as he would often bow down and touch my feet—a gesture I felt humbled by, yet unworthy of.

Vrindavan, with its rich spiritual heritage, is a place where devotion and self-realization converge. My eventual visit, facilitated by Rajesh's guidance and faith in my spiritual journey, marked the beginning of a profound connection with this sacred land.

Rajesh Pandey meticulously arranged my visit to Vrindavan, and I embarked on the journey with Raju, my computer support person, riding my Enfield motorcycle. Upon arrival, we settled into a guest house that Rajesh had kindly reserved for us. After freshening up, he escorted us to the revered Banke Bihari Temple, one of Vrindavan's most sacred shrines. Despite the crowds, we were blessed with a profound *darshan*, experiencing an eye-to-eye connection with the powerful and magnetically charged deity of Lord Krishna. The temple's spiritual energy was palpable, and the *tribhanga* posture of the idol seemed to embody the divine grace of the Lord. After this blissful experience, we returned to the guest house, looking forward to revisiting the temple for the midnight Janmashtami celebrations, which would commemorate the auspicious birth anniversary of Lord Krishna.

As we made our way to the Banke Bihari Temple around 9 pm, the narrow lane was swarmed by an unimaginable crowd, with devotees rushing to catch a glimpse of Lord Krishna. Holding hands to stay together, we navigated through the chaos, but just as we were nearing the temple, I received a clear and direct internal message. It was as though a voice from a higher dimension was speaking to me, saying, *'Tumne abhi abhi to darshan kiya tha, phir kyon chale aa rahe ho? Wapas jao!'* (You had already received a darshan a short while ago. Why are you coming again? Go back!). The message felt like an *akaashwani*—a cosmic sound that left no room for doubt. Without hesitation, I turned around, and my companions, though perplexed, followed my lead. We emerged from the crowd near our parked motorcycles. I didn't elaborate on what had happened but instead asked Rajesh to take me to a quiet place where I could meditate, seeking to process the profound experience that had just unfolded.

We followed Rajesh on our motorcycles, unsure of our destination, until we arrived at a well-lit campus with a majestic temple at its centre. Inside, a vibrant ceremony was underway, celebrating Lord Krishna's birthday through a scriptural narrative delivered by a revered saint. As we sat on the ground, Rajesh briefly excused himself, promising to return soon. With my eyes closed, I slipped into meditation, and almost instantly, my energy began to soar, and my breathing suspended—a state reminiscent of my transformative experiences after 2011. My eyes rolled upward as I entered a profound trance, enveloped in absolute bliss and under the influence of a super divine presence. Though my mind remained active, my senses were largely suspended; the sounds of the ceremony faded into the background. Unaware of when Rajesh returned, he recognized my state of cosmic immersion and gently took hold of my hands. With a knowing glance, he guided me out of the temple to another location within the campus. Still in a state of divine hypnosis, I struggled to walk, relying on Rajesh's support as we moved forward. This experience was a testament to the profound spiritual connections that awaited me in Vrindavan, a city steeped in divine energy and mystique.

Rajesh led us to a small, secluded room in the southern most corner of the ashram campus, a place so deeply enveloped in darkness and isolation that it would have been nearly impossible to find without his guidance. Once inside, the three of us sat in profound silence, surrounded by an atmosphere of deep tranquility. It didn't take long for me to re-enter the intense meditative state I had experienced earlier in the temple, but this time, it deepened significantly, reminiscent of the transformative experiences I had undergone in July 2011.

As we began our meditation session at 11 pm, I felt my breath suspend and a profound sense of senselessness wash over me, lasting for about an hour. By midnight, my internal energy had surged to an extraordinary level, coursing through my crown chakra like a powerful beam shooting upward through my spinal corridor. My entire body heated up, and I sweated profusely as my head tilted slightly backward, my eyes rolled upward, and I felt a supercharged vibration at my *Agya Chakra*—the centre between my eyebrows. Suddenly, there was a dramatic upsurge in energy flow, accompanied by a sensation of something cracking within my spine.

At that moment, I rose to my feet with an uncontrollable cry and rushed out of the room. Overwhelmed by the energy coursing through me, I began embracing trees and lying flat on bushes in the ashram campus. Rajesh noticed my unusual behaviour and came out of his meditation to assist me. Though he tried to hold me and calm me down, I was completely unbound by physical limitations. In a heightened state of divine ecstasy, I ran toward *Matri-Nivas*—the house where Shri Maa Anandamayi once lived—frantically bowing on its staircase and embracing nearby trees.

To Rajesh, my behaviour appeared akin to a nervous breakdown; however, it was far from that. What unfolded was a divinely orchestrated cosmic intervention—a profound spiritual experience that transcended physical understanding. I was merely a witness to this extraordinary event, which unfolded within the charged spiritual atmosphere of Maa Anandamayi's ashram. Rajesh and Raju, who observed this for nearly two hours, were left perplexed by what they had witnessed. It took some time for me to return to a normal physical and mental state after such an intense experience. Once I regained composure, the three of us ventured outside the ashram in search of food at that late hour of the night. This remarkable event left an indelible mark on my spiritual journey, reminding me once again of the mysterious workings of divine grace.

As we sat down for a late-night dinner, the three of us delved into a discussion about the extraordinary incident that had unfolded earlier. Rajesh confessed that he couldn't fully explain the abnormal state he witnessed my body undergo, though he was convinced it was a supernatural phenomenon. He shared how challenging it was to bring me under control and revealed that he had considered seeking medical attention the next morning if I hadn't returned to normal. Rajesh also mentioned his intention to discuss the experience with Shri Shyamal Jee, the key custodian of the ashram, seeking deeper insights.

Raju, still visibly shaken, recounted his own terrifying experience. He described feeling an intense presence of subtle beings while we were meditating in the secluded room, accompanied by a mysterious sound that heightened his fear. He felt paralyzed, unable to move or even lift his body. Interestingly, I had experienced similar phenomena during my meditation, though I hadn't shared it at the time. Rajesh, too, had sensed something unusual but chose to remain silent about it.

Raju only regained his composure after leaving the room and seeing me return to a normal state. The dinner helped ease some of the tension among us, and afterward, we returned to the guest house. However, I remained awake for much of the night, grappling with the powerful aftereffects of the divine experiences I had undergone. This profound event left all of us deeply introspective about the mysteries of spiritual energy and cosmic intervention, each of us processing the encounter in our own way.

The next morning, the three of us returned to Maa Anandamayi's ashram to meet Shri Shyamal Jee and delve into the extraordinary events of the previous night. Still grappling with the profound dimensional shifts I had experienced, I sought to understand if there was something uniquely vibrant about the room where we had meditated. We gathered in the serene open courtyard of the ashram during the early morning hours, sharing my experiences and listening intently as Shyamal Jee spoke about Maa and the ashram's spiritual significance.

Shyamal Jee listened patiently to my account, his demeanour radiating calm and wisdom as he internalized every detail. He posed thoughtful questions about my background, family, profession, and spiritual journey, which I touched upon briefly as our conversation unfolded. His presence was spiritually charged; he seemed to emanate an inner light that resonated with divine energy. During our discussion, he shared that he was an engineer by training from Dhaka University and had been initiated into the spiritual order by Maa Anandamayi herself in 1980, two years before her Mahasamadhi. Since then, he had dedicated himself to the disciplined life of a *Brahmachari*, maintaining celibacy and devoting himself entirely to spiritual practices.

This interaction deepened my understanding of Maa's teachings and her profound influence on those connected to her. Shyamal Jee's insights added a layer of clarity to my own experiences while reinforcing the sacredness of Maa Anandamayi's ashram as a place imbued with divine vibrations.

Our conversation with Shri Shyamal Jee shifted to my experiences in the octagonal room located in the isolated corner of the ashram. Curious about its significance, I asked him to share more about the room's purpose. Shyamal Jee began to explain its spiritual importance and shared a story that highlighted its deep connection to Maa Anandamayi. He spoke about how Vrindavan held a special place in Maa's heart, often drawing her to visit and stay at her residential ashram there. During these visits, she was accompanied by a devoted entourage of close attendants, followers, and numerous visitors. Among them was Deen Bandhu Jee, one of Maa's most devoted disciples, who was deeply dedicated to serving her. He would sit vigilantly outside the room where Maa rested, always ready to respond to her call at a moment's notice.

One evening, Deen Bandhu Jee witnessed an extraordinary event involving Maa Anandamayi that underscored her profound divine connection with the cosmos. As Maa stepped out of her *Matri-Nivas* and walked toward the southern side of the ashram, Deen Bandhu Jee, one of her closest disciples, quietly followed her to see where she was headed. Maa stopped at a secluded spot and stood still for a few moments. Suddenly, the earth in front of her began to palpitate, and a rock started to bulge and rise slightly from the ground.

To Deen Bandhu Jee's astonishment, a subtle human form, milky in appearance, emerged from the stone. The ethereal figure bowed reverently before Maa, who responded with her blessings. After this divine interaction, the form receded back into the rock, but the stone remained elevated, diagonally erect in a shape reminiscent of Mount Kailash—a symbol of spiritual ascension and divine presence.

Maa then calmly walked back to her room, while Deen Bandhu Jee, overwhelmed by what he had just witnessed, followed her closely. Repeatedly asking, *"Maa, wo sab kya tha?"* (Maa, what was all that?), he sought answers to the miraculous event. However, Maa maintained her characteristic silence, leaving the incident shrouded in mystery. This profound occurrence became one of many moments that reflected Maa Anandamayi's transcendental connection with higher realms, leaving those around her in awe of her divine presence and deepening their reverence for her spiritual stature.

Back in her room, Maa finally responded to Deen Bandhu Jee's persistent inquiries. She began by asking him, *"Did you see all that?"* Deen Bandhu Jee confirmed with a simple *'yes'*, as he had witnessed the extraordinary event clearly. Maa then instructed him, *"If you saw all that, go and put a cover around the elevated rock."* Though he obeyed her instructions, he remained unsatisfied and pressed further, asking repeatedly, *"Maa, who was he?"*

After his persistent questioning, Maa finally revealed the truth. She said, *"It was the subtle body of your own previous life. Now go and get that rock covered."* Following her guidance, an octagonal concrete structure was later built around the elevated rock, with the rock at its centre. This sacred space came to be known as Deen Bandhu Kuteer, a place where Deen Bandhu Jee would spend hours in deep meditation, drawn to its profound spiritual energy.

After Maa left her physical form in 1982, Deen Bandhu Jee moved to the upper Himalayan regions, spending much of his time near Uttarkashi in deep spiritual practice. The octagonal room in Vrindavan ashram remains a testament to this divine event, continuing to inspire seekers on their spiritual journeys with its rich history and spiritual significance.

The revelation Maa shared with Deen Bandhu Jee must have left him utterly stunned. To hear that the subtle human form he had witnessed emerging from the stone was his own previous life's subtle body was beyond ordinary comprehension. Such profound truths, as Maa revealed, defy logical interpretation and remind us of the mysterious and unexplainable nature of life. As Shri Shyamal Jee narrated this story, I felt as though Maa herself was revealing her presence to me—a connection that seemed to transcend time and space.

Despite not knowing Maa in my current physical existence, I felt a deep, inexplicable bond with her—a bond that seemed to have been woven across lifetimes. It was as though Maa had orchestrated my journey to her lap at precisely the right moment—on Janmashtami, the sacred day marking Lord Krishna's birth. Though I had never actively sought Maa before, even when my wife Purnima would study writings about her or narrate devotees' experiences with Maa, I now understood that she had chosen this time to bring me closer to her and, ultimately, closer to myself.

Life becomes simpler to understand when we grasp its fundamental purpose: self-realization. As Maa beautifully expressed, *"Bhagwan ko janana swayam ko janana hai aur swayam ko janana Bhagwan ko janana hai"* (Knowing the Creator is to know yourself, and knowing yourself is to know the Creator). These unfolding events left me spellbound and speechless, a testament to the divine intervention that was guiding me toward a deeper spiritual awakening. It was clear that Maa's grace was working through Shri Shyamal Jee, who played a catalytic role in my association with Vrindavan ashram. This profound connection reaffirmed that life's mysteries are not meant to be solved but experienced with faith and surrender.

As I remained bathed in bliss and divine grace, the thought of returning to Delhi seemed almost unbearable. Yet, professional commitments could not be compromised. Before departing Vrindavan, I shared with Rajesh my intention to return the following weekend and requested him to arrange my stay on the Maa Anandamayi Ashram campus.

Rajesh assured me of his full support, and with that settled, Raju and I began our journey back to Delhi.

During the ride, my mind was filled with reflections on the beautifully orchestrated celestial arrangement that had rekindled and reinforced the spiritual connections I had been neglecting in recent months. Distracted by worldly responsibilities, I had not been able to dedicate myself to meditation as I once had. This divine intervention felt like a gentle yet profound reminder to realign myself with the spiritual path.

Raju, too, was lost in thought, recalling his time in Vrindavan and the profound spiritual experiences he had while meditating in the Deen Bandhu Kuteer. He confessed that he had never experienced anything so intense before. However, he also admitted that the fear and awe he felt during those moments left him uncertain about returning to that place again. Raju, though deeply religious, had never been spiritually inclined in a manifest sense and had never practiced meditation before this visit.

For me, this journey back felt like a turning point—a realization of how Maa's grace had drawn me back into her fold at just the right time. It was as if she had designed this experience to bring me closer to myself by reconnecting me with her divine presence. Life's mysteries seemed simpler when viewed through the lens of such divine interventions, where every moment is perfectly timed for our spiritual growth.

With a doubtless mind, I was resolute about revisiting Vrindavan the following week. The magnetic pull of this sacred town was so strong that, soon after returning to Delhi, I began making preparations for my next visit to Maa Anandamayi Ashram. Rajesh had already confirmed that my stay arrangements on the ashram campus had been discussed with Shyamal Ji, which gave me peace of mind. However, regarding Raju's plans, I was uncertain. As the weekend approached, we discussed his intentions. Initially, he expressed discomfort, describing the place as scary and admitting he hadn't felt at ease during his previous visit. Yet, after persistent requests and encouragement from me, he finally agreed to accompany me.

In preparation for the trip, I started gathering essentials—new clothes, clay lamps, oil, and other items—to incorporate rituals into my meditation process. This time, I wanted to deepen my connection with the divine energy of Vrindavan and make my spiritual practices more meaningful. Both anticipation and gratitude filled my heart as I looked forward to returning to this spiritually charged space that had already begun transforming my journey. The thought of immersing myself once again in the sacred vibrations of Vrindavan was exhilarating, and I felt blessed to have the opportunity to reconnect with its profound spiritual essence.

On Friday evening, we arrived in Vrindavan, eager to immerse ourselves in the sacred atmosphere for the full days of Saturday and Sunday before returning to Delhi on Monday. To my surprise, Shyamal Ji had arranged for my stay in *Sadhu Kuteer*, located next to *Deen Bandhu Kuteer*. This was a remarkable gesture, as householders were typically not allowed to stay in these old-style 1960s buildings. For reasons known only to him, Shyamal Ji made an exception in my case. The house where Raju and I stayed was situated in the extreme southern part of the ashram, a secluded area with minimal human activity, providing the perfect setting for introspection.

The stay was nothing short of blissful and unlike anything I had experienced before. It profoundly helped me reconnect with myself, lifting me higher and higher into states of spiritual elevation. My meditation practices during this visit felt uniquely programmed and manifested differently than ever before. Though the external world still existed, it seemed distant and insignificant, allowing me to focus entirely on de-threading my *arjit sanskaras*—the accumulated layers of mental pollutants. A deep realization dawned upon me: to 'de-mind' oneself is to refill with the consciousness of self-realization.

As I delved deeper into meditation, I felt an overwhelming sense of love for the self. My eyes rolled upward and remained fixed as I witnessed my *kutastha* (the center between the eyebrows) awaken and light up. At one point, a radiant Sun appeared in the middle of my forehead, merging the external and internal worlds into one unified existence. In that moment, I became one with the cosmos, and the cosmos became one with me. It was clear that I was receiving a divine blessing—a state of cosmic *Jagriti* (conscious awakening). This experience reaffirmed the profound grace inherent in Maa Anandamayi's ashram and its ability to guide seekers toward spiritual transformation, fostering a deeper connection with the divine within.

During our two-day stay in *Sadhu Kuteer*, Raju and I immersed ourselves in meditation, surrounded by the serene environment of the ashram. Raju proved to be a wonderful companion, and his presence added to the tranquility of our spiritual retreat. On the first morning, as I sat in deep meditation, Raju sat quietly across from me on the other side of the room. The stillness of the space was palpable, and I could sense the room being filled with positive vibrations. A profound state of *ananda* (bliss) began to envelop my entire being, and I was certain that Raju, sitting close by, was also experiencing the same frame of bliss.

When we emerged from the room after our meditation session, Raju turned to me with a look of wonder and declared, "*Meditation occurred to me as well.*" He then shared a vivid narrative of what he had experienced during those moments. As I listened to him speak, a new wave of *ananda* settled within me, and my heart overflowed with emotion. It felt as though I was witnessing a flower bloom before my eyes—a symbol of spiritual awakening and growth.

O Raju! I thought to myself, 'I cannot even express how happy I am for you.' It was clear to me that he had received Maa's blessings, a divine intervention that had touched his life in a profound way. This moment was not just his awakening but also a poignant reminder of how divine grace works in mysterious ways, touching lives in its own time and manner. Witnessing Raju's transformation filled me with joy and gratitude, reinforcing the belief that Maa's presence was always guiding us toward spiritual growth and self-realization.

From August 2017 onward, my journey into devotional surrender deepened, and my visits to Maa Anandamayi's Vrindavan Ashram became more frequent. Every weekend, I found myself irresistibly drawn to the ashram, where I began to feel an indelible connection with its sacred environment. The ashramites, too, welcomed me with open hearts, embracing me as one of their own. Shyamal Ji's unwavering support and cooperation made every visit seamless—whether I arrived late at night or during odd hours, my food was always kept ready in my room, and an attendant was there to assist me with a warm smile.

As time passed, companions from Delhi began joining me on these spiritual journeys. Among them was Devis Saha, a young professional in the supply chain domain, who became a regular part of my weekend travels. Together, we meditated late into the night, often past 9 pm, before having a simple dinner and retiring for the day. These meditations were profound, bringing forth subtle and transformative experiences for both of us. Rajesh also occasionally joined us for meditation in the *Deen Bandhu Kuteer*, adding to the depth of our shared spiritual exploration. Later, two of my younger colleagues from public health, Mohit Sharma and

Sanjay Rai, became part of these visits, further enriching our collective journey of self-discovery.

The ashram became a sanctuary where devotion and self-discovery intertwined seamlessly. Each visit deepened my connection with Maa's divine presence and strengthened the bonds with those who accompanied me on this path. It was as if Maa's grace orchestrated not only my journey but also the journeys of those who were drawn to her through me, weaving a tapestry of love, light, and spiritual growth that transcended the boundaries of time and space.

Since 2017, my numerous visits to Maa Anandamayi's ashrams have enriched my journey of self-realization with a wealth of profound experiences. These travels have not been limited to Maa's Vrindavan Ashram but have also included visits to Almora, Dhaulchheena, Rajgir, Delhi, Varanasi, and Vindhyachal ashrams—each imbued with its unique spiritual essence. While the auras of these ashrams reflect their dimensional diversity, Maa's blissful presence is a constant that can be felt across all of them, weaving a thread of continuity through the diverse landscapes. Though it is impossible to compare Maa's ashrams, I found the Almora, Dhaulchheena, Vindhyachal, and Vrindavan ashrams to be particularly potent centres of high-intensity subtleties, where the constant churning of energy forces creates an atmosphere conducive to profound spiritual experiences.

The Rajgir Ashram holds a special place due to its historical and spiritual significance. Maa often chose this ashram for her secluded stays. When someone asked her about why she considered constructing an Ashram there, she replied: *"This place is very important. After killing Jarasandh, the then King of Magadh, Shri Krishna, along with Arjun and Bheem, rested here briefly during their onward journey."* This revelation outlined the ashram's connection to ancient tales of valour and devotion.

On the other hand, Maa referred to the Dhaulchheena Ashram as a *tapovan* (a meditational retreat), offering seekers a serene space for deep contemplation amidst nature. Dhaulchheena Ashram is located 26 kilometres off Almora on Pithoragarh road.

The Almora Ashram is uniquely positioned near the ancient Pataal Devi temple and around the spiritually significant Kasaar Devi area. This region has long drawn spiritual seekers and wanderers due to its rich history and natural beauty. Swami Vivekananda himself stayed at Kasaar Devi, where he was deeply inspired by its geomagnetic anomaly—one of only three such places in the world (the others being in the UK and Peru). Sister Nivedita, his disciple, also spent significant time in Almora, further enriching the spiritual legacy of the area.

Each visit to these ashrams has been transformative, offering me new dimensions of spiritual growth and self-discovery. Whether it was meditating in the tranquil surroundings of Dhaulchheena or feeling the historical vibrations at Rajgir, every experience has brought me closer to Maa's divine grace and further along my path of self-realization. These journeys have not only deepened my connection with Maa but have also illuminated the interplay of all these sacred spaces, each serving as a gateway to profound spiritual awakening.

Between August 2017 and March 2020, my life underwent a profound transformation as I embarked on a journey of spiritual exploration. During this period, Vrindavan became my spiritual sanctuary, essentially my second home, where I found solace and deepened my connection with the divine. The town, steeped in the legends of Lord Krishna and Radha, offered numerous opportunities for spiritual growth and introspection.

This transformative journey also included Himalayan expeditions, which were carefully planned with specific spiritual objectives in mind. These expeditions, set against the majestic backdrop of the Himalayas, provided a unique setting for meditation and self-reflection, further enriching my spiritual quest. The combination of Vrindavan's devotional atmosphere and the Himalayas' serene majesty created a powerful synergy that propelled me toward profound spiritual experiences and realizations.

This period of intense spiritual exploration laid the groundwork for further adventures and insights, which I will delve into in the following chapter. The journey was not just about physical travel but a deep dive into the realms of consciousness, where every moment was a step closer to understanding the mysteries of the universe and the depths of my own soul.

During the nationwide lockdown declared by the Government of India in March 2020, life came to a standstill as strict restrictions confined people to their homes to curb the spread of Covid-19. For nearly three months, I was confined to my small apartment in Delhi, grappling with the challenges of isolation while the nation faced a high-intensity phase of the pandemic. Inter-state travel was severely restricted, and my traveller's spirit struggled with this enforced stillness. However, by July 2020, as restrictions began to ease and inter-state travel was permitted with precautions, I saw an opportunity to return to Vrindavan.

When I discussed my plans with Shyamal Ji at Maa Anandamayi Ashram, he granted permission with the condition that I would remain mostly within the ashram premises. With his approval, I quietly made my way to Vrindavan and became the only outsider allowed to stay in the ashram during that time. The experience was surreal; while the world outside suffered under the weight of the pandemic, I found myself in a state of blissful seclusion. The ashram provided a sanctuary where I could retreat from the chaos and reconnect deeply with myself.

Vrindavan itself was transformed by the lockdown. The city was unusually quiet, with minimal human activity. The skies turned a deeper shade of blue, and the Yamuna River appeared cleaner than ever before. The chirping of birds filled the air during the day—sounds that had long been drowned out by urban noise. Reports of wild animals venturing into human settlements across various regions highlighted how nature was reclaiming its space. Yet, amidst this natural rejuvenation, humanity faced immense loss as countless lives were cut short by the pandemic. Families mourned fathers, mothers, brothers, and sisters who were untimely recalled to their cosmic homes.

(With Devis Saha during Vrindavan Parikrama)

The cosmos seemed to manifest itself differently during this period, as if reminding us of its power and play. While suffering and loss were widespread, I felt blessed to have been enveloped in Maa's grace at Vrindavan Ashram—a space where peace prevailed even amidst global catastrophe. It was a time of profound reflection and spiritual awakening for me, set against the backdrop of a world grappling with unprecedented challenges. The stillness of the ashram and the tranquility of Vrindavan provided a stark contrast to the turmoil outside, allowing me to delve deeper into my spiritual journey and find solace in the divine presence that surrounded me.

After spending around 10 days at Maa Anandamayi's Vrindavan Ashram, I decided to return to Delhi to attend to my official assignments. That morning, as I prepared to leave, my wife Purnima asked if I could bring back a Gopal Ji (child Krishna) idol from Vrindavan. Since I had no prior connection with Gopal Ji and felt unmotivated to handle such matters, I politely refused, citing the lockdown restrictions as an excuse. However, shortly after, an unexpected and strong urge arose within me—a compelling desire to visit Govardhan. Though I had never been there before and none of my close companions from Vrindavan were available to accompany me, the pull was so robust that I couldn't deny it.

By the afternoon of September 5th, amidst a complete lockdown and curfew-like situation, I somehow reached the entrance of Govardhan. Stopping for tea at a half-closed shop, I asked the young boy selling tea whether it was possible to drive through the town despite the restrictions. With remarkable confidence, he replied, *"Go, go on, no one will stop you."* His assurance erased any doubts from my mind, and I began driving through the by-lanes of Govardhan along its *parikrama marg*.

For those familiar with the holiness of Govardhan, its *parikrama* (circumnavigation) is a deeply revered spiritual practice spanning approximately 22 square kilometres. Day and night, devotees undertake this sacred journey with unwavering devotion. As I drove through this divine space amidst the stillness of lockdown, it felt as though the cosmos itself had orchestrated this moment for me—a unique opportunity to connect with Govardhan's sacred energy in solitude. The silence and emptiness of the streets only heightened the spiritual intensity of the experience, allowing me to immerse myself fully in the mystical aura of Govardhan.

As I embarked on the *Parikrama Marg* around Govardhan, the sacred mountain revealed its beauty on my right—blocks of deep brown stones naturally lodged together, with parts of the *Parvat* (mountain) visible amidst the dense forest covering its lower fringes. While admiring this divine sight, my attention was unexpectedly drawn to a small half-open shop on my left, prompting me to stop my car spontaneously. I stepped out and approached the shop, which was manned by a young boy selling religious articles, books, and idols. Among the items on display, a Gopal Ji idol caught my eye, and I found myself inexplicably drawn to it. Without hesitation, I uttered a flat statement to the boy: *"Please pack him for me"*.

The boy began packing the idol of child Krishna as I paid him the amount he requested. Despite my actions, I couldn't fully comprehend why I was doing what I was compelled to do—it felt beyond logic or understanding, as if guided by an unseen power. When the boy asked if I intended to dress and ornament the Gopal Ji idol as per tradition, I declined, stating it wasn't necessary. Placing the packed idol on the back seat of my car, I resumed my journey along Govardhan's Parikrama Marg.

The *Parikrama*, spanning approximately 22 square kilometers, is a revered practice for devotees who circumnavigate Govardhan day and night in devotion.

Despite the lockdown and curfew-like conditions that prevailed, I completed my first car-bound *Govardhan Parikrama* without hindrance. As I returned to my starting point, I realized that this sacred journey had gifted me something extraordinary—the advent of Gopal Ji in my life. It felt like a divine return gift from Govardhan itself, marking a new chapter in my spiritual journey with profound significance. The unexpected arrival of Gopal Ji in my life seemed to symbolize a deeper connection with the divine, one that transcended the ordinary and entered the realm of the mystical.

As I began my drive back to Delhi, Gopal Ji, still wrapped in a piece of paper, lay quietly on the back seat. Just as I exited the Govardhan catchment area, Mohit Sharma, one of my colleagues, called to inquire about my whereabouts. I updated him on my journey and shared the unexpected arrival of Gopal Ji in my life. Mohit was both delighted and surprised by this development. However, he immediately expressed concern about how I was handling Gopal Ji. When I mentioned that he was lying wrapped in paper on the back seat of my car, Mohit disapproved and emphasized the importance of treating Gopal Ji with proper reverence.

Mohit's guidance felt like the transcendental world unfolding itself through him, peeling away layers of ignorance and novice understanding within me. He provided detailed instructions on how to dress and ornament Gopal Ji appropriately, which I listened to with humility and submission. As part of my onward journey, Mohit suggested two options: returning to Govardhan or heading straight to Mathura. Although returning to Govardhan seemed simpler, I felt an inexplicable pull toward Mathura—as if the decision wasn't mine but HIS.

Upon reaching Mathura, I found the city in complete shutdown due to the lockdown, with only a few shops partially open. I drove around the main road searching for a suitable shop to acquire items for Gopal Ji but was met with disappointment at every turn. Frustrated and considering heading to Vrindavan instead, I realized that even this decision wasn't mine to make—it was HIS. The unfolding events felt guided by a divine force beyond my comprehension, leading me deeper into a spiritual journey where surrender and faith were becoming my compass. It was as though I was being gently nudged toward a path that would reveal itself in due time, with each step orchestrated by a higher power.

Unexpectedly, as I drove along the *Krishna Janmabhoomi Marg* (Shri Krishna's Birth Place Road), I noticed a tiny shop open at the corner where the lane began. I parked my car nearby, took Gopal Ji from the back seat, and approached the shop. Within minutes, an extraordinary transformation unfolded. Gopal Ji was adorned with a beautiful set of clothes, ornaments, a flute, and even a throne to sit on. The entire process felt magical, as if it happened in flashes and sparks before my eyes.

In the midst of a total lockdown, when people were avoiding even visiting each other's homes, Gopal Ji had chosen to visit mine and stay with me forever. With great reverence, I placed him on the passenger seat next to me as though he were my co-traveller and began driving back to Delhi. As I neared my residential colony, it started raining heavily, creating a flood-like situation just as Gopal Ji entered my complex. The timing felt symbolic, as if nature itself was marking his arrival with a celestial welcome.

Since that day—September 5, 2020—Gopal Ji has become an inseparable part of my life, and I have become a part of his. Instinctively, I treat him like my son and have named him Keshav. In our home, he is always the first to be fed before the rest of the family eats. This bond continues to grow stronger each day as I write about him now. His presence in my life feels like a divine blessing that brought joy and purpose during one of humanity's darkest times. The way he seamlessly integrated into our family's daily rituals has been nothing short of miraculous, filling our home with love and light.

My spiritual journey, intertwined with the arrival of Gopal Ji and the teachings of my Guru, reflects a profound transformation. The coincidence between my spiritual name and the name Gopal Ji assumed for himself feels like a divine alignment, emphasizing the truth that our true essence often lies hidden beneath layers of ignorance. As Maa Anandmayi beautifully put it, *"Knowing the self is to know the divine."* Through divine grace and consistent effort, I began peeling away the veil of darkness, moving closer to self-realization.

Living with Gopal Ji in Delhi brought a new rhythm to my life. Despite being duty-bound to remain in Delhi for work, the presence of Gopal Ji significantly increased my visits to Vrindavan. With the Covid-19 lockdown still in place and remote work becoming the norm, I found myself spending more weekends at Maa Anandamayi's ashram in Vrindavan—a sacred abode that became my sanctuary during those challenging times.

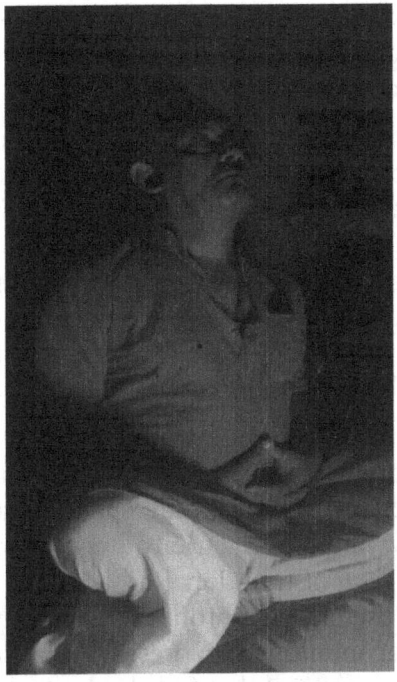

(Mid-night transcendence at Maa Anandmayi ashram, Vrindavan)

Vrindavan during the lockdown was a transformed city. Its streets were quiet, its air and water purified, and its nights serene. The Yamuna River sparkled with newfound clarity, and the chirping of birds filled the air. I found solace on its banks, especially during evenings and late nights, where the stillness allowed me to connect deeply with myself. The holy town's isolation became a blessing, offering me an environment where my own self became a blissful companion, guiding me through its sacred corridors.

This period of introspection and devotion deepened my connection with both Gopal Ji and Vrindavan, reinforcing my spiritual journey and anchoring me in divine grace. As I navigated the challenges of the pandemic,

Gopal Ji's presence and the tranquility of Vrindavan became my guiding lights, illuminating the path to inner peace and spiritual awakening.

In the midst of my spiritual journey, my heart remained filled with enormous bliss as I was surrounded by the sacred atmosphere of Vrindavan. The ashramites and Shri Shyamal ji Brahmachari, the Ashram administrator, provided me with warm hospitality and support during the challenging times that the world was facing. They ensured my physical and spiritual well-being, taking care of my stay, food, and spiritual health with utmost care.

During the evenings, I would drive to Tatia Sthal, a unique and vibrant location in Vrindavan that has maintained its primitive charm. This ashram, spanning acres, remains untouched by modern electricity, relying instead on the soft, ethereal glow of traditional oil lamps to illuminate its grounds. The use of brass, bronze, and clay utensils further emphasizes its commitment to preserving ancient traditions, creating an environment that feels both timeless and deeply spiritual.

The sanctum sanctorum of Tatia Sthal houses captivating Radha Krishna idols, whose eyes seem to draw visitors into a profound spiritual connection. This sacred space was nurtured by Swami Haridas himself during medieval times, and its essence remains unchanged to this day, exuding a sense of historical and spiritual significance.

Tatia Sthal is known for its distinctive trees, which appear to be in a state of deep meditation, especially after dusk. The atmosphere becomes particularly mystical in the dark hours, creating an environment that both intrigued and slightly intimidated me. I would venture a few meters into the campus after nightfall, experiencing a mix of fascination and apprehension that prevented me from exploring deeper into the grounds. The stillness and darkness seemed to heighten the spiritual energy of the place, making it feel as though the trees themselves were guardians of ancient secrets and wisdom.

This unique setting, with its historical significance, natural beauty, and spiritual ambiance, provided me with a profound connection to Vrindavan's rich spiritual heritage, allowing me to immerse myself in the timeless traditions of devotion and meditation. It was as if time stood still in Tatia Sthal, offering a glimpse into a world where the past and present blend seamlessly, and the divine presence is palpable in every moment.

Maa Katyayani Peeth, nestled in the sacred city of Vrindavan, is a revered Shakti point that embodies the essence of divine feminine power. Established by Shri Keshvananda, a direct disciple of the illustrious Shri Lahiri Mahashaya, this temple is one of the most sacred sites for Shakti worship in Vrindavan. Its historical significance is further underscored by the legend of Shri Mahavatar Babaji, who is said to have appeared in his physical form and sat on the stairs while Shri Keshvananda was still alive.

The temple's sanctum sanctorum houses a mesmerizing idol of Maa Katyayani, whose eyes are renowned for their profound, transformative effect on devotees. Her gaze is described as both protruding and deeply captivating, capable of transforming one's atomic field into a superlative form. This experience is often likened to receiving eternal fulfilment, as if the divine energy emanating from her presence transcends the boundaries of human comprehension.

While the temple is frequently visited by many, the most potent spiritual experiences are said to occur during quieter hours when fewer people are present. It is during these moments that the concentrated, unbroken prevalence of energy around the temple allows for a deeper connection with the divine. Maa Katyayani Peeth is not just a place of worship but a gateway to the mystical realms of Shakti, where cosmic interventions weave an embroidery of spiritual awakening that transcends the limits of human understanding.

While I was blissfully residing in Vrindavan and occasionally traveling to Delhi for official work, I noticed a boil developing on my back. Initially dismissing it as a minor issue, I paid little attention until it began growing in size and causing significant discomfort, particularly while sleeping. Positioned near the centre of my back, close to the spinal cord, it was difficult for me to see or assess the boil myself. Concerned about the pain, I sought advice from Rajesh Pandey, a long-time resident and Yogi of Vrindavan's sacredness, who visited me along with Devis Saha, a companion who had recently recovered from Covid-19.

Rajesh recommended consulting a surgeon at Ramakrishna Mission Sevashrama Hospital, conveniently located opposite Maa Anandamayi Ashram in Vrindavan. The hospital, renowned for its charitable services and advanced facilities, was easily accessible. Upon examination, the doctor advised immediate surgery due to the boil's severity and suggested performing the procedure at his private clinic nearby to avoid lengthy formalities. That very afternoon, accompanied by Rajesh and Devis, I underwent surgery at the private clinic under local anaesthesia. The doctor removed a boil the size of a table tennis ball—a sight that left me startled and uneasy.

The doctor recommended sending the extracted mass for a biopsy test. At this point, Rajesh reassured me with profound spiritual insight, stating to the doctor: *"He is a Yogi; such issues won't matter much to him. He must have taken someone else's ailment upon himself. He will be fine soon."* Rajesh's words carried the weight of his deep spiritual understanding and unwavering faith—a reflection of his own blessed connection with Vrindavan's holiness.

Rajesh Pandey himself is an extraordinary Yogi who has lived in Vrindavan for many years, deeply rooted in its sacred energy. His presence during this challenging time provided both practical support and spiritual reassurance, reminding me of the transformative power of divine grace even amidst physical trials. His unwavering optimism and faith in the divine healing process were a beacon of hope, illuminating the path to recovery and spiritual growth.

After returning to the ashram with my post-operative open wound, I embarked on a challenging journey of recovery. The doctor had deliberately left the wound open, avoiding stitches to allow it to heal naturally over time. While this approach was necessary, it caused significant discomfort, especially at night when sleeping became painful. During the day, I remained consciously careful to avoid aggravating the wound. Alone in my ashram room, I managed my recovery with minimal assistance, though Rajesh Pandey visited periodically to check on me, and the ashram boys offered their support when needed.

Despite the physical pain, Gopal Ji's presence provided immense solace. As a devoted caretaker, I continued serving and attending to him in every way, treating him as one would care for his/her own child. After a couple of days in the ashram, I travelled back to Delhi for official obligations. Although Covid-19 restrictions were still in place, travel had become more relaxed. The wound required dressing every four days, but visiting a hospital or nursing home posed risks due to the pandemic. To address this, I trained Sonu, a young boy from my apartment complex, to handle the dressing process. Remarkably, he performed the task with great care and precision.

After spending a few days in Delhi, I decided to undertake a 1,100-kilometer drive to my hometown. The journey was daunting given my unhealed wound and occasional pain, but the gracious presence of Gopal Ji on the front seat beside me made it possible. His divine companionship turned what could have been an arduous journey into one filled with strength and reassurance. Every step of this recovery period felt guided by grace, reminding me of the resilience that faith and devotion can instil even during difficult times. The journey itself became a testament to the transformative power of spiritual companionship, where the divine presence not only alleviates physical pain but also illuminates the path forward with hope and courage.

Chapter - 14

First Visit to Shri Mahavatar Babaji Cave

My first journey to visit the sacred Mahavatar Babaji Cave in Dunagiri, Uttarakhand, was preceded by two earlier attempts that, despite their promise, ultimately fell short. In 2006, while enroute to Badrinath and Kedarnath, I coincidentally arrived in Dwarahat but only managed to inquire about the cave, unable to proceed further. My second attempt in 2011, while traveling beyond Almora, was similarly guided by an inner pull toward Dwarahat, with the hidden destination in my mind being Babaji's Cave. However, fate had other plans, and I couldn't reach the cave on that occasion either.

In the months leading up to the Covid-19 lockdown, I found myself enveloped in a vortex of mental anguish, triggered by the challenges of my physical world. Living in Delhi with my son, Padmanabh, I sought his consent to embark on a motorcycle trip to Uttarakhand's Corbett National Park. Although we didn't plan to enter the park due to the lack of prior permits, we hoped to explore its buffer zones. We spent a night and two days in Ramnagar, a place familiar to me from my early years of passion for wildlife.

On the night of October 29, 2019—Diwali, the festival of lights—we decided to visit my cousin Bibhuti in Haldwani. As we conversed that evening, my long-held desire to visit Mahavatar Babaji's Cave resurfaced. I inquired about the journey, and Bibhuti, with his characteristic warmth, assured me that he would arrange everything. He made a few phone calls, and it was decided that we would set out early the next morning in a four-wheel-drive vehicle.

The next day, October 30th, we began our journey before dawn, ensuring we reached the cave at the recommended time. This marked the beginning of a deeply transformative spiritual journey to one of the holiest sites in Uttarakhand—the cave where Mahavatar Babaji initiated Lahiri Mahashaya into Kriya Yoga. The journey itself felt like a divine calling, a chance to reconnect with my inner self amidst the serene beauty of the Himalayas.

As we began our trek to Mahavatar Babaji's Cave at around 11 am, the journey itself felt like a pilgrimage. It took us about an hour to ascend the one-kilometre path, and upon reaching the cave, I felt an overwhelming sense of returning home—a feeling that resonated deeply within me. Initially, I had planned to change into a fresh set of clothes before entering the cave for meditation, but the powerful energy emanating from it was too compelling to resist. I asked my son and cousin to wait outside while I entered the cave, allowing my body to surrender to its blissful pull.

The cave, with its conical shape narrowing down at its end, seemed to envelop me in its sacred space. Upon entering, I noticed a gentleman seated at the farthest point, which my mind seemed to be drawing me toward. Initially, I didn't feel the need to move closer and sat where space was available. There was another young man with long hair in the cave, who occasionally shook his head, perhaps lost in his own meditative state. As soon as I settled into meditation, I sensed that the person in the corner was preparing to leave. Seizing the opportunity, I took my mat and moved further inside to occupy the seat, feeling an intense spiritual connection as I did so.

This moment felt like a culmination of my long-held desire to visit the cave, a place where Mahavatar Babaji had imparted profound spiritual teachings to Lahiri Mahashaya. The energy within the cave was palpable, and every step felt guided by a divine force, leading me deeper into a state of meditation and spiritual awakening. The experience was transformative, as if the cave itself was embracing me, welcoming me to a realm of profound peace and inner connection.

The experience I had in the cave that afternoon was more profound than I could have ever imagined. I transcended my physical form, entering a dimension where nothing else existed. For about an hour, I was almost breathless, immersed in transcendental bliss. A beam of energy coursed from my navel to the crown chakra, ascending into space. The cosmic sound resonated through my body as my internal ears began to perceive it. My spine remained erect, my head tilted backward with my eyes rolled upward, and my body received one of the most divine blessings imaginable. The cells of my physical body were activated, while my breath, suspended in a wonderful state, pulled my energy upward.

(In a transcendental state during one of my early visits to the cave)

Seated in a state of both being and non-being, I lost track of time, and one and a half hours passed before I returned to my normal senses. However, I was unable to speak, still under the profound cosmic influence. As I opened my eyes to gaze at the outside world, I burst into tears, crying uncontrollably. The man in front of me, a stranger until that moment, looked at me with deep reverence. When our eyes met, he kneeled down and placed his head at my feet. I was taken aback by his gesture, unsure of how to respond.

In that moment, I sought guidance from my Guru, Shri Mahavatar Babaji. The message I received was clear: I should bless him. I placed my hands on his head and offered my blessings. As I rose to my feet and exited the cave, he followed me, seeking my contact information. My son shared it with him after I nodded in agreement. This gentleman, Dr. Aman Singh, a plastic surgeon from Hyderabad, became a good friend over time. I met him on a couple of occasions in Hyderabad in the following years. His wife, Dr. Kanupriya, was also a spiritual seeker, and our paths crossed in a beautiful convergence of destiny and divine connection.

This experience in the cave was not just a personal spiritual awakening but also a moment of profound human connection, transcending words and explanations. It reminded me of the deep bonds that can form between strangers when touched by the divine, and how such encounters can lead to lasting friendships and shared spiritual journeys. The memory of that day remains etched in my heart, a testament to the transformative power of spiritual experiences and the unexpected ways in which they can weave lives together.

As we descended from the holy cave, I found myself enveloped in a profound silence, my heart and mind still resonating with the transformative experiences I had just encountered. Though accompanied by two close companions—my son and cousin—I spoke only when necessary, as if the depth of my emotions and thoughts couldn't be fully expressed in words. I couldn't help but reflect on how blessed my son was to have had the darshan of the sacred cave at the tender age of 19. Despite struggling with a cold and cough that day, he seemed genuinely happy to have visited the cave, a testament to the spiritual impact it had on him. My cousin Bibhuti, too, appeared deeply moved by his first visit, though he kept his feelings private, allowing the experience to unfold within him.

As hunger eventually brought us back to the physical world, we hadn't eaten lunch and decided to stop on our way back to Haldwani to grab a meal. Yet, even while eating, my thoughts lingered on the cave and the meditative experiences I had within. A realization dawned upon me that this was not my spirit's first visit to the cave—it felt like a home-coming after lifetimes. The overwhelming sense of fulfilment and peace that accompanied this thought confirmed that my long-cherished dream had finally been realized.

This journey was more than just a physical pilgrimage; it was a spiritual awakening that left an indelible mark on my soul. The sacred energy of the cave continued to resonate within me, reminding me of the eternal connection between the seeker and the divine. The experience felt like a culmination of past and present, weaving together threads of destiny and spiritual longing in a way that transcended words and explanations.

In February 2020, I had the privilege of returning to Mahavatar Babaji's Cave, this time accompanied by Dharmendra, a friend of my younger brother Sudhakar. As we arrived at the sacred site, I was struck by the stark contrast from my previous visit. The cave's interior was now fully wet, with water dripping from the ceiling and flowing out through its base. Despite being the only two visitors at the time, I hesitated to lay down my meditation mat due to the damp conditions, fearing it would get soaked. However, with no alternative, I placed it down and prepared for meditation.

As I sat in the middle of the cave to avoid the water flow, I began to transcend slowly and gradually. Before long, I was no longer anchored to the physical plane. My consciousness shifted to another dimension where I experienced astral travel and encountered cosmic beings. Human-like figures appeared before me—elderly individuals with glowing faces, long hair, and beards—each staying for a few seconds before disappearing. Some lingered longer than others, but I couldn't discern who they were or their purpose in coming close to me. It felt like meeting passersby during a journey through an unfamiliar realm.

This second experience in the cave was equally enthralling but more settled compared to my first visit. Remarkably, when I concluded my meditation after about an hour, I found that my mat remained completely dry despite the damp conditions inside—a wonder that left me in awe. When I stepped outside and reunited with Dharmendra, who had already exited the cave, we discussed this extraordinary occurrence.

This visit deepened my connection with the sacred space and reaffirmed its profound spiritual energy. The encounters during meditation reminded me of the limitless possibilities of consciousness and left me with a sense of wonder and gratitude for such divine experiences. The cave, once again, proved to be a portal to the unknown, guiding me through realms beyond the physical, and cementing its place in my heart as a site of profound spiritual awakening.

In late April 2020, I embarked on a return journey to Mahavatar Babaji's Cave, accompanied by a group of dear companions: Rajesh Pandey from Vrindavan, Sanjay Rai from Delhi, and my cousin Bibhuti from Haldwani. We stayed at Maa Anandamayi Ashram in Almora and began our day early, setting out toward the cave. Along the way, we stopped at Joshi Guest House in Kukuchina for a cup of tea. It was there that Joshi Ji kindly requested us to escort a mother and her daughter from Agra, who were visiting the cave for the first time. We gladly agreed, welcoming them into our group.

As the lead trekker, I guided the group through the dense forest trail toward the cave. The path, though marked with signs, is not straightforward and involves numerous twists and turns. After crossing a small river stream, I inadvertently turned left instead of right, confidently believing I was on the correct path. The others followed me without hesitation, trusting in my guidance. Soon, we found ourselves navigating through an unmarked section of the forest with no clear signs or path to follow.

This unexpected detour highlighted the challenges of trekking to Babaji's Cave, where even seasoned visitors can lose their way amidst the dense foliage. However, the experience also underscored the spirit of exploration and the shared camaraderie among us as we sought to reconnect with this sacred site. Eventually, we corrected our course and continued toward our destination with renewed focus and determination, our collective energy fuelled by the anticipation of reaching the cave once again.

As we trekked upward, covering about 600 meters, I began to sense that we were not on the correct path. My mind felt clouded—while I intuitively recognized something was amiss, I couldn't discern the right direction and continued climbing. It was during this moment of uncertainty that I distinctly felt the presence of a supernatural being walking beside me. The sensation was vivid and undeniable, yet accompanied by an apprehension of a lurking leopard nearby. Suddenly, my cousin Bibhuti came running toward me, urging me to stop and informing me that we were indeed on the wrong route. His words snapped me back to my senses, and I reluctantly acknowledged my mistake.

I felt deeply sorry and embarrassed for the inconvenience my fellow trekkers had endured due to my misjudgement. However, there was an inexplicable force driving me toward the wrong path—a feeling so strange that it left me pondering its significance. As we descended to correct our course, my mind was flooded with unanswerable questions: Who was the being I felt walking alongside me? Why did he appear? Was I retracing a path from a previous life? These thoughts lingered as we resumed our journey toward the cave, each step filled with a mix of curiosity and introspection.

When we finally reached the cave, its main entrance was shut due to Covid-19 restrictions. Instead, we all sat outside on the concrete platform. Though unable to enter, the energy of the place remained so vibrant, reminding us of its sacredness and leaving each of us immersed in quiet reflection. This experience added another layer of mystery and spiritual depth to my connection with Mahavatar Babaji's Cave, a reminder that sometimes the journey itself holds as much significance as the destination.

One of the most unexpectedly delightful revelations I encountered during my meditative experience outside Mahavatar Babaji's Cave was witnessing my own energy manifest in a humanly materialized form resembling Maa Durga. She appeared vividly between my two eyebrows, radiating a serene smile and a sandy black-and-white hue. I caught glimpses of her three times in short intervals, each time lasting just a few seconds. This vision filled me with an indescribable transcendental bliss, as if my physical being was merging into the vastness of the cosmos, becoming an undivided part of universal reality.

As I sat with my back resting against the outer wall of the cave, a magnetic current coursed through my body, and time seemed to dissolve entirely. My consciousness shifted to a realm beyond the comprehension of space, leaving me in a state of profound unity with the infinite. The experience was deeply transformative, reinforcing the sacred energy of the cave and its ability to connect seekers with higher dimensions of existence. In that moment, the boundaries between self and universe blurred, and I felt the cosmos embracing me as an integral part of its vast expanse.

As we sat outside the closed cave, most of us, including the two ladies, wore expressions of profound peace and tranquility. We were all undergoing self-realizations, each at our own level, as if the sacred energy of the place had awakened a deep sense of inner calm within us. After witnessing my eternal energy form reflect, I was left speechless and found it challenging to lift my body from its seated position. We spent more than two hours in this meditative state before beginning our descend.

(In transcendence outside Shri Mahavatar Babaji cave during partial lockdown)

As I walked down the trek, I felt enveloped in a state of complete compassion and love for myself, reflecting on the blessed experiences I had been given to undergo and witness. The journey back to Almora was a significant one, as I was the sole driver. The distance from Kukuchina to Almora is approximately 90 kilometres, winding through the picturesque curves of the mid-Himalayan terrain. The drive requires caution due to blind turns and steep slopes, but the breathtaking views of the Himalayas made it a memorable experience.

On our way back, we stopped at Joshi Guest House for lunch. It was fascinating to learn that Joshi's father was a great devotee of Shri Mahavatar Babaji and had settled in Kukuchina, building the guest house there. The road from Dwarahat to Kukuchina became motorable only about 15-20 years ago, making it easier for travellers. Previously, visitors had to endure difficult road conditions up to Kukuchina, which remains the last point of the motorable metallic road. Beyond this point, the path continues for about two kilometres over a bumpy patch of boulders and sand, followed by a trek of approximately one and a half kilometres to reach the cave.

This journey not only deepened my spiritual connection but also highlighted the challenges and transformations that travellers have faced over the years to reach this sacred site. The experience was a testament to the enduring allure of Mahavatar Babaji's Cave and the profound impact it has on those who visit. The journey back to Almora was a time for reflection, allowing me to process the profound experiences I had undergone and to appreciate the beauty of the Himalayas that cradled this sacred place.

Our journey this time included visits to Kasaar Devi, Jageshwar Dham, Dhaulchheena Maa Anandamayi Ashram, and Golu Devta Temple. We explored these sites over the following days of our stay at Maa Anandamayi's Ashram in Almora. As mentioned earlier, Maa's ashram is situated between Kasaar Devi on the upper side and Patal Devi on the lower side. From the ashram courtyard, one can enjoy the breathtaking, escalating views of the northern Himalayas. Maa Anandamayi had a deep affection for Almora and often travelled there to stay. Locals from Almora would frequently visit the ashram to seek her darshan and blessings.

(In a dialogue with the sky outside Maa Anandmayi ashram in Dhaulcheena, Almora)

One of Maa's closest disciples, Jyotish Chandra Roy, also known as Bhaiji, has his final resting place there. His samadhi, topped with a Shivlinga, is a revered site within the ashram. Although the ashram is part of the Almora city area, it is nestled in a quiet corner, providing a serene atmosphere for spiritual reflection and connection with nature.

In 2020, I had the privilege of visiting Shri Mahavatar Babaji's Cave multiple times, each visit unfolding differently as cosmic consciousness revealed itself in unique ways. By April 2021, one of my seniors and former colleagues, Usha Kiran, had expressed a strong desire to visit the cave. At the time, she was battling the final stages of Carcinoma. Although we hadn't seen each other in years, we had reconnected over the past six months. She would often follow my Facebook updates about my Himalayan expeditions, which fascinated her deeply.

Despite her challenging physical condition, which made planning difficult, Usha shared her intention to visit the cave with me toward the end of March 2021. She requested that I accompany her on this journey, as she planned to travel to the Himalayas with her sister Lakshmi. This request touched my heart, and I was eager to support her in fulfilling her spiritual aspiration, despite the challenges she faced.

Usha arrived in Delhi toward the end of the first week of April, and the three of us set off in a car for Ranikhet, eventually heading to Joshi Guest House in Kukuchina. By the time we reached the guest house, it was already around nine in the evening. The Himalayan nights are distinct from those in the plains, with darkness that can be intensely overwhelming. This darkness is often accompanied by a fear of nocturnal creatures, especially in areas like Kukuchina, which is known to be leopard-infested. It's crucial to exercise caution when venturing out at night.

After checking into our rooms, we had dinner and attended to Goapl ji, ensuring he was fed before being put to sleep. He follows a daily routine similar to that of a human being, which made his care a bit more predictable. Despite the challenges of navigating through such a dark and potentially dangerous environment, we were determined to continue our journey to Mahavatar Babaji's Cave, driven by a deep spiritual aspiration.

The next morning, we began our trek to Shri Mahavatar Babaji's Cave, filled with excitement and anticipation. Usha was particularly thrilled, as her long-cherished dream was about to be realized. Despite her fragile health—having undergone fifteen rounds of chemotherapy in Hyderabad—I was slightly apprehensive about her ability to manage the trek. Her family had been hesitant about her undertaking such a strenuous journey, but as we progressed, I saw her handling herself remarkably well. Our driver accompanied us to provide support, and I was glad he could partake in the divine blessings of this sacred journey.

We reached the cave just as it was being unlocked for visitors. Each of us took our respective seats, with me settling into my usual spot and placing Gopal Ji beside me. Basic rituals, such as lighting the lamp, were performed before we began our meditation. As soon as I sat down, I delved deeply into my eternal realms, synchronizing myself with higher states of consciousness. Since 2011, my spiritual experiences had evolved significantly, often marked by an abrupt shutdown of physical consciousness and a suspension of corporeal breathing. The sensation of transitioning swiftly into unworldly dimensions never ceased to amaze me.

While immersed in meditation, I remained unaware of the states Usha and her sister Lakshmi were experiencing. Our driver sat at the entrance and occasionally snored, a reminder that every spirit's journey is uniquely pre-programmed and beyond intervention. This trek was not just a physical journey but a profound spiritual voyage for each of us, offering glimpses into the infinite realms of cosmic consciousness.

After returning to our normal states, I observed that Usha looked profoundly content, as did her sister Lakshmi. It was evident that both had experienced something deeply transformative, enough to bring them to a state of inner stillness. Later, during our conversation, Usha shared that she had been guided through a divine realm, not just for this lifetime but for many more to come. Lakshmi expressed similar sentiments, noting that her health conditions had allowed her to be more fully absorbed in her meditation.

(In the cosmic frame outside Shri Mahavatar Babaji Cave with Usha Kiran and others)

We descended the trek in contemplative silence, each of us lost in our own reflections. Along the way, we stopped for a cup of tea at Meena Agri's house, which serves as the base camp for the trek. Meena Agri, an elderly and deeply pious woman, lives there with her family. Her home is strategically located at the starting point of the trek, making it a place every visitor passes through. Meena is known for her love of meditation and her strong spiritual connection. She once shared with me some of her meditative experiences, revealing how she often saw herself floating outside her body while meditating.

Hearing her stories, I was convinced that she carried Mahavatar Babaji's blessings; otherwise, it seemed unlikely she would be placed at such a significant location—the entrance to the holy cave's trek route. Her presence and devotion add a unique spiritual charm to the journey, making every visit even more memorable. The tranquility and peace that enveloped us during our descent were a testament to the profound impact of our experiences at the cave.

After returning to the guest house that afternoon, we savoured a simple yet delightful Himalayan lunch, which added warmth and comfort to our spiritually charged journey. As I reflected on the day's events, I felt like a spectator in a grand play orchestrated by the intricate web of karma—a predestined set of actions and reactions that bind us to our present existence. What we perceive as reality often feels like a mirage in the desert, with physical appearances merely reflecting the karmic roles we are meant to perform within the illusionary framework of time and space.

Usha and I had shared a professional relationship for years, interacting only for official purposes since she was one of my superiors. The required distance between us back then made it impossible to foresee how dramatically time would alter our roles. Now, she was in the Himalayas seeking spiritual connection with herself, while I was given the role of her guide and facilitator for this sacred journey. Just a few years ago, neither of us could have imagined such a turn of events.

Every evening during our stay, Usha and her sister Lakshmi would join me in my room for an hour-long meditation session before dinner. In these moments, I found myself playing the role of a Hierophant, offering guidance and answering their spiritual questions. While Usha spoke fluent English and had many questions about spirituality, Lakshmi, who only spoke Telugu, had fewer queries that Usha translated on her behalf. Remarkably, answers to even the most intricate spiritual questions seemed to flow through me effortlessly, as though someone else was working in the background to provide clarity. I didn't know these answers from scriptures or prior knowledge; they simply emanated from within, reinforcing my belief in the divine orchestration of such moments.

This experience was a profound reminder of how karma shapes not only our relationships but also the roles we are destined to play in each other's lives. It highlighted the linkages of our journeys and how divine forces work through us to fulfil higher purposes beyond our comprehension. The journey with Usha and Lakshmi was a testament to the mysterious ways in which life brings people together, weaving their paths into a tapestry of shared experiences and spiritual growth.

On the second day of meditation at Shri Mahavatar Babaji's Cave, as I emerged from my session still carrying the lingering effects of deep introspection, Usha approached me with a firm declaration: she intended to revisit the cave the next morning. This decision meant deferring our planned third-day visit to Almora and Maa Anandamayi Ashram, but I accepted her resolve without hesitation. Adjusting our plans required some logistical coordination, which I managed smoothly with all concerned parties.

On our way back from the cave, Usha expressed a heartfelt desire to spend time with Meena Agri at the basecamp. There, she joined a group of village women who were sipping tea and chatting. Usha thoroughly enjoyed their company, engaging in lively conversations and capturing group photographs with them. Watching her interact so warmly, I couldn't help but marvel at the divine play of consciousness manifesting through her.

Despite battling the final stage of carcinoma and enduring 15 rounds of chemotherapy, Usha displayed remarkable vitality and resilience. She trekked, talked, ate, and mingled with people with a strength that belied her physical conditions. Her immense love for Shri Mahavatar Babaji seemed to fuel her determination and endurance. It was clear to me that without Babaji's grace, it would have been impossible for her to undertake such a challenging journey through the Himalayan terrain.

I witnessed in Usha an extraordinary transformation—a rigid being softening into a state of profound self-surrender. The endurance, physical strength, compassion, love, and commitment she displayed were nothing short of cosmic blessings bestowed upon her. Through her journey, I saw the divine hand at work, orchestrating her evolution and bringing her closer to Babaji's essence. For me, it was a humbling privilege to witness this play of consciousness and the transformative twists and turns of a human life devoted to spiritual pursuit. In that moment, I saw an evolved Usha Kiran—a soul deeply touched by grace, her spirit elevated by the profound experiences she had undergone.

On the third and final day of our stay at the guest house, I woke up early, around 6:30 a.m., and felt an inexplicable pull to step out into the long corridor where Usha and Lakshmi were staying. Normally, I wouldn't venture there so early, but something beyond my understanding guided me to do so. As I entered the corridor, I noticed a tall, young man standing silently, gazing toward the Dunagiri hills in the direction of the holy cave. Intrigued, I approached him and introduced myself. He identified himself as Shri Amar Singh from Ayodhya, Uttar Pradesh, and his calm demeanour immediately struck me.

(With Amar Singh, Usha Kiran and Lakshmi outside Shri Mahavatar Babaji Cave)

Curious about his presence, I asked about the purpose of his visit, though I already had an inkling. He explained that he had attempted to visit the cave the previous day but had arrived too late, finding it locked. Amar Singh also mentioned that he was scheduled to return to Ayodhya that evening and had a train to catch from Haldwani. For reasons I couldn't fully explain, I felt compelled to urge him to revisit the cave that day instead of leaving without experiencing its sanctity. I assured him it was worth deferring his return journey for such a rare opportunity. There was an undeniable divine synchronicity between us that morning, and Amar Singh readily agreed to join us for the trek.

I shared this unexpected encounter with Usha and Lakshmi so they could prepare to welcome another spiritual seeker into our group. We reached the cave on time and settled inside for meditation. Amar Singh had brought along a companion who waited outside, capturing photographs of the serene surroundings. That day's meditation session was unlike any other—it was profoundly uplifting, deeply soothing, and charged with an extraordinary magnetic energy that words cannot fully convey.

During my meditation, I felt my atomic field being recharged with a higher energy frequency, elevating me to a deeper level of realization. For the first time during my visits to the cave, I had a vivid vision of Shri Mahavatar Babaji himself. He appeared standing on a rock outside the cave, wearing a white dhoti up to his knees and a short white kurta. In his right hand, he held a tall bamboo stick. The vision was so clear and powerful that it left me in awe.

(A beam of light dawns upon me outside Shri Mahavatar Babaji Cave)

When we concluded our meditation after two hours and stepped outside the cave, I instinctively looked toward the rock where Babaji had appeared in my vision moments before. My eyes filled with tears as I reflected on this divine blessing. Amar Singh was equally amazed by his experiences that day, visibly moved by what he had witnessed.

That evening, back at Joshi Guest House where we decided to stay for one more night, we spent hours discussing our profound experiences from the last three days at the cave. As we sat in my room sharing reflections, Amar Singh called me unexpectedly. His voice was filled with awe as he asked if I had seen the photographs he had shared on WhatsApp. Due to poor network connectivity in the area, I hadn't yet viewed them. He hinted at something incredible captured in those pictures but refrained from revealing details, only adding that we would be mesmerized when we finally saw them.

This series of events left us all deeply humbled by the divine play of consciousness unfolding before us—a reminder of how grace works in mysterious ways to connect souls and elevate them toward higher realms of spiritual realization. The journey was a testament to the relationship of our lives and the profound impact of shared spiritual experiences on our paths.

As we embarked on our return journey to Hairakhan Baba's Cave via Neeb Karori Ashram in Kainchi, we stopped for breakfast at Dwarahat. It was there that my WhatsApp finally began downloading the photographs Amar Singh had shared earlier. As we viewed them, we were astonished by their extraordinary nature. Every group photograph was enveloped by a large, moon-like ball of energy, a phenomenon that left us speechless. In two of my individual pictures, the same radiant orb hovered above my head, and in one, a beam of light descended onto me, illuminating my face with a cosmic glow.

The sight of these images left us all awestruck, unable to express the depth of our emotions. We could only exchange glances, overwhelmed by the magical manifestation of the cave's divine energy. Seeing ourselves surrounded by this celestial light filled us with immense joy and reverence. For me, it felt like a continuation of my vision during meditation—when I had seen Babaji—and now he seemed to be revealing his presence through this extraordinary phenomenon.

(Within the frame of the cosmic circle outside Shri Mahavatar Babaji Cave with Usha Kiran and others)

The photographs were a testament to the sacred energy of the cave and its surroundings, offering us a tangible glimpse of the divine grace we had been blessed to experience. It was a moment of profound realization that left us deeply humbled and spiritually uplifted. The experience reinforced our belief in the interconnectedness of our lives and the profound impact of shared spiritual experiences on our paths. Though words cannot fully capture the essence of such moments, they remain etched in our hearts as reminders of the divine forces that guide us.

After breakfast, we continued our journey toward Kainchi Dham, a sacred haven associated with Neeb Karori Baba, a saint whose teachings have deeply resonated with my spirit since my first visit in 2018. Every time I travel to Shri Mahavatar Babaji's Cave, stopping at Kainchi Ashram has become an integral part of my pilgrimage, a ritual that feels both necessary and enriching. By noon, we arrived at the ashram and spent about half an hour immersed in its serene ambiance and darshan, allowing ourselves to absorb the profound spiritual energy that pervades this place.

Usha and Lakshmi were equally eager to visit, drawn by the spiritual allure of Shri Neeb Karori Baba and the stories of his divine presence. Nestled along the highway, the ashram is easily accessible yet feels like stepping into a different realm—a tranquil oasis that envelops visitors in peace and tranquility. A short descent from the road leads to this sacred space, surrounded by lush greenery and infused with divine vibrations.

The ashram houses a tiny cave where Neeb Karori Baba meditated during his early years. This humble cave, barely four feet in size under a large extending rock, served as his initial place of residence, a testament to his simplicity and devotion. Below the ashram flows a small stream that swells dramatically during monsoon, adding to the mystical charm of the place and reminding us of the ever-changing yet eternal nature of life.

My connection with Shri Neeb Karori Baba extends beyond Kainchi Dham to his Vrindavan Ashram on Parikrama Marg, where he was cremated and where his Samadhi now stands. I often ponder the depth of this bond, believing it is Shri Mahavatar Babaji's grace that guides me to these sacred spaces. This divine orchestration also applies to my connection with Maa Anandamayi and her ashrams.

These associations feel intricately designed rather than coincidental, reinforcing my belief in the relationship of spiritual journeys and the unseen forces that shape them.

Kainchi Dham remains a testament to Neeb Karori Baba's teachings of love, devotion, and service, drawing seekers from across the globe to experience its profound spiritual energy. Each visit to this ashram is a reminder of the transformative power of faith and the enduring legacy of saints who have walked among us, leaving behind trails of light for us to follow.

We arrived at Hairakhan Baba Ashram around 4:30 p.m. in the evening. The ashram is situated about 35 kilometres from Haldwani, nestled deep within the remote Himalayas. Despite its proximity to Haldwani, the journey was challenging due to poor road conditions. The village of Hairakhan is renowned for a mystical young man who appeared in one of its caves, believed by many to be the reincarnation of Shri Mahavatar Babaji. This extraordinary figure emerged in 1970 and left his body in 1984. His devotees referred to him by various names, including Bhole Baba, Treymbak Baba, and Maha Munindra Baba, though he never claimed a name for himself.

During his time, he primarily resided in Haidakhand but also travelled extensively. In Hairakhand, he established an ashram on the banks of a wide river. On the opposite side of the ashram lies a narrow cave, and parallel to it are a series of temples dedicated to different deities. The entire setting is breathtakingly beautiful, captivating visitors with its unique ecosystem and environmental subtlety. The ashram's serene ambiance and spiritual energy make it a must-visit destination for those seeking a profound connection with nature and the divine.

Due to the partial Covid-19 lockdown still in place, we were unable to secure accommodation within the ashram. Instead, we stayed as paying guests with a local household nearby, whose family were devoted followers of Shri Babaji. As soon as we checked into their home, they kindly arranged to take us on a tour of the area, including the cave across the river. The three of us visited numerous sites where Babaji had conducted rituals or resided. One of the most significant places was a room where an *'akhand dhuni'* (unextinguished fire) had been lit since Babaji himself ignited it. This room was filled with high energy that seemed to invigorate one's vitality.

Nearby, under the open sky, stood a Shiv Lingam surrounded by several massive Peepal trees. To reach the riverbank, we descended using the extended stairways. The river, though wide, had low water levels, making it easy to cross. However, during monsoon season, the water level rises significantly. Our host's family shared stories and insights about Babaji's life and teachings, enriching our understanding of this sacred place and its spiritual significance.

After refreshment, we headed toward the Hairakhand Baba Ashram, a sacred site nestled in the Himalayas. The entrance to the cave there is quite narrow, and the inner space can accommodate only four people at a time. Inside, there is an even smaller compartment where only one person can sit, but the limited oxygen levels make it challenging to stay for long. The three of us managed to sit in the narrow inner area for a while but soon moved to the larger outer cave, where we meditated for an hour. The experience was deeply spiritual and bore striking similarities to our time at Shri Mahavatar Babaji's Cave, filling us with a sense of peace and connection to the divine.

By 8:30 p.m., we concluded our meditation and took a brief tour of the temple area, meeting a few residents along the way. The ashram was home to several permanent residents, many of whom were foreigners—mostly women—who had devoted themselves to Babaji's teachings. Unfortunately, due to time constraints and our need to return to the guest house, we couldn't engage in long conversations with them.

That evening marked the conclusion of our week-long Himalayan journey, a journey that had been filled with profound spiritual experiences and deep connections. Back at the guest house, our host served us a delicious local vegetarian meal, which we thoroughly enjoyed. The stay was not only comfortable but also economical. Usha and Lakshmi expressed their contentment at having visited the consecrated seat of Haidakhand Babaji, feeling spiritually fulfilled as we prepared for our departure to Vrindavan the next morning. The visit to Hairakhand had been a fitting end to our Himalayan sojourn, leaving us with memories and reflections that would stay with us forever.

The next two days of our journey were dedicated to Vrindavan, where we stayed at Maa Anandamayi's ashram. The serene and spiritually charged atmosphere of Vrindavan, known as the sacred playground of Lord Krishna, added a fitting conclusion to our week-long pilgrimage. After spending two peaceful nights there, it was time to return to Delhi. Usha and Lakshmi departed for Hyderabad, their hearts full of gratitude and contentment.

Usha shared that the Himalayan journey had been one of the most enthralling experiences of her life, a journey that felt like the physical manifestation of her long-cherished dreams. Remarkably, she felt better than ever after the trip, leaving her family in disbelief at how she managed such a strenuous journey despite her health challenges. For me, it was clear that this journey was guided by divine will. Witnessing Usha trek through rough Himalayan terrains—covering nearly ten thousand steps over four days—was nothing short of miraculous. The pathways we traversed were among the most inaccessible plains, yet she completed the journey with strength and determination that seemed almost supernatural.

This pilgrimage was a testament to the transformative power of faith and divine grace, which not only facilitated our travels but also brought us closer to ourselves and the divine energies surrounding us. It was a journey that will remain etched in our hearts as a profound spiritual awakening—a reminder of the mysterious ways in which life can be transformed when guided by a higher purpose.

Until a month after our Himalayan trip, Usha remained remarkably fit and active back in Hyderabad. She resumed her household chores, visited her farmhouse, and even engaged in some professional activities. We stayed in regular touch, often revisiting her Himalayan experiences, which she considered a divine miracle. Meanwhile, I continued to reside in Delhi, visiting Vrindavan whenever my schedule permitted. The month of May 2021 passed smoothly, but in the first week of June, Usha reported a resurgence of her physical troubles and requested that I visit her in Hyderabad. I couldn't refuse her plea.

Upon arriving in Hyderabad, I noticed that she had begun to weaken and decline. The doctors seemed to have limited options left to help her. I continued to pray for her early recovery and stayed with her at her home. One of my primary duties was to meditate for her every evening in her room. Despite her acute pain, she found solace and stability whenever I meditated. Her desire for self-awareness was so strong that even in her state of physical suffering, she would close her eyes and sit in meditation alongside me on the floor.

(With Dr. Kanupriya at Mt. Sambhala near Hyderabad)

(In a higher state seated on the Skull Rock at Mt. Sambhala, Hyderabad)

During my stay, I took her to a Tibetan therapist in Delhi for a day. The doctors who examined her confided in me that the chemotherapy had likely compromised her condition. They expressed doubts about the effectiveness of their treatments after she had undergone 15 rounds of chemotherapy. Our collective hopes began to dwindle, but we continued to hold onto the spiritual strength and resilience that had sustained her through her journey.

In the first week of July, I returned to Delhi and embarked on another journey to Shri Mahavatar Babaji's Cave. One of my primary intentions was to meditate and pray for Usha's early recovery, seeking divine intervention in her health. I spent two days at the cave, joined by Mohit Sharma, my ex-colleague, and his family. Despite the Himalayan region experiencing monsoon rains, our journey remained smooth and unaffected by the weather. After completing the visit, I returned to Delhi and maintained regular contact with Usha and her family, though I couldn't visit Hyderabad again due to my commitments.

Over time, Usha's condition visibly deteriorated. She had stopped eating and appeared pale and weak, her once vibrant spirit now struggling against the physical challenges she faced. Her decline weighed heavily on me, especially as I was in the midst of joining a new assignment that required frequent travel and kept me away from her side. On the night of July 23rd, while travelling for work, I received the heartbreaking news from a colleague that Usha had passed away. The shock and grief overwhelmed me as memories of our shared Himalayan journey flooded back—the courage she displayed and her unwavering longing to visit Shri Mahavatar Babaji's Cave three times during that trip.

For me, witnessing her determination and spiritual devotion was a testament to the divine manifesting itself through human resilience. Though Usha's physical journey had ended, I felt deeply that her cosmic ascent had just begun—a transition into higher realms guided by the divine grace she had sought so fervently. Her journey was a reminder of the profound impact of faith and the mysterious ways in which life can be transformed when guided by a higher purpose.

As I continued my professional journey in Bihar, traveling the length and breadth of the state to engage with health officials and strengthen systems, I would often find myself drawn to the Himalayas. Whenever time permitted, I would sneak away for a brief 2-3-day visit to Shri Mahavatar Babaji's Cave, immersing myself in the spiritual energies that elevated my consciousness to higher dimensions. The pull toward the sacred cave was so profound that it compelled me to cover two thousand kilometres back and forth drive without feeling fatigued—a testament to the transformative power of the divine.

During these journeys, I encountered a diverse group of individuals—wanderers, trekkers, and divine explorers—each on a quest for something beyond the mundane. Interacting with them expanded my perspective and deepened my understanding of the world. Age seemed irrelevant in this realm; young and old alike came seeking eternal peace and harmony with nature. Many trekked through the rugged Himalayan terrains for days before returning to their worldly lives, yet none appeared tired. Instead, they carried an unwavering energy and had their plans for the next morning already drawn.

These encounters reinforced the profound impact of the Himalayas—a place where physical limitations dissolve and spiritual aspirations take precedence. The journey to Mahavatar Babaji's Cave is not just a trek through breathtaking landscapes but a gateway to inner transformation, where seekers connect with divine energies and rediscover themselves. It is a testament to the enduring allure of the Himalayas, where the boundaries between the physical and spiritual blur, and the journey itself becomes a path to enlightenment.

"In late 2021 and early 2022, my wife, Purnima, joined me on a journey to Shri Mahavatar Babaji's Cave, marking her entry into the spiritual terrain of the Himalayas. Her readiness had ripened, and she began exploring this sacred landscape with awe and reverence. Purnima often shared how worldly thoughts would diminish as she walked through the Dunagiri hills, traversing the moist curves of patchy land layouts. The subtlety of the realm, where divine consciousness seemed to prevail over the mind's physical programming, left her deeply moved.

Together, we ventured to Pandu Kholi for the first time—a location four kilometres vertically above the base where the trek begins. This place, diagonally and vertically above Babaji's Cave, is accessible via two routes: a direct but challenging trek from the cave or a longer yet slightly easier trail. While younger trekkers find it manageable, those above forty may find it more demanding. Pandu Kholi is often referred to as Swargashram (heavenly abode), a 'top of the world' destination surrounded by dense forests on one side and sharply edged slopes on the other. The area is dotted with natural Shiv Lingams made of rough rocks—some small and others tall—scattered across the plains. It has long been a meditational retreat for many spiritual Masters who associate themselves with Shri Mahavatar Babaji.

Hidden within this sacred space is a disguised cave that is nearly impossible to spot unless pointed out. The site also features tiny temples, a small ashram, and a guest house inhabited by a few renunciates. On my first visit to Pandu Kholi, something extraordinary happened. As soon as I reached its plains, I lay down on the grassland and instantly fell into a deep meditational consciousness—a state beyond ordinary meditation or sleep. My mind seemed to cease entirely, and I remained in this elevated state for over an hour before returning to regular consciousness. When I awoke, I found Purnima exploring the upper part of the area. Though I tried to regain normalcy, I continued dwelling in an upper dimension for some time.

(At Pandukholi, up above the earthly plains)

We stayed at Pandu Kholi for about two hours before trekking back down to Kukuchina. The experience was transformative for both of us—a profound reminder of the sacred energies that permeate these Himalayan realms and their ability to elevate human consciousness beyond worldly limitations. Pandu Kholi stands as a testament to the enduring allure of the Himalayas where, nature and spirituality blend seamlessly, inviting seekers to explore the depths of their own consciousness.

During one of my previous trips to the cave, a profound desire emerged in my mind—to acquire a small patch of land near the sacred site. I shared this aspiration with my companions, including Bibhuti, who frequently accompanied me on these spiritual journeys. He began exploring possibilities with local residents, and in early 2021, we started making progress on this vision. On March 2, 2022, I successfully registered a small patch of land just below the cave. Remarkably, the purchased land turned out to be centrally located within the village panchayat that encompasses the cave.

(During one of the cave trekking)

My next endeavour is to establish a spiritual resource centre for the global community that visits this remote region. This centre will serve as a haven for seekers, offering a space for meditation, reflection, and connection with the divine energies that permeate the Himalayas. It is a testament to the transformative power of faith and the mysterious ways in which life can be shaped by divine intervention.

On July 12, 2022, a significant milestone was achieved with the official registration of Ananda Initiatives Trust in Ranikhet, with its registered office located in Ratkhal village. The following day, July 13, held special significance as it was both my birthday and Guru Purnima—a day revered for its spiritual importance. To commemorate this occasion, Purnima and I visited Shri Mahavatar Babaji's Cave and immersed ourselves in meditation together. During this profound session, I experienced a series of extraordinary spiritual visions.

While seated in deep meditation, I had three distinct visions of Shri Mahavatar Babaji. Two of these visions resembled the familiar images often associated with him. However, in the third vision, he appeared as a large-faced figure with long, flowing hair cascading below his shoulders. This figure was dark-skinned rather than fair and exuded an immensely divine aura. Though I wasn't entirely certain if it was Babaji himself, it was clear that this being was a supremely divine companion of the great Guru.

In the same meditative state, I had my first vision of Shri Neeb Karori Baba during my Mahavatar cave meditation. He appeared vividly in his temporal form, seated and smiling at me with a celestial glow. He wore white clothing and radiated a blissful presence. Additionally, I encountered a recurring phenomenon—two mysterious eyes without a face. These penetrating eyes seemed to hold immense energy within them and appeared to be just a meter away from me before phasing out after a few seconds. Their presence has always been enigmatic and deeply powerful.

The combination of these mystical visions, the overwhelming meditational bliss, and the sense of realization moved me to tears. I wept openly in the cave, unmindful of the strangers around me. It took some time for me to return to my normal state, but the experience left an indelible mark on my spiritual journey—a profound reminder of divine grace and connection on such an auspicious day.

Visits to Shri Mahavatar Babaji's Cave were profoundly re-engaging, re-energizing, and spiritually cultivating—experiences so profound that words often fall short of capturing their essence. Each visit felt like a home-coming, as though I was returning to a sacred place I had been away from for far too long. During meditative discourses in the cave, I would often witness beings passing through my inner vision. These figures, mostly unworldly and seemingly historical, appeared as if emerging from another dimension. While I could not recognize most of them, their appearances were crystal clear—some lingered for a while, while others vanished within seconds. Occasionally, familiar figures would also manifest but in forms larger and more majestic than I had ever imagined.

For instance, Lahiri Mahasaya would appear in a grand form with curly white hair covering his head. Similarly, Shri Yukteswar would often stand before me, gazing piercingly into my soul from close proximity. The presence of Shri Mahavatar Babaji was felt on multiple occasions. Once, I saw him standing outside the cave on a rock visible from the staircase below. He wore only a loincloth up to his knees and held a long stick in one hand, his upper body uncovered. On other occasions, he would appear so vividly that it felt as though he was just inches away from me. His presence was often accompanied by a cloud of radiant light that engulfed my entire being with an indescribable fragrance. In those moments, my body underwent intense internal vibrations and shivering that culminated in an unexplainable state of bliss.

These experiences were transformative and deeply humbling, leaving me immersed in divine grace and wonder. The cave itself seemed to be a portal to higher dimensions—a sacred space where the boundaries between the physical and spiritual dissolve, allowing seekers to connect with the infinite. Such moments of divine communion reaffirmed the timeless wisdom and energy that Shri Mahavatar Babaji continues to impart to those who seek him with devotion and sincerity. The cave remains a testament to the enduring allure of the Himalayas, where nature and spirituality blend seamlessly, inviting seekers to explore the depths of their own consciousness and experience the divine in its purest form.

While seated inside the cave, each meditative discourse with myself unfolded into a unique set of experiences. Some elements remained consistent across visits, but the formats during meditation discourses kept evolving. At times, the upward flow of energy was intensely palpable, and I could sense it rising higher and higher into space. A powerful pull from above seemed to uplift my prana, as if urging it to transcend my physical form. Once inside the cave and seated, the stillness of breath and mind would occur swiftly. Most of the time, a bee, though unseen, would arrive from somewhere and hover around and over my head, making a humming sound. Occasionally, I would feel as though it had pierced and bitten me around my neck.

In these moments, I could experience my own energy passing through the top of my head, leaving me feeling blank and completely empty. This was accompanied by a parallel sensation of breathlessness and bodylessness—a state I would describe as a transcendental shift of consciousness. Sometimes, the cosmic sound of Omkar Naad would permeate and prevail, and in response, a similar physical sound of Omkar would spontaneously erupt from my navel, continuing for at least a minute. The eternal sound would then repeat itself in close frequencies. The fellow meditators seated around could hear the sound emanating from me.

(While seated inside the cave someone placed a rose flower in my lap)

With such profound experiences unfolding inside the cave and around me, I found it challenging to return to normal human existence. It would take some time to bring my senses back to the physical world. The intensity of these experiences left me deeply moved and connected to the divine energies that permeate the Himalayas—a reminder of the transformative power of meditation and the sacred spaces that facilitate such profound spiritual connections.

Chapter - 15

An Interface with Shri Neeb Karori Baba

In the early months of 2018, I faced significant professional challenges. In March, I accepted the role of Executive Director at a Delhi-based not-for-profit organization focused on juvenile justice, which had been established and promoted by the late Mrs. Indira Gandhi. Upon joining, I took on management and administrative responsibilities as per the mandate of an Executive Director. The organization was responsible for the care of approximately

100 juvenile children, ensuring their education, health, food, and nutrition needs were met. Additionally, we conducted outreach activities in the peri-urban areas of Delhi. I also served as the ex-officio Manager of a government-run school associated with the organization.

Given my natural inclination toward passionate commitment to assigned tasks, I began setting up systems and procedures in my role as Executive Director. People management was one of my primary responsibilities, and I immersed myself in the workload, starting at 9 a.m. and continuing until 7 p.m. each day. Living alone in Delhi, I also had to manage personal responsibilities such as cooking, washing clothes, and maintaining a clean-living space. Despite the challenges, I was driven by divine inspiration and held high aspirations for the role I had accepted.

However, as time passed, I began to sense misalignment between my spirit and the organizational environment. The Chairperson of the organization—a retired IAS officer who had served as a Secretary in the Government of India—was excessively interfering in my role as Executive Director. She was authoritative, argumentative, and often rude. Her behaviour reflected a sense of entitlement, treating the organization as her personal fiefdom and its staff as mere subordinates. Misappropriation of organizational resources for personal pursuits further compounded the negativity.

She frequently expected me to act as a signatory for orders she dictated, undermining the autonomy of my role. This constant interference made it increasingly difficult for me to align myself with the toxic environment surrounding me daily. Despite my initial enthusiasm and commitment, I realized that this was not the right place for me—a realization that challenged both my professional aspirations and spiritual equilibrium.

One fine morning, I decided to tender my resignation and move on from the organization. I did so pleasantly and felt a deep sense of relief. The Chairperson also accepted my decision, likely recognizing that my presence would have hindered her ability to continue misappropriating resources without scrutiny. With no professional assignments in hand, I returned home, but this didn't worry me much. What brought me joy was the opportunity to reconnect with myself. I spent my days meditating, cooking, eating, and searching for better opportunities.

I had developed friendships with a group of well-wishers from my former organization, and they would often visit me. We would discuss familiar topics, but I found myself wanting to distance myself from the past. To break free from these memories, I planned a trip to Jim Corbett National Park with some of my former colleagues. None of them had visited Corbett before, and they were eager to join. We set off in a large car, and I arranged for us to stay in a government accommodation at Ramnagar, a place I was familiar with from past experiences. The trip offered a chance to reconnect with nature and leave behind the negativity of my recent past.

In the early 2000s, my passion for forests had become one of the first manifestations of spirituality in my life. Between 2000 and 2006, I visited Jim Corbett National Park twenty-five to thirty times, often driving through its wilderness in my personal vehicle during a time when self-driven four-wheelers were permitted with prior permission from the Forest Department. These journeys were not mere excursions but profound engagements with nature's cosmic energy. Corbett's dense forests and grasslands offered an unparalleled experience of serenity and connection.

Dudhwa National Park in Uttar Pradesh was another destination I frequented, staying in remote forest guest houses within core zones where visitors rarely ventured. Unlike Corbett, Dudhwa required self-sufficiency; I carried raw food, vegetables, and essentials to prepare meals amidst the solitude of the jungle. The absence of human contacts heightened the spiritual essence of these stays. Dudhwa's unique twenty-seven square-kilometre grassland—a haven for tigers—was particularly captivating. These grasslands, where trees don't grow, exude a cosmic vibrancy that aligns with Sanatan culture's concept of Van-vaas (forest dwelling) as a preparatory phase before Sanyas (renunciation).

The jungles provided an immersive experience filled with unpredictability and occasional danger, yet they were brimming with life forces that nourished my spirit. Haunted yet enchanting, the remote guest houses became sanctuaries for introspection and cosmic alignment. These memories remain etched in my heart, and while I could write endlessly about them, I'll reserve those reflections for another time.

After completing our jungle explorations at Ramnagar, a persistent thought began to surface in my mind: what would it take to visit Kainchi Dham on our way back to Delhi? This thought struck me with such intensity that I felt compelled to share it with my colleagues and seek their opinions about altering our route. Why the thought of visiting Kainchi was so dominant in my mind, only Baba Neeb Karori himself could explain. My rational mind could not decipher it.

Interestingly, I had no prior personal connection with Baba Neeb Karori. While I had read about him and heard stories of his divine presence, he was not someone I had deeply explored or known in his physical frame. Yet, when I looked at Baba's image, I felt an inexplicable familiarity, as if my spirit had known him for lifetimes. His presence seemed to pull me in—a magnetic force that placed me in a state of profound stillness and connection. It was as though he was not new to my cosmic consciousness, even if he was unfamiliar to my worldly understanding.

This sense of being "pulled in" by Baba's image and energy was deeply moving, leaving me with the feeling that my journey to Kainchi was not just a physical detour but a spiritual calling orchestrated by forces beyond comprehension. The thought of visiting Kainchi became an irresistible urge, a call from the divine that resonated deeply within me.

On a serene morning in early July 2018, I found myself at the feet of Baba Neeb Karori at Kainchi Dham. For reasons beyond my understanding, everyone in my group seemed unusually happy and at ease in the ashram, despite not knowing Baba deeply. The ashram exuded an extraordinary vibrancy, nestled beside a gentle stream of a Himalayan River. Despite its proximity to the highway connecting Ranikhet and Almora, the ashram remained remarkably insulated from external noise, creating an atmosphere of profound peace.

Kainchi Dham holds immense spiritual significance as one of the primary ashrams associated with Baba Neeb Karori. Baba spent considerable time here before departing for Vrindavan, where he shed his mortal frame. His samadhi is now enshrined in a temple of silence at Vrindavan. At Kainchi, Baba initially lived in a small cave that still exists today—a modest space large enough for just one person to lie down. This cave, along with the entire ashram, radiates a cosmic energy that is almost palpable.

The spiritual vibrations of the ashram are deeply transformative. Once inside, the charged atmosphere seems to suspend the mind and dissolve thoughts into stillness. The experience is one of profound connection and transcendence, making Kainchi Dham not just a place of pilgrimage but a sanctuary for seekers yearning for divine communion with Maharaj-ji's eternal presence. The ashram's serene ambiance and spiritual potency create a space where the boundaries between the physical and spiritual worlds blur, inviting all who enter to immerse themselves in the timeless wisdom and love that Baba Neeb Karori embodied.

Neeb Karori Baba, affectionately known as Maharaj-ji, spent considerable time at Kainchi Dham, transforming it into a spiritual haven in the Kumaon hills of Uttarakhand. During his lifetime, the ashram became a magnet for enlightened beings and seekers from various walks of life. Maharaj-ji was revered for his omnipresent nature and supernatural abilities, with many devotees recounting instances of him appearing in two places simultaneously—a testament to his divine presence.

One of the most iconic stories associated with Neeb Karori Baba is that of Richard Alpert, who later became Ram Dass. A Harvard professor of psychology, Alpert travelled to India in 1967 and had a transformative encounter with Maharaj-ji at Kainchi Dham. This brief meeting profoundly changed his life, as Baba gave him the name "Ram Dass," meaning "Servant of God," and guided him toward self-realization. Upon returning to the West, Ram Dass became a spiritual teacher and mentor, helping countless individuals navigate the complexities of modern life through his teachings on mindfulness, love, and service. His influential book *"Be Here Now"* introduced Eastern spirituality to Western audiences and remains a foundational text in modern spiritual literature.

Kainchi Dham continues to attract devotees from around the world, including notable figures like Steve Jobs and Mark Zuckerberg, who sought inspiration at the ashram. The serene environment of Kainchi Dham—nestled amidst lush greenery and flowing rivers—offers a space for meditation, introspection, and spiritual awakening. Even after Maharaj-ji's physical departure in 1973, his presence is deeply felt by those who visit this sacred place, a testament to the enduring legacy of his love and wisdom.

Since July or August 2018, I have lost count of the number of times I have visited Kainchi Dham. My first visit left an indelible mark on my spirit, as though my atomic field had aligned with the super-magnetic energy of Baba Neeb Karori's ashram. Every journey to Shri Mahavatar Babaji's cave naturally included a stopover at Kainchi, which became an integral part of my spiritual pilgrimage. Many of my fellow travellers also had the opportunity to visit Kainchi with me, often sharing in the inexplicable peace and connection the ashram offers.

(Outside Neeb Karori Baba's Kainchi ashram)

To my spirit, Baba Neeb Karori felt like someone I had known for lifetimes. His image evoked a profound sense of familiarity, as though I was reuniting with a beloved presence. Often, I would sit on the staircase near the veranda where Baba used to sit, overcome with emotion and shedding tears of devotion. Carrying my Gopalji with me, I would sit there in silent communion before continuing my onward or return journey. The energy of Kainchi Dham, its serene surroundings, and Baba's eternal presence have made it a sacred anchor in my spiritual path—a place where my soul feels truly at home. Each visit to Kainchi has been a journey of rediscovery, a testament to the enduring bond between my spirit and the divine love that Baba embodies.

Kakrighat, situated on the way to Almora from Kainchi, is a serene and spiritually significant site. It is renowned as the place where Sombari Baba, one of the revered predecessors of Shri Neeb Karori Baba, lived in profound seclusion. Sombari Baba maintained a life of complete isolation, avoiding interactions with the outside world, and resided near the upper segments of a beautiful river that takes an L-turn at Kakrighat. He often stayed by a banyan tree and a nearby temple, living a simple life devoid of worldly comforts. The subtle spiritual energy of Kakrighat can only be truly experienced by visiting the place, where the essence of his ascetic life still resonates.

Kakrighat also holds historical significance as Swami Vivekananda is believed to have spent substantial time there during his travels in 1890. It is said that this was one of the places where Swamiji had profound realizations about eternal truth before continuing his journey through Almora. Among the many places Swamiji visited for self-enquiry, Kasaar Devi stood out as one of his favourites.

Kasaar Devi, about 10 kilometres from Almora, is renowned for its unique geomagnetic properties due to its location within Earth's Van Allen Belt. This phenomenon creates a cosmic energy field similar to those found at Machu Picchu and Stonehenge. The area has long attracted spiritual seekers, including notable figures like Swami Vivekananda, Bob Dylan, and D.H. Lawrence. Meditation at Kasaar Devi often leads to extraordinary experiences due to its charged energy field. Visitors frequently report heightened states of awareness, faster breathing followed by body-lightness, and a sense of transcendence.

(At Kasaar Devi, Almora)

My own experiences meditating at Kasaar Devi have been transformative. Each session brought an intense sense of physical lightness as my breathing suspended and my spiritual being seemed to ascend outwardly and upwardly. In these moments, my sense organs entered a blackout state, leaving me immersed in profound stillness and connection with the cosmic energy that permeates this sacred place. Both Kakrighat and Kasaar Devi continue to stand as timeless sanctuaries for seekers on their spiritual journeys, offering a profound connection to the divine and the eternal wisdom that resides within these sacred landscapes.

(In a meditative state at Kasaar Devi)

Coming back to Neeb Karori Baba, and as I mentioned before, Kainchi had become a point of spiritual connection for me which would transmit a substantial amount of cosmic energy that helped fostered my spiritual journey mindfully well. I could make a balance with my grihastha (householder) life, the outer world and my divine pursuits. I could never even understand what I was looking for and where I was headed but I was always sure that the path I was given to walk on, the rambling was being made blissful. I liked to indulge in spiritual journeys and hold discourses that related to the divine, a dimension not much known to any. As it was foretold by my Guru, *'tum adhyatmik yatrayen karoge'* (you will undertake spiritual journeys), I was comprehending, I was realizing the prophecy. I had become a shuttle between one spiritual point to reach out to so many other dots in a short span of time. In Vrindavan, when my interface with Maa Anandmayi ashram got established, it became surprisingly so obvious that Baba Neeb Karori's ashrams's darshan became a natural part of my visits there.

In Vrindavan ashram, there is a big room with a high platform, supposedly the seat of Shri Baba where he used to rest and meet with devotees. This room is filled with a lot of positive energy and vibrations. Several devotees are seen to be doing Japa, meditation and conducting prayers inside. People from across geographies flock to receive celestial solace which one gets in abundance in the ashram there in Vrindavan. I too have visited this ashram a number of times that I can really remember now. My journey there is still on. There is a pull-force that drives me to this ashram. I still have clear memories of my first time visiting Baba's Vrindavan ashram. Rajesh Pandey, my spiritual companion who I have talked about in previous chapters lives and works out of Vrindavan holy city. He was the one who had accompanied me to this ashram sometime during 2017. On reaching the Samadhi Mandir of Shri Baba, we met with a Mauni Baba (a man in his early forties who maintains complete silence and does not speak). This Baba is the caretaker of Samadhi Mandir (Samadhi Mandir is where Baba's body was cremated). When I saw him looking at me, his looks were penetrative. And he smiled, as if trying to convey to me *'O, you have finally arrived. Welcome!'* And then he kneeled down to take something out of the front drawers. A picture of Shri Baba he was holding in his hand which he handed over to me. Inscribed on the back of the pic was Ram in Devnagari script. I humbly took that divine gift and held that to my heart for a few seconds before seeing Rajesh requesting the Mauni Baba for a similar pic for himself. His request was honoured by the Mauni Baba.

(In a blissful state inside Neeb Karori Baba's Samadhi Ashram at Vrindavan)

Sometimes, during the evening visit to the ashram, Mauni Baba would speechlessly communicate that I should eat dinner in the kitchen after my meditation and before I left. Normally, I live and dine out of Maa Anandmayi ashram but sometimes I take the exception and enjoy the simple yet so delicious Roti and Sabji at this other ashram. I also feel that the dining request coming from Mauni Baba on some special days has special significance. But how do I understand that and read between the lines, remains an unanswered proposition. My meditational experiences of Neeb Karori Baba ashram in Vrindavan have mostly been transcendental in nature. Even though visitors keep coming in and moving out of the room, once the physical breathing has transitioned to the cosmic one, and the spirit has elevated to the cosmic plains above, it would hardly make a difference if physical activities are being undertaken in the outer world. Post my meditation session in the ashram, I would become speechless for some time. It would take me time to return to normalcy. My companions would also sense that phenomenon at times. As far as my own personal experiences go, both these ashrams in Kainchi and Vrindavan are places of high spiritual energy. In Kainchi, Shri Baba had spent substantial time. He would visit Vrindavan periodically and stay at the present place of the ashram.

I considered every visit an opportunity to Baba's ashram granted as Baba's greatest gift and grace to me in my own spiritual endeavours. It made my journey smoother. Handling life dilemmas was made easy. Both sukha and dukh came out to be balanced well enough through the ultimate realization that all of these were part of the temporariness of the temporal body. Allowing life anomalies and materialistic fervours to carry themselves forward is perilous as far as the onward journey of the spirit is concerned. Over the years I have realised how important it is to walk on a path that leads to divine realizations. Self-realization is to realize the divine and to realize the divine is to realize the self. How simple? Yet, how complicated we really understand the whole divinity to be. Today, my mind can think of these subjects pertaining to spirituality and self-realization is certainly a great gift which I graciously received from my Guru in 2011. And always recount on his prophecy *'tum adhyatmik yatrayen karoge'* (you will undertake spiritual travel). In one sentence, the rest of my life was comprehended. I was about forty-year-old, when I received that prophecy. Today I am about fifty-seven-year-old and have been living out the same forecast for the last sixteen years.

The blessing I received marked the beginning of a life-changing journey toward self-realization. Reflecting on my life, I am deeply grateful to have experienced such grace at a pivotal age—around forty years old—when my focus shifted from materialism to embracing self-realization as the prime goal of my life. Over the past sixteen years, this journey has been incredibly blissful and benevolent, overshadowing other phases of my life that were filled with volatile events.

Hardships have been an integral part of my life, often intertwined with painful human relationships where trust and emotions have faced cataclysmic outcomes. My mother was the only true friend I confided in, offering a cool, kind, and humanly considerate presence. Her early departure, when I was about 37-38 years old, left me shattered for years. Though I hid my pain, I suffered deeply. As her legacy, I carried her unfulfilled dreams, which she could not realize due to living within a traditional rural setting without modern amenities. Despite being born in a rustic village, my mother instilled in me elements of sophistication that I continue to draw upon in my daily life.

This journey of self-realization has not only helped me navigate life's challenges but also allowed me to honour my mother's legacy by living the life she envisioned for me. Her influence remains a guiding light, reminding me of the strength and resilience that has carried me through life's trials. The spiritual path I embarked upon has been a transformative journey, one that has brought profound peace and understanding, even in the face of adversity. As I look back, I realize that the blessings and challenges have intertwined to create a tapestry of growth, each thread weaving together to form a life of purpose and fulfilment.

Chapter - 16

The Quiet Mystic of Goner

I have been associated with Shri Gurudev since December 1995, the year I first had the privilege of his darshan at Jaipur's Amer Ashram. Coincidentally, this was also the year I got married, and my wife's family had a long-standing connection with the ashram. My father-in-law was initiated by the revered Guru and Avadhoot Shri Pahari Baba (Hariharanand Giri), who's ardent disciple is now known as Gurudev Shri Bhuvneshwaranand Giri ji. At the time of my first meeting with Shri Gurudev, I was around 27 years old and had no understanding of spirituality. Accompanying my wife to the ashram during my visit to Jaipur for an interview at a prominent public health institute in the southern part of the city, I had no idea that this encounter would mark the beginning of a profound spiritual journey in my life.

My first impression of meeting the saffron-clad man was not unlike encountering any ordinary Sadhu. To my eyes, he did not seem particularly remarkable—he was a thin, bearded man dressed in saffron robes, living as a brahmachari (celibate). His demeanour was quiet; he spoke little and refrained from discussing religious doctrines or spiritual subjects. Yet, despite his simplicity, he was surrounded by a diverse group of serious seekers from across India and abroad, all drawn to him with reverence and belief in his spiritual elevation.

At the time, I could not fully grasp what inspired such devotion among his followers. Instead, I observed the activities within the ashram while adhering to Purnima's guidance on the dos and don'ts of conduct there. This marked my first interface with an ashram—a setting that would later become significant in my spiritual journey.

This initial encounter highlights the enigmatic nature of true spiritual figures, whose impact often transcends outward appearances and conventional understanding. While their simplicity may obscure their profound essence at first glance, their presence and energy gradually reveal themselves to those who seek with sincerity. As I reflect on that moment, I realize that the seeds of my spiritual awakening were sown in that very ashram, amidst the quiet yet powerful presence of Shri Gurudev.

Following my interview, I was thrilled to receive confirmation of my selection from the committee. We returned to the ashram, filled with joy, to seek Shri Gurudev's blessings before embarking on our journey back to Delhi. I was asked to join the position as soon as possible, and upon returning home, we packed up and left Delhi to begin a new chapter in Jaipur. Looking back, I now realize that this period of my life was cosmically orchestrated, allowing me to spend invaluable time in the proximity of an ascetic of the highest spiritual calibre.

At the time, however, I was largely unaware of the significance of this opportunity. Coming from a family that adhered to religious traditions and rituals but lacked a deep orientation toward spirituality, I had little understanding of what lay ahead. My upbringing in a rural village, where I spent the first 11 years of my life, was rooted in simplicity and traditional customs. Festivals were celebrated with fervour, and rituals were performed diligently, but the deeper dimensions of spirituality remained unexplored.

This transition to Jaipur marked not just a geographical shift but also a profound spiritual awakening. Though I could not comprehend it fully at the time, my exposure to Shri Gurudev and the ashram environment sowed the seeds for a journey that would eventually transform my understanding of life and its higher purpose. What began as a move for professional advancement turned out to be a divinely guided step toward self-realization and spiritual growth. As I reflect on that period, I am reminded that life's most significant transformations often unfold when we least expect them, weaving together seemingly ordinary moments into a tapestry of profound spiritual awakening.

Almost every week, we would visit the ashram to meet Shri Gurudev, and I would often sit quietly in the hall where people from various walks of life gathered for his darshan. Devotees came not only from different states of India but also from western countries, drawn by his spiritual presence. I remained a silent observer of the events that unfolded there. Many people sat close to him, sharing their troubles and seeking guidance, while others sat quietly in corners with their eyes closed, immersed in meditation or reflection.

Upon arrival, everyone was offered a platter of prasad, usually consisting of fruits and sweets—a tradition rooted in the ethos of service and hospitality established by Shri Gurudev's Guru. For those traveling long distances, lunch was also served as part of the ashram's practice of feeding everyone, a principle deeply embedded in its values. I don't recall how many times I had the opportunity to partake in this prasad, but it always felt like a blessing.

Although we had set up our residence in the city and rarely stayed overnight at the ashram, my time there remains vivid in memory. Occasionally, when Shri Gurudev was not surrounded by others, he would ask me questions about my work, showing genuine interest in its details. Interestingly, he never spoke to me about spirituality, meditation, or God directly. Even with others, his conversations often revolved around worldly matters—life, living, and topics prompted by those seeking his reflections.

The ashram was more than a place of worship; it was a sanctuary where people found solace and connection. Shri Gurudev's simplicity and approachability created an atmosphere where profound spiritual energy coexisted with practical wisdom. Though I may not have fully understood the depth of those interactions at the time, they planted seeds of introspection and growth that continue to shape my journey today. As I reflect on those moments, I realize that Shri Gurudev's presence was not just about imparting knowledge but about fostering a sense of community and compassion, reminding us that true wisdom lies in living harmoniously with the world around us.

Shri Gurudev's daily routine was marked by simplicity and consistency. In the early hours, he would remain in his room, emerging around 9 a.m. to take his seat and begin reading newspapers one by one. Occasionally, he would glance at those seated nearby before returning to his reading. His demeanour was always soft-spoken and humble, a quality that remained unwavering over time. Even when raising his voice to call someone, it was mild and direct, reflecting his composed nature.

Shri Gurudev's approach to guiding people was deeply practical. For health concerns, he would advise consulting a good doctor; for legal matters, he recommended seeking a capable lawyer. His solutions were rooted in worldly pragmatism, yet they carried an undeniable sense of clarity and wisdom. People often followed his advice with unwavering faith, and many believed they succeeded because of the path he suggested.

What stood out most among those who visited him was their complete surrender. They believed wholeheartedly in him without questioning or rationalizing their faith.

This simple act of surrender seemed to create a profound connection between Shri Gurudev and his followers, enabling them to find solace and solutions in his presence.

The ashram was not just a place for spiritual discourse but also a space where practical wisdom met deep faith. Shri Gurudev's ability to address worldly concerns while maintaining an aura of humility and compassion made him a beacon of guidance for people from all walks of life. His presence was a testament to the power of simplicity and faith, reminding us that sometimes, the most profound truths lie in the simplest of actions and beliefs.

In the early days of my association with Shri Gurudev, I often found myself questioning the behaviour of those who came to seek his guidance. My rational mind struggled to understand why people acted with such child-like reverence toward him. Observing how visitors interacted with him, I noticed that most arrived without any pretence or ego—they left behind their worldly burdens and surrendered completely. Some were initiated by Shri Gurudev or his Guru, yet all displayed the same degree of respect and devotion.

Now, with hindsight and deeper understanding, I am able to grasp why people behaved the way they did. Shri Gurudev's presence seemed to evoke a sense of humility and surrender in everyone who came to him. His ability to connect with individuals on a deeply personal level, offering practical solutions to their problems while embodying spiritual wisdom, created an atmosphere of trust and faith. People believed in him wholeheartedly, not because of rational analysis but because of the profound impact his guidance had on their lives.

This complete surrender was the cornerstone of their devotion—a rare quality that transcended logic and allowed them to experience the transformative energy of Shri Gurudev's presence. It is this unshakable faith that continues to inspire me and countless others who have had the privilege of being in his proximity.

To me, he initially appeared as a spiritual being primarily because of his saffron attire and long beard. However, when he spoke, he discussed worldly affairs with simplicity and humility. His way of life was remarkably consistent and unchanged, yet it drew people from all walks of life to the ashram. The devotees around him believed him to be a Yogi of the highest spiritual order, attracting both old followers ordained by his Guru, Shri Hariharanand ji (Pahari Baba), and those he himself had initiated into the path of divinity.

I often observed a few foreigners visiting the ashram, including a lady from Italy and another from the U.S., who would return annually and stay near the ashram. They spent their days within the ashram's serene environment, basking in blissful tranquility. This blend of worldly simplicity and profound spiritual energy made Shri Gurudev a beacon for seekers from diverse backgrounds, all drawn to his presence without needing him to overtly display his spiritual stature. As I reflect on those moments, I realize that Shri Gurudev's influence was not just about his teachings but about the sense of peace and unity he fostered among those who encountered him, transcending cultural and geographical boundaries.

Shri Bhuvneshwaranand Giri has been holding the Yogic seat at the Amer Ashram since 1974, following the passing of his Guru, Shri Hariharanand Giri, also known as Pahari Baba. The ashram, situated at the foothills of the Amer Hills on the northern edge of Jaipur, was established by Pahari Baba in the early 1970s. When Pahari Baba first entered the building, a traditional haveli (as it is called in Rajasthan), it was in a dilapidated state. Despite its condition and the surrounding area being largely forested with minimal habitation, Pahari Baba insisted on staying there. His decision was based on a profound revelation he shared, saying, *"Main to yahan pahle kai baar aa chuka hoon. Aur ab main yahin rahunga*" (I have come here several times before, and now I will stay here), referring to his spiritual connection with the place from past lives.

Pahari Baba also revealed that Jaidev, the medieval saint and author of the celebrated Geet Govind, had once stayed at this very location and composed verses of his epic work there. This historical and spiritual significance added a profound aura to the ashram, which became a centre for seekers drawn to its deep-rooted sanctity and connection to divine energies.

Over time, the Amer Ashram underwent significant renovations, transforming it into a more liveable space with modern amenities both inside and outside. On special occasions such as Guru Purnima and Chaitra Navaratri, the ashram would see a steady stream of devotees arriving from Jaipur, across Rajasthan, and other parts of the country. The purity, piety, and unwavering devotional commitment of those performing the rituals during these celebrations were unlike anything I had experienced elsewhere.

Shri Gurudev would sit quietly in his seat, offering humble yet precise instructions to the devotees managing the events. One of the most remarkable aspects of these gatherings was their serene atmosphere. Despite the presence of hundreds of people, there was an extraordinary sense of order and silence—no public announcement systems were ever used. The harmony and calmness often made me feel as though I was participating in something beyond this world.

In the midst of all this activity, Shri Gurudev remained seated in his chair, observing everything with a calm yet attentive demeanour. His ability to oversee every detail while maintaining a composed presence was extraordinary. The steadfast devotion of those managing the events reflected their deep faith in him, creating an environment that was both spiritually uplifting and profoundly peaceful. As I reflect on those moments, I realize that the ashram was not just a place of worship but a sanctuary where spirituality and serenity coexisted, reminding us of the beauty of simplicity and the power of collective devotion.

During Guru Purnima celebrations at the ashram, thousands of devotees would visit Shri Gurudev to seek his blessings. Remarkably, each individual received his personal attention and blessings, a testament to his extraordinary endurance and Yogic discipline. From morning until late evening, Gurudev would remain seated in one place, unshaken and unchanged in posture, embodying the resilience and focus of a true Yogi. Devotees would come, offer their prayers, and leave, while Gurudev maintained an aura of calm throughout the day. To me, this was a profound manifestation of the endurance and spiritual depth of a realized being.

Observing these events often left me deeply contemplative. Coming from a background where the Guru-Parampara was not followed, I found myself grappling with questions about the magnetic pull that drew so many people to Gurudev. At just the age of twenty-eight, I was trying to reconcile my logical mindset—shaped by contemporary education systems rooted in ideologies like Marxism and egalitarianism—with the sheer devotion and surrender I witnessed. The rational framework I had absorbed during my studies in Delhi seemed ill-equipped to explain this phenomenon.

What struck me most was the unwavering faith of the devotees. They worshipped him with complete surrender, leaving behind all notions of logic or scepticism. Retrospectively, I realize that my exposure to writings on Indology by scholars like Max Weber provided an intellectual lens but fell short of capturing the experiential depth of what unfolded before me. Those moments at the ashram were unlike anything I had encountered—a dimension beyond reason, where devotion transcended intellect and touched something far more profound.

As I reflect on those days, I am reminded that true wisdom often lies beyond the confines of logic and rational thought. The ashram was a place where spirituality and devotion merged, creating an atmosphere that was both humbling and transformative. It was there that I began to understand the power of faith and the profound impact it can have on one's life, even for someone like me, who was initially grounded in rational thinking.

As I continued to observe the events at the ashram, I found myself in a state of passivity, unable to translate my thoughts into action. This period of introspection was soon interrupted as my stay in Jaipur came to an end, and I embarked on a new assignment in Bihar. My wife and I relocated to Patna, where our first child, Parijat, was born in 1997. Life seemed to unfold with its own momentum, navigating through the complexities of the material world, which I likened to a 'Maya-market.' This journey highlighted the dual nature of human existence—on one hand, the glory of being born as a human, with the potential for spiritual growth and self-awareness; on the other hand, the pity of remaining unaware of our true consciousness, trapped in the illusions of the material world.

As I reflect on those moments, I realize that life's experiences, both mundane and profound, serve as catalysts for introspection. The birth of my child and the transition to a new city were not just life events but also opportunities to ponder the deeper truths of existence. The concept of maya, or illusion, became more relatable as I navigated the complexities of life, seeking to balance the demands of the material world with the pursuit of spiritual awareness. It was a journey of discovery, one that gradually revealed the importance of recognizing and transcending the veil of maya to uncover the true nature of our being.

My annual journeys to the Jaipur Ashram became a cherished tradition, often coinciding with official visits to the city. Yet, no trip felt complete without the darshan of Shri Gurudev. During times of immense suffering, Gurudev was my sole refuge, a presence to whom I could redirect all the burdens I carried. He seemed to absorb everything, leaving me unencumbered by the emotional "leftovers" that might otherwise weigh heavily on my mind. His patience and fatherly consolation were unwavering, often concluding with his gentle words, *"Achha beta"* (Alright, my son).

I vividly recall moments of vulnerability when I cried before him, openly requesting his grace—a rare act for someone who seldom asks for favours, not even from gods in temples. This act of asking marked a turning point in my spiritual journey, though its significance remains beyond logical explanation. Gurudev's pervasive influence in my life was steeped in mysteries that defy narration or comprehension.

Over time, as my life gained momentum, I began receiving transcendental signals—experiences that I have elaborated upon in earlier chapters. Whenever I shared these metaphysical encounters with Gurudev, he graciously listened with undivided attention. All my highs and lows were discussed with him; every act of good and bad was credited by him with equal grace. His blessings extended beyond my individual spiritual path and touched my family life as well, offering divine guidance at every turn.

Reflecting on these experiences highlights the profound role Gurudev played—not just as a spiritual guide but as a source of unconditional support and wisdom. His presence bridged the gap between worldly struggles and transcendental understanding, fostering a connection that continues to shape my journey in ways both tangible and mystical. As I look back, I realize that Gurudev's impact was not just about the moments we shared but about the enduring sense of peace and clarity he instilled in me, guiding me through life's complexities with a gentle yet profound touch.

Shri Gurudev has recently relocated his physical abode to Goner village in Jaipur district, Rajasthan, where he continues to graciously guide people on their spiritual journeys and help them navigate life's challenges. The present-day ashram, situated away from the distractions of city life, provides a serene environment that attracts spiritually inclined individuals who come to immerse themselves in meditation and silence. On occasions, devotees from outside India visit the ashram, some staying for months while observing maun (silence) and dedicating themselves to meditational practices. This tranquil setting allows seekers to disconnect from worldly responsibilities and reconnect with their inner selves.

Shri Gurudev's approach remains profoundly humble—he neither claims mastery nor engages in advocacy but operates with an aura of simplicity, lightness, and love. His presence is magnetic, drawing seekers who find solace and spiritual growth under his guidance. For those who take leave from their regular lives to spend time at the ashram, it becomes a sanctuary for introspection and transcendence. I feel immensely blessed to be connected with such an advanced Yogi whose influence transcends conventional understanding and continues to illuminate my path with grace and wisdom. As I reflect on this connection, I am reminded that true spiritual growth often occurs in the simplest and most unassuming of settings, where love and lightness are the guiding principles.

I am uncertain about the nature of my connection with Shri Gurudev in this life, but I am convinced it is beyond being 'normal and casual.' Occasional insights have led me to contemplate that our relationship spans multiple lifetimes, with the present being one of them. It seems he has been playing a silently special role in ensuring I remain under his observation, supplementing the necessary guidance and support whenever needed. In the grand tapestry of life, every event is interconnected and part of a pre-designed plan. My relationship with Shri Gurudev illustrates this principle, as I find myself drawn to the ashram in Jaipur whenever direct contact is warranted, regardless of the context.

As I walk the spiritual path, I have come to realize that his periodic interventions are part of a larger pre-programmed journey, with him serving as the Master Enabler. This connection transcends rational understanding, operating on a level that is both profound and mysterious. The inability to fully comprehend this bond is natural, as it is rooted in a dimension beyond logic and linear thought. Embracing this connection with openness and trust, I continue on a path of self-discovery and spiritual awakening, guided by his subtle yet profound influence.

In reflecting on this journey, I am reminded that significant relationships often carry over lessons, unresolved karma, or shared goals from previous lives to aid in our evolution. Shri Gurudev's presence in my life embodies this principle, offering not just guidance but also a sense of being part of something much larger than myself. His role as a spiritual guide underscores the idea that nothing in life happens by chance; every interaction and relationship serves a purpose within the grand design of our existence."

One of the profound insights that emerges is that human relationships are inherently karmic, suggesting that they should not be viewed through the lens of emotional attachment. This understanding serves as a catalyst for the journey of self-realization. Detachment plays a crucial role in facilitating this shift, allowing individuals to navigate their paths with greater clarity and freedom.

In this context, detachment does not mean a lack of love or care but rather a release from the entanglements of ego and expectation. It allows us to engage with others from a place of compassion and understanding, while maintaining a deep connection to our inner selves. As we journey through life with this awareness, we begin to see that every relationship, whether joyful or challenging, contributes to our growth and self-realization, ultimately leading us toward a deeper understanding of ourselves and the universe.

This journey of self-discovery, guided by the principles of karma and detachment, reminds us that life is a tapestry woven from the threads of past, present, and future. Each moment, each relationship, and each experience are a part of this intricate design, leading us toward our highest potential. By embracing this perspective, we can move through life with greater ease, grace, and wisdom, recognizing that everything unfolds as it should, in perfect harmony with the cosmic plan.

Chapter - 17

The Covid-19 Pandemic's Hidden Gift: A Shift in Consciousness

The Covid-19 pandemic can be seen as a karmic consequence of humanity's collective actions, reflecting the imbalance we have created in nature through our relentless pursuit of material wealth and disregard for spiritual values. From a spiritual perspective, this global crisis serves as a wake-up call, urging us to reconnect with cosmic consciousness and recognize the incorporation of all life. Vibrations transcend physical boundaries, and the universe remains sensitive to human actions, reacting in ways that often elude our understanding due to the veils of ignorance clouding our minds.

The pandemic has highlighted humanity's insensitivity to the larger *prakriti* (nature) we are part of. Post-industrialization, advancements in science and technology have fuelled material desires and attachments, leading to wealth accumulation and environmental degradation. This imbalance has driven humanity toward destruction, as our actions increasingly ignore the theological virtues described in sacred texts like the Bhagavad Gita. These virtues—fearlessness, purity, compassion, honesty, non-violence, and detachment—are essential for right action and spiritual growth but are largely absent in contemporary society.

The teachings of the Bhagavad Gita emphasize detachment from material emotions and outcomes while fostering qualities such as peace, loyalty, modesty, and clarity. The absence of these values in modern life has contributed to the karmic repercussions we face today. Covid-19 serves as a reminder of impermanence (*aniccā*), suffering (*duḥkha*), and interdependence—the three marks of existence described in Buddhist philosophy. It challenges us to transcend ego-driven pursuits and embrace a higher consciousness rooted in compassion, unity, and self-realization.

Ultimately, Covid-19 is not just a health or economic challenge but a spiritual battle—a call to realign humanity's priorities with cosmic harmony. It invites us to reflect on our actions, embrace theological wisdom, and cultivate virtues that lead to collective healing and evolution. By recognizing this crisis as an opportunity for transformation rather than merely a challenge, we can foster a global shift toward higher consciousness and sustainable living. This journey of self-discovery and spiritual awakening is a path that requires patience, resilience, and a willingness to embrace the unknown, but it promises a future where humanity thrives in harmony with nature and itself.

The period between 2020 and 2022 was a transformative and tumultuous time for humanity, marked by unprecedented challenges that shook the world in ways few could have anticipated. The Covid-19 pandemic claimed countless lives, even in countries with advanced healthcare systems, leaving families and individuals to grapple with profound physical and emotional setbacks. In India, life came to a standstill as people endured some of the worst suffering in recent history. While the pandemic disrupted the normal world order for several months, it also had an unexpected effect: nature began to flourish as human activity decreased, revealing the intricate balance between human and natural systems.

Despite the chaos, many people experienced a profound shift in their energies. For some, this period marked a turning point, allowing them to develop a deeper connection with their true selves. Those who had struggled to advance in meditation found this time conducive to making significant progress. Personally, I made sincere strides on the path of self-realization during this period. Spiritual leaders and those with Himalayan wisdom viewed this era as a *khand-pralay* (partial cosmos), a phenomenon that does not destroy everything at once but affects life and living in a partial yet profound manner. This perspective highlights the pandemic's role as a catalyst for spiritual growth and introspection, offering a unique opportunity for individuals to reconnect with themselves and the world around them.

In reflecting on this period, it becomes clear that the pandemic served as both a challenge and a blessing. It forced humanity to pause, reflect, and reevaluate priorities, fostering a global shift toward greater empathy, resilience, and spiritual awareness. As we navigate the aftermath, we are reminded that even in the darkest moments, there lies the potential for transformation and growth. The journey through this *khand-pralay* has been a testament to human resilience and the capacity for spiritual evolution, guiding us toward a future where we may live in greater harmony with nature and ourselves.

In November 2019, following my transformative visit to the cave, I was guided to officially travel to Kolkata and then Guwahati. During my time in Kolkata, I was blessed with the opportunity to visit the Dakshineswar Kali Temple, where I attended the *Sandhya Aarti* (evening prayer) in the Kali temple. Afterward, I sat in meditation in Sri Ramakrishna Paramahansa's room for about an hour, experiencing a profound state of transcendental tranquility reminiscent of my in-cave meditation. As I meditated, a bell rang at 8:30 pm, signalling the end of my time there. Upon standing, I noticed a photograph of Shri Mahavatar Babaji hanging above my seat, precisely in front of the bed where Paramahansa used to rest. This moment of synchronicity left me in awe, and

I attempted to share my amazement with Mohit Sharma, a colleague who had accompanied me to the shrine.

My journey continued in Guwahati, where I visited the revered Maa Kamakhya Temple. There, I received the divine grace of meditation while standing near the sanctum sanctorum. In a state of deep absorption, I found my body seemingly stuck to a rock wall for a significant period. With my eyes closed, I experienced a loss of physical consciousness until my colleague gently touched me to indicate it was time to leave. Reflecting on these spiritual visits, which occurred shortly before the first outbreak of Covid-19 in India, I wonder if they were cosmically designed as preparatory endeavours to help me face the pandemic. While the answer remains unclear, these experiences undoubtedly deepened my spiritual connection and resilience, equipping me to navigate the challenges that followed.

In March 2020, as India implemented a nationwide lockdown to combat the Covid-19 pandemic, my life in Delhi came to a standstill. Confined to my apartment, I adhered to the strict movement restrictions and followed all prescribed protocols. However, this period of isolation unexpectedly gifted me with an abundance of "me time," which I devoted to self-reflection and meditation. Even amidst daily routines like cooking, I dedicated over an hour during the day to meditation, and my evenings were similarly dedicated to deep introspection. These meditative practices often led me to a state of profound blissfulness that transcended verbal expression—though those who have mastered the art of breathwork may understand the eternal highs and lows of energy I experienced.

As the days turned into weeks, the forced detachment from routine life began to feel less burdensome and more pleasurable. I found myself enjoying my own company, with no external obligations or visits disrupting this newfound solitude. This period also marked the beginning of my journey's account writing. Bit by bit, I started documenting my life's experiences into chapters, reflecting on my spiritual and personal growth. During this same time, I also completed compiling my Hindi poems, which culminated in the publication of my first book, *O Aharnish Pyass* (2021), by Bodhi Publication in Jaipur, followed by another coffee table poetry publication *"Tum Reet Gayi, Main Beet Gaya"*, from Shwetwarna Prakashan in 2023.

In retrospect, the lockdown, while challenging for many, became a transformative phase for me—a time of inner exploration, creativity, and spiritual progress. It taught me the value of stillness and self-reflection in a world that often moves too fast to pause. Through this journey, I discovered that solitude can be a powerful catalyst for growth, allowing us to reconnect with ourselves and our creative potential. As I reflect on those months, I am reminded that sometimes, the most profound transformations arise from the unexpected pauses in life.

The Covid-19 lockdown in India, implemented in March 2020, was a complex phenomenon with both positive and negative outcomes. On the one hand, it was remarkably successful in saving lives by slowing the spread of the virus and preventing the healthcare system from being overwhelmed. Studies suggested that the lockdown averted a significant number of cases and deaths, making it a crucial measure in controlling the pandemic. However, the economic and social consequences were severe. Millions of people, particularly those from economically weaker sections, faced immense hardship as businesses shut down, leading to widespread job losses. Migrant workers were forced to return to their native places, often undertaking arduous journeys on foot with their families due to the suspension of transportation services.

The lockdown also highlighted the stark disparities in society, as those who were most vulnerable suffered the most. Despite these challenges, the resilience of the Indian people and the government's efforts helped mitigate some of the damage. From a spiritual perspective, the pandemic was seen by some as a karmic consequence of humanity's actions, a reminder of nature's role in regulating the balance of life on Earth. While the physical origins of the virus were attributed to China's wet markets, others viewed it as part of a larger cosmic design, underscoring the linkage of life and the need for harmony with nature.

Interestingly, despite India's high population density, its death rate remained relatively lower compared to many Western nations—a phenomenon that invites deeper reflection on factors beyond conventional reasoning. This disparity raises questions about the role of cultural, spiritual, and environmental factors in influencing the pandemic's impact. Ultimately, the lockdown served as a catalyst for introspection and spiritual growth for many individuals, highlighting the importance of balancing material pursuits with sensitivity toward nature and collective well-being.

During the lockdown, I adhered to the prescribed norms, maintaining social distancing and staying in isolation. My days were filled with activities such as cooking, reading, writing, and active meditation. One of my evening rituals included lighting an oil lamp outside my flat, a practice that has continued to this day. An hour of meditation each evening led to uninterrupted and fearless sleep, providing a sense of peace and tranquility.

In the late evenings, I would often engage in conversations with Mohit Sharma, a close colleague from the program management unit I led, and his family. They would ask me a range of questions related to religious science, spirituality, and existential inquiries about the self and the existence of God. Our discussions gradually became more frequent and intense, often lasting for hours. I shared my knowledge and insights to the best of my ability, and these interactions deepened our connection and understanding of spiritual concepts.

Around the same time, my first cousin, Bibhuti, who was based in Haldwani with his family, began incorporating meditation into his daily routine. He would often meditate with his five-year-old daughter, while his wife, though not interested in meditation herself, supported their practice. Bibhuti would occasionally share his meditational experiences and pose thoughtful questions, reflecting on his journey.

Inspired by the growing interest in spirituality around us, we decided to create a WhatsApp group called 'Samvad Darshan,' which translates to 'the philosophy of words.' This group was designed to host weekly discourses, fostering a community where we could explore and discuss spiritual ideas and experiences together. The creation of this group marked a significant step in our collective spiritual journey, providing a platform for sharing wisdom and insights during a time of global uncertainty.

During the challenging months of the Covid-19 pandemic in 2020, as lockdowns persisted and restrictions eased slightly by August, I formed a close bond with Devis Saha, a young colleague who had recovered from the virus but was struggling with depression. Amid our frequent conversations, we devised a plan to travel to Vrindavan in my car, seeking solace and spiritual rejuvenation through meditation. By the grace of Shri Shyamal Jee Maharaj of Vrindavan Ashram, we were granted permission to stay for extended periods while adhering to the "work from home" norm. This time allowed us to immerse ourselves in meditation and self-reflection, fostering a deeper connection with our inner selves.

Our days were spent meditating in serene corners of the ashram, often choosing Deen Bandhu Kuteer as a favourite spot for late evening sessions. Devis, though young, carried a deep spiritual lineage from past lives, evident in his meditational depth. Occasionally, we visited Shri Neeb Karori Baba Ashram to delve further into our inner journeys. One of the most profound experiences for me occurred outside Rang Mahal in Nidhi Van—a sacred site shrouded in mystery and divine energy. Sitting under the shade of tree branches on an extended platform near Rang Mahal, I would meditate for hours, experiencing states of suspended breathing similar to those I had encountered in Shri Mahavatar Cave in the Himalayas.

The caretaker of Rang Mahal would offer me *pan* (betel nut), leftover from divine offerings placed the night before—a phenomenon unique to Nidhi Van, where all offerings appear mysteriously consumed by morning. The district administration prohibits human presence inside Nidhi Van at night, adding to its mystique. My meditations outside Rang Mahal were marked by extraordinary experiences that transcended physical consciousness, reaffirming the existence of an unknown dimension that prevails upon my being.

Reflecting on this period, often termed the "Corona catastrophe," I see it as a time of profound spiritual growth and bliss. It was a phase that deepened my connection with myself and the cosmos—a reminder that even amidst global adversity, moments of spiritual awakening can emerge as gifts of grace. Through these experiences, I came to understand that life's challenges can serve as catalysts for inner transformation, guiding us toward a deeper understanding of ourselves and the universe.

During the Covid-19 pandemic, I began to sense a profound transformation in the collective consciousness of humanity. People from different corners of the globe were connecting with each other in a spontaneous and effortless manner, transcending geographical boundaries. One such moment of spiritual resonance occurred during my stay at the Vrindavan Ashram, where I encountered Maria Lieber, a devoted follower of Shri Maa Anandamayi. Her radiant presence, clad in a simple white saree, immediately drew my attention as she walked into the ashram. Our meeting felt like a union of two spirits, witnessed by the sacred Chhalia temple behind us.

Maria, an American with Russian roots, lived a life of deep devotion in Vrindavan and Govardhan, offering *seva* (service) in various ways. From our very first conversation, it felt as though we had known each other across lifetimes. We often sat together by the serene banks of the Yamuna River, engaging in profound discussions about non-physical subjects like life's deeper meanings and spiritual facets. Her unwavering commitment to spirituality was inspiring; her glowing face and humble demeanour reflected her profound connection with Shri Maa Anandamayi's teachings.

During her time in Govardhan, we undertook the sacred Govardhan *parikrama*, walking twenty-square kilometres throughout the night—a deeply transformative experience that connected us on a spiritual level. Maria's past-life connections to India seemed evident in her devotion and ease with the people she mingled with here. She frequently travelled to Omkareshwar for extended stays before returning to Vrindavan or Govardhan.

Interacting with Maria has always been a blissful experience—a reminder of the divine essence that can manifest in human form. Her humility, piety, and spiritual depth continue to inspire me, making our connection a unique and cherished part of my journey during this transformative period of global awakening. Through our conversations and shared spiritual experiences, I have come to realize that some connections transcend time and space, reflecting a deeper cosmic design that brings souls together in unexpected yet meaningful ways.

As the 'Samvad Darshan' group welcomed new members, it gained momentum, evolving into a vibrant community of spiritual seekers. We initiated the 'Saturday Satsang,' a weekly spiritual discourse held every Saturday evening from seven to eight. This platform became a sacred space for sharing experiences, raising questions, and seeking clarifications on a wide range of subjects, including spiritual practices, their scientific aspects, the cosmos, and the lives of Yogis. What made this group truly unique was its diversity—members from different age groups, backgrounds, and geographical origins came together, many of whom I had never met before except through divine grace.

The growth of 'Samvad Darshan' reflected the collective yearning for spiritual exploration during uncertain times. It became more than just a group—it transformed into a sacred space for connection, introspection, and shared wisdom, bringing together individuals who were magnetically drawn toward their meditational journeys and spiritual growth. Through these interactions, we discovered that spiritual connections can transcend physical boundaries, often emerging through unexpected encounters that feel guided by a higher purpose.

In mid-2021, as the Covid-19 pandemic's intensity waned and life began returning to normal, I felt an inexplicable pull to return to my home state. By July 2021, I embarked on a new assignment with an organization, working on a health systems strengthening of the Bihar state government. Among my key responsibilities was overseeing post-graduate medical education promotion initiatives across all thirty-eight districts of Bihar—a role that not only allowed me to contribute to public health but also became a catalyst for deepening my spiritual journey.

Traveling extensively for work, I made time to visit places of immense spiritual significance, some familiar and others new to me. Revisiting sacred sites like Bodhgaya, Rajgir, Pawapuri, and Nalanda profoundly impacted me, stimulating what felt like the atomic essence of my being. These visits often reminded me of my Guru's prophecy: *"Tum aadhyatmik yatrayen karoge"* (You will undertake spiritual journeys). Each day on the road affirmed this vision, as I felt guided by an unseen force.

What struck me most during this period was the boundless energy I experienced. Despite covering distances of two to three hundred kilometres daily, I never felt fatigued and was always ready for the next journey by morning. It often left me wondering: who or what was truly traveling in my body? The answer remains elusive, yet the realization that something beyond physicality was at play became increasingly clear.

These travels not only deepened my connection with Bihar's rich spiritual heritage but also reaffirmed the profound interplay between work and inner growth. The sacred sites—like the Mahabodhi Temple in Bodhgaya, where Lord Buddha attained enlightenment; Jal Mandir in Pawapuri, where Lord Mahavir achieved nirvana; and the ancient ruins of Nalanda—served as powerful reminders of humanity's timeless quest for truth and transcendence. Reflecting on this period, I see it as a divine orchestration, blending duty with spiritual evolution in ways that continue to inspire and transform me. Through these experiences, I came to understand that life's journey is not just about destinations but about the profound transformations that occur along the way.

Traveling across the country allowed me to connect with a diverse array of people, an experience that felt like mingling with the totality of existence. It was a grace that filled me with an eternal sense of fulfilment, as if I were soaring through the open sky, unencumbered and free. From bustling cities to rural villages, each journey was a testament to the beauty of human connection and the vastness of our shared experiences. During my travels, I would often stop at roadside eateries for a bite, then continue on my way, feeling invigorated by the simplicity of these encounters. My physical energy seemed to align with the frequency of my journeys, as if the more I travelled, the more energized I became. This phenomenon was both intriguing and reassuring, a reminder that sometimes, our bodies respond to the rhythms of the universe in ways that transcend conventional understanding.

One of the most memorable experiences was during my visit to Kaimur district. Locals shared with me the significance of various religious sites in the area, including 'Gupt-dham,' a mystical place nestled deep within the Vindhya Mountain range. To reach it, I had to traverse about twenty-five kilometres of rugged terrain. Gupt-dham is a cave with a wide opening that extends into a dark tunnel about 100 meters long. Water drips from the ceiling, creating an ethereal atmosphere. Inside, several Shiv Lingams are naturally formed, with water droplets pouring over them from above. In one corner, I saw a large Shiv Lingams positioned near the ceiling, and there were formations resembling beehives that seemed active, radiating a strange, star-like light.

Locals would often visit this site with deep reverence, though it was interesting to note how such places sometimes lose their spiritual essence and become more ritualistic. I yearned to meditate there for a while, to immerse myself in the mystical energy that permeates the space. However, local officials advised me to return before nightfall for safety reasons. I hope to return to this cosmically charged site again, to delve deeper into its mysteries and connect with the beings that dwell beyond the physical realm.

This journey not only deepened my connection with the natural world and its spiritual dimensions but also reminded me of the beauty in exploring the unknown and the profound experiences that await us on the path less travelled. Through these encounters, I came to realize that traveling is not just about reaching destinations but about the transformative moments that occur along the way— moments that can awaken us to new perspectives and deeper connections with ourselves and the universe.

The district of Kaimur is also famed as the sacred seat of Maa Mundeshwari, believed by many to be the site of one of the oldest surviving temples in the world. It is here that the unique ritual of *"Rakt-Rahit Bali"* (bloodless sacrifice) is reverently offered to the Mother Deity—a sacred observance which I have been privileged to witness on numerous gracious occasions.

This venerable temple, perched upon the hierophanic summit of the Vindhyachal range, stands without a roof to this day, yet commands the unwavering devotion of countless pilgrims from distant regions. The same demonic cult that once laid waste to Nalanda also wrought destruction upon this hallowed shrine. Yet, the inherent sacredness and sanctity of the land have remained inviolate and unblemished through the ages.

Within the 'Garbhgriha'—the sanctum sanctorum—a lofty, multi-faced Shivlingam occupies the center, while Maa Mundeshwari herself resides in a revered corner of the same sanctum, bestowing blessings upon all who seek her grace.

The Deo Sun Temple, situated near Gaya in Bihar, is a testament to India's ancient architectural brilliance and spiritual heritage. Dedicated to Surya, the Sun God, this temple is unique among sun temples as it faces west toward the setting sun, unlike the traditional orientation toward the rising sun. The temple's origins are steeped in legends and historical narratives, with some accounts tracing its construction to the Treta Yuga, the era associated with Lord Ram. However, historical records suggest it was built by King Bhairavendra Singh of the Chandravanshi dynasty during the medieval period.

The temple's architecture is awe-inspiring, featuring a hundred-foot-tall pyramid-shaped *shikhara* adorned with intricate carvings and motifs that reflect Nagara and Vesara styles. The sanctum houses idols of Vishnu, Surya, and Avalokiteswara, though these are not the original presiding deities. Outside the sanctum, broken sculptures of Surya with seven horses, Uma-Maheshwara, and Vishnu are kept as relics of its storied past. The temple complex also includes sacred water tanks like Rudra Kund and Surya Kund, believed to possess healing properties for ailments such as leprosy.

Despite enduring invasions and periods of neglect, the Deo Sun Temple has retained its spiritual significance and architectural grandeur. Its intricate stone carvings showcase the advanced craftsmanship and scientific knowledge of ancient Indian architects—skills that rival modern engineering techniques. Visiting this temple evokes a sense of wonder about how advanced ancient civilizations were in blending spirituality with technology.

The experience of visiting Deo twice was deeply enriching for me. Observing the temple's timeless beauty and cosmic energy reinforced my belief in the enduring legacy of India's spiritual and architectural heritage. It serves as a reminder that ancient knowledge often surpasses what we term "modern science," blending art, devotion, and engineering into masterpieces that continue to inspire awe even today. Through these visits, I gained a deeper appreciation for the harmony between human creativity and the divine, a balance that ancient cultures seemed to achieve with remarkable precision.

Maa's ashram in Rajgir holds immense spiritual significance for me, serving as a personal pilgrimage site during my travels across the Magadh region of Bihar. This ashram, closely associated with Maa Anandamayi, is where she would retreat for *agyatvas* (solitude).

The campus exudes an energy that transforms into peace and tranquility, enveloping all who visit. A small temple housing Shiv Lingams adds to the spiritual aura of the ashram. Maa's room on the first floor has always been a source of profound spiritual elevation for me; meditating there consistently takes me to higher dimensions. Divine design seemed to orchestrate my daily routine perfectly—I would complete my official duties visiting various districts and return to Rajgir each evening to freshen up, meditate in Maa's room for an hour, and have dinner at the ashram.

Rani Maa, a lady ordained in Maa's order, serves as both caretaker and cook at the ashram. She also looks after Shri Patit Pawan Ji Maharaj, the in-charge of Maa's Rajgir ashram. Maharaj Ji has served Maa Anandamayi for many years and has lived in several of her ashrams across India, including Dehradun, Varanasi, and Rajgir. Listening to Maharaj Ji speak about Maa and her teachings has always been a blessing for me. His love and affection encouraged me to spend more time at the ashram, deepening my spiritual connection and understanding of Maa's divine presence.

This sacred space in Rajgir not only revitalized my spirit but also reaffirmed the profound harmony between duty and devotion. It stands as a testament to the timeless wisdom and energy that permeates places touched by divine grace. Through my experiences at the ashram, I came to understand that spiritual growth often unfolds in the most unexpected ways, weaving together moments of solitude, connection, and service in a fabric of profound meaning and purpose.

Mandar Hill, located in the Banka district of Bihar, is a site of immense spiritual, mythological, and historical significance. Rising approximately seven hundred feet high, this sacred hill is steeped in legends and serves as a pilgrimage destination for Hindus and Jains alike. It is believed to be the *Mandarachal Parvat* mentioned in Hindu scriptures, used as the churning rod during the *Samudra Manthan* (churning of the ocean) by gods and demons to extract the nectar of immortality. Lord Vishnu, in his Kurma (tortoise) avatar, supported the hill during this cosmic event, making it a symbol of divine intervention and harmony.

During my second visit to Mandar Hill, I trekked to its summit and meditated there for over an hour. The experience was transformative—a surge of energy coursed through me, elevating my consciousness beyond the physical realm. For that brief period, I transcended my bodily existence, entering a state of breathless stillness and profound transcendence. It felt as though I was revisiting a past life—a life that unfolded before me with vivid clarity but was not tied to my current existence. Such moments are beyond words; they can only be felt deeply within.

Mandar Hill's physical formation itself is awe-inspiring. Its structure resembles a human figure lying on its back with its head elevated—a natural wonder that boggles the mind. The hill is dotted with narrow caves and ancient carvings that add to its mystique. Exploring these caves revealed a sacred energy that seemed to resonate with the hill's mythological past. The summit houses temples dedicated to both Hindu and Jain traditions, including rare sculptures of Lord Vishnu and Jain Tirthankara Vasupujya, who attained *nirvana* here.

One of the most fascinating aspects of Mandar Hill is its connection to cosmic energy shifts. The Papaharni Sarovar at its base is believed to cleanse sins, while marks on the rocks are said to be remnants of Vasuki, the serpent used as a churning rope during *Samudra Manthan*. The hill also bears footprints attributed to Lord Vishnu as Madhusudana after defeating the demons Madhu and Kaitabh.

My meditation at Mandar Hill left me with an unparalleled sense of fulfilment. It felt as though this visit had been cosmically ordained, waiting for the right moment in time. The energy I experienced there continues to resonate within me, reminding me of the profound spiritual dimensions that lie hidden in such sacred spaces. Mandar Hill is not just a geographical marvel but a timeless bridge between mythology, spirituality, and human consciousness—a place where one can truly connect with the divine essence of existence.

Life, in its essence, is a manifestation of the divine, woven from the same elemental consciousness that pervades all existence. Some individuals possess the awareness (*drishti*) to perceive and decode this reality, understanding the evolutionary movements of life, while others remain veiled in ignorance, unaware of their intrinsic connection to this universal truth. This ignorance—both within and outside—is not imposed by external forces but arises from our own delusions. It traps us in cycles of *sukha* (pleasure) and *dukkha* (suffering), perpetuated by our lack of understanding.

The journey to awakening often involves the arrival of a Guru or teacher—a messenger who dispels the darkness of ignorance (*gu*) and illuminates the path to wisdom (*ru*). The role of a Guru is not merely to impart knowledge but to facilitate an inner transformation, guiding seekers toward self-realization and spiritual awakening. As described in Hindu tradition, the Guru serves as a mirror reflecting the divine within us, helping us transcend ego-driven delusions and align with our true essence.

Interestingly, not all Gurus are physically present. Some operate from unseen realms, subtly influencing and awakening individuals when the time is ripe. This process often involves a shift in consciousness—a moment of divine grace that opens new dimensions of understanding. However, maintaining this awakened state requires personal effort and balance. As spiritual traditions emphasize, divine grace can initiate transformation, but it is through our own perseverance that we sustain it.

The Guru-disciple relationship is one of profound trust and surrender. A true Guru embodies divine wisdom and compassion, offering guidance tailored to each seeker's unique journey. Whether through direct teachings or subtle influence, Gurus help individuals navigate the complexities of life and uncover their inherent divinity. In this way, they act as beacons of light, dispelling ignorance and fostering a deeper connection with the cosmic order.

Ultimately, life itself is a spiritual journey—a process of awakening to our divine nature. The presence of a Guru, whether seen or unseen, plays a pivotal role in this evolution. Yet, it is our responsibility to embrace this guidance with humility and dedication, allowing it to transform us from within. Through this interplay of grace, effort, and guidance, we move closer to realizing the eternal truth that life is not separate from the divine but a reflection of it in its purest form. This realization empowers us to transcend the cycles of suffering and joy, embracing a life of profound peace and understanding.

During the Covid-19 pandemic and its aftermath, I observed a profound shift in consciousness both in myself and others. This transformation manifested in diverse ways, reflecting the varied paths individuals took toward spiritual growth and introspection. For instance, Dharmendra Thakur, an IT professional and a friend of my younger brother Sudhakar, became deeply devoted to Maa Anandamayi and began believing in the divine existence of Shri Mahavatar Babaji. He would often travel to Vrindavan and other Maa's ashrams during his free time and started practicing meditation. His quiet demeanour during *Dhyan Darshan* sessions revealed the unfolding of divine energy within him.

Similarly, Pawan Rana, a young IT professional from Himachal Pradesh living in Chandigarh, demonstrated remarkable spiritual growth. An exceptional meditator, Pawan would immerse himself deeply during our Saturday meditational discourses. He often shared those spiritual discussions rejuvenated him, triggering an upward flow of energy within him. His curiosity about his meditative experiences led him to ask insightful questions that enriched our collective understanding.

This shift in consciousness aligns with broader observations during the pandemic, where existential anxiety and uncertainty prompted many to seek meaning and spiritual growth. The pandemic highlighted the inter-play of humanity and the importance of global cooperation, fostering a sense of global consciousness that transcended national boundaries. Through these experiences, individuals like Dharmendra and Pawan exemplified how the pandemic catalysed a global shift in consciousness, encouraging deeper introspection and spiritual exploration amidst adversity. Their journeys underscore the potential for transformative growth during challenging times, illustrating how crises can become catalysts for profound personal and collective evolution.

This period seemed to awaken deeper existential inquiries in many, as was evident in individuals like Shri Prasoon Pandey. Hailing from the holy city of Ayodhya, Prasoon is deeply self-exploring individuals. Despite his physical youth, Prasoon is profoundly evolved on the planes of consciousness, with a mind deeply attuned to seeking answers to existential questions. He would often reach out to me with inquiries that transcended the ordinary, reflecting his quest for higher understanding.

Prasoon has been a regular participant in the *Samvad Darshan* discourses and weekly meditation sessions. Formally initiated by Sri M., he embodies a spiritual enthusiasm that inspires others on similar paths. Two of his *Guru-Bhais* (co-disciples), Arnab Nandi and Ashok Kumar, have also joined *Samvad Darshan* through his encouragement. Prasoon is deeply charged with spiritual energy—reading, meditating, and engaging in discussions about creation and the Creator. His dedication to spiritual growth is both inspiring and humbling.

For me personally, knowing such spiritually inclined individuals has been a blessing. They not only enrich my journey but also provide subtle yet profound support that feels guided by dimensions beyond the physical. Their presence reminds me of the linkages of all seekers and how divine grace often manifests through others to keep us steady on our path. Without such companions, the risk of faltering or losing direction could easily arise.

This period of transformation has underscored the importance of collective spiritual exploration and mutual encouragement among seekers. It reaffirms that spiritual growth is not an isolated endeavour but one supported by shared wisdom, divine guidance, and the uplifting presence of kindred spirits like Prasoon and his companions. Through these interactions, I have come to understand that spiritual journeys are often intertwined, with each person playing a role in guiding others toward deeper understanding and enlightenment.

During the Covid-19 pandemic and its aftermath, my journeys became incredibly frequent and speedy, to the point where I felt as though I embodied speed itself. Traveling through all thirty-eight districts of Bihar, I discovered places of profound spiritual significance that I had never known existed. These visits were guided by a prophecy that foretold my journey to such sites. Wherever I went, I would meditate and internalize the vibrations of these sacred spaces, feeling my energy field expand immensely.

One of the places that fell on my path was Parsarma in the Supaul district of north-eastern Bihar. This village is the birthplace of the renowned Yogi Shri Lakshminath Gosain, who lived there before moving to Bangaon, a nearby location where the Kosi River flows. Lakshminath Gosain was known for his extensive travels across India and Nepal, and he shared some contemporary years with Shri Shyama Charan Lahiri, suggesting they might have interacted. His spiritual legacy continues to inspire seekers today.

I felt magnetically drawn to Parsarma, visiting it multiple times over a short period. During one of these visits,

I had the opportunity to meditate inside a tiny settlement housing a Vishnu idol believed to have been installed by Shri Lakshminath Gosain himself. The idol is depicted in Shambhavi Mudra with eyes twisted upward, and meditating there was a captivating experience. I am grateful to my friend Dr. Anant Kumar Ji for facilitating these visits to Parsarma and Bangaon. Anant ji, One of the Deputy Collectors in present-day Bihar administration happens to be quite an evolved spirit born to an equally elevated mother.

(With Dr. Anant Kumar at home)

These journeys not only deepened my spiritual connection but also underscored the profound impact of visiting places imbued with spiritual energy. Each visit felt like a divine orchestration, guiding me toward deeper self-awareness and inner peace. Through these experiences, I came to understand that life's journey is not just about destinations but about the transformative moments that occur along the way—moments that can awaken us to new perspectives and deeper connections with ourselves and the universe. This realization has been a blessing, reminding me of the close associations of all spiritual seekers and the role that sacred sites play in our collective journey toward enlightenment.

During my visits to Bangaon and Mahisi, I found myself at a historically and spiritually significant sites, renowned as the location of the great theological debate between Shri Mandan Mishra and Shri Adi Shankaracharya. This debate, which also involved Mandan Mishra's wife, Ubhaya Bharati, stands as a monumental event in Indian philosophical history. It revolved around the contrasting philosophies of *Dvaita* (Duality), championed by Mandan Mishra, and *Advaita* (Non-Duality), expounded by Adi Shankaracharya. The discourse reportedly lasted for months, with Ubhaya Bharati serving as the impartial judge.

According to legend, when reverend Ubhaya Bharati challenged Adi Shankaracharya to debate her after her husband's defeat, she posed questions on household life and worldly experiences. To answer comprehensively, Adi Shankaracharya is said to have temporarily left his body and entered that of a king to gain firsthand experience of a householder's life before returning to his original form. This extraordinary episode highlights the depth and rigor of spiritual inquiry during that era.

Adjacent to this site is the Maa Ugratara Temple, adding to the sacredness of the location. While there, I felt an inexplicable sense of familiarity, as though I had visited this place in past lives. Unfortunately, due to time constraints on my official trip, I could not meditate there as I had intended. However, even a brief visit left me deeply moved.

In Bangaon, I also came across a Sun Temple dating back to the Pal dynasty. This discovery expanded my understanding of Bihar's rich architectural and spiritual heritage, as Sun Temples are relatively rare in the region. Reflecting on my experience, I felt magnetically drawn to these sacred sites, as if guided by a higher force. These visits not only deepened my spiritual connection but also enriched my awareness of India's profound philosophical and cultural legacy.

During my travels in the region, I had the opportunity to meet Shri Chandra Shekhar Jha, a senior bureaucrat in the Bihar administration, stationed in Madhepura district. Although we had spoken over the phone previously, this was our first in-person meeting, which took place in January 2023 near a small temple dedicated to the great Yogi Shri Lakshminath Gosain, whose spiritual legacy I have mentioned earlier. At the time, I was immersed in meditation when Mr. Jha arrived, accompanied by Dr. Anant Kumar, a young officer of the same cadre.

Later that evening, we gathered at Dr. Anant's residence and engaged in an enriching discussion on *Advaita* (non-duality). It felt particularly significant to delve into this profound subject in a region historically tied to the celebrated debate on *Dvaita* (duality) and *Advaita* between Shri Mandan Mishra and Shri Adi Shankaracharya. Mr. Jha spoke extemporaneously on non-duality with such clarity and depth that it felt as though Brahma himself was speaking through him. His words left me speechless, resonating deeply with my own transcendental experiences. At one point, he turned to me and asked if my meditative experiences aligned with what he had described. I nodded affirmatively, feeling an unspoken connection.

Mr. Jha has been associated with the *Samvad Darshan* team for a few months, but this was my first opportunity to interact with him one-on-one. I would describe him as a *Gyan Yogi* (seeker of knowledge), who shared with me his aspiration to transition into *Dhyan Yog* (the path of meditation). I assured him that his desired transformation would soon begin to manifest. We met on several other occasions afterward, each interaction further deepening my respect for his spiritual insight.

This encounter reaffirmed the linkages of seekers on the spiritual path and reminded me of how divine grace often orchestrates such meetings to facilitate mutual growth and understanding. It was a privilege to engage in meaningful dialogue with someone so deeply rooted in knowledge yet earnestly striving for meditative transcendence. Through these interactions, I came to understand that spiritual journeys are often intertwined, with each person playing a role in guiding others toward deeper understanding.

My coming back to Bihar was accompanied by so many revisits to those sites I had already visited in my past lives. Traveling back and forth to places containing immense vibrations was part of the official entourage. Whichever district I travelled, significant locations would fascinate me and I would make sure to visit. And these visits would happen in short frequencies. Traveling was happening with faster speeds, as never envisaged. In some months, for instance, I would travel almost twenty-five days. On some other occasions, without being tired, I would myself drive for seventeen hours and reach up to my new Himalayan abode. Staying there for three-four days would help my consciousness to uplift amidst the walk I would undertake in thick forests and go uphill to reunite with the cosmic subtleties I originally belonged. So much recharged energy I would feel I gained during the stay there. Probably, equal amounts of emptiness too, I gained, as if to get reminded that I didn't belong to the world of physical attachments but to the divine. Holy cave visits were part of all such Himalayan trips. I saw life's magic in manifestation in several ways than just one. Were it all subjected to being assigned to one particular factor or a bunch of them that provided so much of impetus to self-searching, I can't say. No one can say that! Therefore, it's always good to talk about the patterns of life, the journey upward, while conducting all mandatory duties of physical existence.

Priyabhishek Sharma, a college teacher from Himachal Pradesh, has been traversing the spiritual path for many years. In our conversations, he shared a remarkable encounter with a Himalayan *Saadhu* whom he never met again. This chance meeting profoundly altered his life, as he began to dwell in dimensions beyond the earthly realm. Despite being a householder and teacher by profession, Priyabhishek developed a sense of detachment from the socio-physical order and started meditating for hours, worshiping Shakti. His experiences are vivid and incomparable.

Priyabhishek has been in touch with a great Himalayan Master from Himachal Pradesh who closely follows the teachings of Shri Mahavatar Babaji. When discussing my journeys to the holy Mahavatar cave, he expressed a deep desire to visit it. Soon after, he devised a plan to drive to the cave, and I served as a virtual guide for him. Since then, he has visited the cave twice, experiencing profound bliss. Additionally, Priyabhishek has been encouraging me to complete writing this book, so that others may gain insights into what a householder's spiritual journey can look like. He challenges the common perception that a spiritual being must don saffron and detach from the mainstream world, highlighting that true spirituality can thrive in any lifestyle.

In recent times, a significant development has unfolded, one that I believe is deeply connected to the divine design and manifestations of past lives. My spiritual friend, Shri Priyabhishek Sharma, whose journey I have mentioned earlier, expressed his desire to purchase a piece of land near my abode in the same village where the holy cave is located. His spiritual thirst was evident, and I witnessed its materialization within a remarkably short span of time. Interestingly, the same landowner, Shri Bahadur Singh, from whom I had acquired my land, offered another patch of land in close proximity. The purchase process began and concluded seamlessly in less than three months.

Together, we are envisioning the creation of small dwelling units for spiritual seekers who wish to spend time near the holy cave. Currently, there are no free accommodations or food services available in this remote area. For meals and lodging, travellers must rely on Joshi Guest House in Kukuchhina, which is the most accessible option. However, it requires a journey from the site. Alternatively, there is a wooden resort named 'Vanprastha' located below my land and home. While it offers comfortable accommodations, its high costs make it unaffordable for many travellers.

Our shared vision aims to provide an affordable and serene space for seekers to immerse themselves in spiritual practices without financial constraints. This initiative feels like an extension of the divine energy that surrounds the holy cave and its surroundings. It is our hope that these efforts will create a nurturing environment for those on their spiritual journeys, allowing them to connect deeply with the vibrations of this sacred place while experiencing the simplicity and peace it offers. Through this endeavour, we aspire to bridge the gap between spiritual aspiration and practical accessibility, fostering a community that can thrive in harmony with nature and the divine

In addition to Priyabhishek, there are others who want to buy land out there and get their respective huts built. I was seeing such spiritual interests rise in this post-Corona period. A rise in consciousness to relate to the self, was something significant to witness. People I would see inclined to travel, hold spiritual discourses and read books. They would often ask questions spiritual in nature. These people I am talking about came from different age-groups, religious following and caste backgrounds. Common to all of them was that they were all seeking their 'selves'.

Manish Mathur, a long-time colleague and a friend from Bhopal expressed his desire to visit the holy cave in the recent past. He was trapped under a behavioural deformity he wanted to get rid of. His wife too spoke with me at some point. Accepting such requests posed by people came to me as a divine mandate being conferred upon me. I honoured his request and drove him to the cave from Delhi. I had planned to initiate some work at my place out there, painting and carpentry to be precise. But the first target of every such visit was to visit the cave, meditate out there and then indulge in other activities. Manish accompanied me to the cave and sat inside with his eyes closed and mind centred around the self. He informed me later that he stayed in that position for almost half an hour.

Shri Amar Singh's spiritual journey has been profoundly influenced by his first visit to the holy cave on April 9, 2020. Upon returning, he intensified his practices and deepened his divine commitment by finding a young Kriya teacher who guided him in the right techniques. This teacher would conduct rituals attended by a small group of followers, including Amar Singh, and they would occasionally visit the holy cave together. Since 2020, Amar Singh has revisited the cave at least four times, reflecting his growing spiritual engagement.

Amar Singh's spiritual exploration has been both captivating and extensive. He has travelled to various places of spiritual significance, including one important site associated with the Kriya tradition. Located about hundred kilometres from Ayodhya in a place called Magahiya, this site is an ashram founded by one of Lahiri Mahashay's direct disciples. The ashram is notable for housing one of Yogiraj's leg bones, which is considered a sacred Samadhi. Amar Singh has often invited me to visit this place for a night stay, though I have not had the opportunity yet. I am interested in visiting in the future, which would allow me to experience the spiritual vibrations of this sacred site firsthand.

Bibhuti, I still remember, wasn't a spiritual being at all. He might have been a religious believer but certainly didn't hold on to Dhyan or meditation. On my first visit to the cave, he accompanied me. I saw him sitting outside the cave but wasn't inclined to be inside and meditate at that high dimension. I didn't tell him to do that either. My son and he sat outside. However, within a few weeks after that visit, he himself started to share with me that he had begun to meditate regularly and also made his five-year-old daughter sit with him. As per him his daughter and he himself were gaining momentum bit by bit. He also talked about how slowing down of his breathing had begun and that he started to feel internal alignments. Bibhuti, I am witnessing a fast transition in, both personally and professionally.

For some days, there was a thought that would appear in my mind with periodic frequency that I should organise a feeding party for the children around the area that Swami Lakshmi Nath Gosain's ashram was located in. This thought was quite powerful in its cosmic decadence. It would appear again and again. One fine morning, while I talked with Anant ji, I shared a few words about a divine will I was being given to actualise. And I was convinced about it. Anant ji heard me quietly and assured that he would get that organised. He also added that the proposed function could be organised on an auspicious evening. In two-three conversations we held about it and a Purnima evening was decided for the function to be held outside the ashram. The distant family members of Shri Gosain were readily available to organise the children feeding event. About four hundred children from the local area were invited to join the feast. Elderly people and women of the local communities too joined and ate alongside the children.

Three-four government officials were present in highest reverence for Swami ji. For me, witnessing a divine thought actualise on the ground was to see the divine forces making me carry forward some of their own mandates. I wasn't even a doer, instead, I was seeing how different beings were pulled together to carry different tasks forward. Within about four hours, about four hundred stomachs were fed with good food in that remote rural area, a village about fifteen kilometres off from an Eastern Bihar district town. I could not really figure out why I received that message that I was made to actualise within a short span of time on a Purnima (full moon) night. I believe being aware brings synchronisation of mind and spirit.

Such frequently happening new events have been ever changing. New, never thought-of places are being visited again and again as if my body has been pulled under a magnetic influence. I try to figure that out at times, but I reach nowhere. While I was still at Supaul district circuit house, it was a Sunday morning. Anant ji had informed me of a great householder Yogi who lived nearby in a village on the banks of Kosi River. We planned to visit Him that Sunday morning. To reach the reverend Yogi's village, we had to leave our vehicle on the northern banks of Kosi and then take a boat to cross over and walk a kilometre further to reach his house. His name, as we were told, was Shri Visheshwar Yadav. Locals fondly called him 'Mahatma Baba'. The Mungrar village we were seated at, was where, 'Mahatma Baba' was born in, sometime in 1945. His father was Shri Mahanti Yadav. On the physical plains, 'Mahatma Baba' was a typical householder with 6 children, 4 sons and 2 daughters. He was a retired government teacher, who mostly served in a school in Pipra Hari village not at much distance from the Supaul district headquarters. In earlier days, Supaul district used to fall under Saharsa district, which is one of Bihar State's divisional headquarters.

Within a short span of our arrival, he appeared to us from his abode nearby. The moment I looked at him, as he walked towards us, he sent across vibrations that sensationalised my being. We were given to sit under a mango tree. He was around eighty years of physical age and had leaned down because of aging. He sat down and we started to chat. I was made to be mindful of being a close observant. Anant ji was the one who asked him several questions, mostly pertaining to his life journeys with special reference to his spiritual quests. He appeared to be illuminated and cosmically charged and that reflected on his face. He came out candidly and spoke about how his spiritual inclinations started and evolved. He spoke in Maithili, the local language. It wasn't difficult for me to understand Maithili as my own mother tongue was Maithili. My mother came from a village which was located around sixty kilometres south of where we were seated.

Mahatma Baba gave us the understanding that he came in contact with his Guru Shri Ram Adheer Mahto ji, who himself was a teacher. His meeting with his Guru was quite interesting. One of those early years during the late 1950s, Koshi had flooded the area. His entire village had been rehabilitated to another village close to Supaul district headquarters. His family too was resettled. Mahatma Baba was around nine or ten years of age during that time period. For studies, Shri Mahanti Yadav, the father of Mahatma Baba took him to Shri Ram Adheer Mahto. However, Mahatma Baba wasn't interested in studies. People used to mock Mahatma Baba's Guru Shri Mahto saying it wasn't difficult to make a parrot learn how to recite 'Sita Ram' but it wasn't possible to educate that child. In response to those who mocked, Shri Mahto made a prophecy about Mahatma Baba and reassured, *"Visheshwar will not only learn how to recite Sita Ram in the next fifteen days, but will also prove to be a great Yogi in time to come".*

On another occasion, Shri Lakshmi Nath Gosain (the reverend Yogi who I have already talked about in preceding pages), appeared to him in a subtle form and said *"everyone is dear to me but you are my beloved one"*. While we kept talking under that mango tree that Sunday morning in the open space outside his house, he continued to be candidly humble in his presentation. At some point, we heard him say *"Maa Katyayni once appeared to me during one of my meditation sessions and expressed her desire to stay here. Since then, she has been putting up with me here".* He encouraged us to visit his place of meditation. That was a simple one room space with a bed-like structure made on the floor which was covered with hundreds of red-lotus flowers. That room was pulsating to say the least. While he talked, I was speechless. My letters had ceased to exist. For about an hour, I was a silent listener and an observer. Anant ji was the only one in dialogue with him. Aseem, another friend and a Saadhak (meditator) himself was also present, but was quiet. We were told that several senior officials from government and other walks of life visit him from time to time seeking his blessings.

Soon after my eastern Bihar trip and meeting with 'Mahatma Baba', I was taken to Bhagalpur region. Holy Ganga flows through Bhagalpur. On the banks of the river, Shri Maharshi Mehi's ashram is located. Shri Maharshi Mehi was among the most revered saints and a Yogi of high acumen who lived for around ninety-nine years. He instituted Gurudham which I was revisiting yet another time. Previously too, I was made to visit the ashram but wasn't able to sit and meditate there (which I normally do at such places). Anant ji's parents have been initiated under Shri Mehi's tradition. Anant ji visits the ashram along with his parents from time to time.

He knew people who would guide me to sit and meditate at an appropriate location. I was given to understand that there was a clay-cave there that was distributed into several under-the-earth compartments and was made of multiple layers. The last layer touched the Ganga banks. Though the cave remained locked and was limited to access. However, if special permission was obtained, it could be opened for a limited period of time for meditation. One of our Dhyan Darshan group members, Arpit, a young Yogi who lived out of Bhagalpur, had also agreed to meditate with me in the cave. Therefore, he was there that morning when I revisited the ashram. The visit was well coordinated and allowed our access to the cave.

At first glance, the clay cave was an incredible sight, crafted entirely from natural clay through meticulous digging and skilled techniques. The main entrance led to a descending path that opened onto a lower platform, which further branched into left and right wings. The cave was thoughtfully designed with dedicated spots for meditation, creating an inviting space for seekers.

Upon entering the cave, the caretaker informed us that he would lock the entrance from the outside and return after an hour to reopen it. Both Arpit and I settled into meditation, immersing ourselves in the exclusive energy of the cave. For me, this was a first-time experience—meditating in a clean and serene clay cave. The body quickly tuned into cosmic frequencies with minimal effort, a process that usually takes about half an hour in other settings but happened in just five minutes within the cave.

(Inside Maharshi Mehi's Mud-cave at Bhagalpur, Bihar)

Despite the presence of insects like cockroaches, which were abundant and visible as they crept into the cave, we remained focused on our meditative pursuits. Over two consecutive days, we were fortunate enough to enter the cave and explore its depths, each visit deepening our connection with its sacred vibrations. This experience not only highlighted the cave's natural beauty but also its potential as a transformative space for spiritual growth and introspection. The cave's unique energy seemed to amplify our meditative experiences, allowing us to connect more deeply with our inner selves and the cosmic forces that surround us.

On my fourth visit to Mandar Hill, I arrived at its base around 4 pm after completing official work at the Civil Surgeon's office in Banka. Though a ropeway has been installed for ease of access, I preferred to walk up, as the journey itself feels like a spiritual ascent. The hill, primarily a large stone boulder with expansive dimensions, emanates escalating energy that synchronizes deeply with one's inner self. Its layered structure adds to its mystical allure, and from a distance, all seven high points are clearly visible.

During this visit to Mandar Hill, I felt cosmically guided to meditate at Shankh-Kund. Arriving at the pond late in the afternoon around 4:30 pm, I was drawn by an irresistible spiritual pull despite the intense heat radiating from the base stone. Overcoming physical discomfort, I sat and meditated for about forty-five minutes. The experience was transformative. The first image that emerged in my consciousness was of Shri Lahiri Mahashaya, whose subtle presence felt unmistakably clear. My awareness shifted swiftly into a transcendental state, where cosmic sounds resonated deeply within me, leaving an intoxicating effect even after emerging from meditation.

At the shell-tank, (Shankh-Kund), on top of Mandar Hill, Banka, Bihar

The energy of Shankh-Kund seemed to synchronize effortlessly with my being. Though I could not physically see the massive conch shell submerged in the pond, its presence created an undeniable synergy that enveloped my entire consciousness in blissfulness. This profound experience reminded me of how sacred spaces like Mandar Hill serve as conduits for spiritual transformation, allowing seekers to connect with higher dimensions and cosmic vibrations.

The Madhusudan Temple, situated about a kilometre north of Mandarachal (Mandar Hill), is a site of profound historical and spiritual significance. Dedicated to Lord Vishnu, the temple houses a unique mobile idol of Madhusudan, which was retrieved from Mandarachal itself. This idol is believed to have survived the destruction of ancient temples atop Mandar Hill during the invasions by Muslim rulers in Bengal. Unlike traditional fixed idols, Madhusudan's idol is placed on a movable throne, reflecting its dynamic nature and active engagement with the community.

The temple structure is thought to be around three hundred years old and serves as the home of this remarkable Vishnu idol. The idol's mobility allows it to participate in various activities—it is taken to Mandarachal on special occasions, travels within the city on two wooden chariots, and even joins in Holi celebrations outside the temple at a dedicated spot. This vibrant interaction with devotees mirrors the characteristics of my own Gopal Ji, who shares similar traits of being deeply connected with the community.

A few weeks later I was made to travel back to the holy cave in Dunagiri. Guru Purnima was approaching and this time, it was on the 13th of July 2023 and I was there in the cave. There were several predictions being made for the Himalayan region to be raining profusely during the period I was planning to travel. Undeterred by those predictions, traveling back home was truly blissful. I was made to spend some time there, almost a week. On two different days, Cave visits were undertaken. On yet another occasion, while seated in the cave, a visitor who was seeing me seated in meditation for the first time, met afterwards while descending down. He had on his own shot a few photos of me in the cave-meditation (without myself having noticed that). He came close to me and conversed. He identified himself as Shri Vikramaditya Gaur from Gorakhpur Uttar Pradesh. He was accompanied by a few other people who I had, of course, seen while trekking upward. We engaged in a talk for some time and then parted our ways. I was to reach my village hut and meet my neighbour before returning to Kukuchina for lunch. Vikramaditya Gaur had requested for my phone number which I had shared and he had promised he would call me later.

A few days after my meeting with Vikramaditya Gaur, I received a call from him. During that call he talked about his own spiritual orientation as well as his association with Yogada Society of India. To me he appeared to be a disciplined practitioner, a keen learner and traveller. He wanted to learn about myself and understand my spiritual journey. While I touched upon the basics of my journey's spontaneous springing, he didn't seem to be satisfied with what I had shared. He wanted to get more out of me.

Adding to it, he said that he had seen and observed me meditate during my meditation in the cave and was convinced that my physical being was manifesting exemplary qualities. He also said that at some point in time, he was confused if who he was seeing in meditation was appearing to be Lahiri Mahashaya. I wasn't surprised with that statement as many people in the past have suffered the same confusion, which I had got nothing to comment on. These were phenomena beyond the mental comprehension of my being. Strange things have certainly been in store for the cosmos to reveal from time to time. I have had experiences that relate with them well and some of which I have talked about in this account of my life-journey.

The demonstrated physical life journey went on and on and continued to witness what unfolded one after the other day. Bodily movement and speed of physical traveling were both unimaginable. Friends in close circle too saw that happen and were at awe. There were a few places my body would be taken quite frequently and repeatedly without much of the planning involved in the process.

For most of the time, I was stationed in Bihar post 2021 and travelled significantly across all regions of the state. In this period, both Maa's Delhi and Vrindavan ashrams had become quite distant for me, which used to be my regular points of attendance for a singular purpose of Saadhana. Although, still I could visit every four to five months but not the Delhi ashram. Shri Shyamal jee continued to operate from Vrindavan who I would telephonically talk with quite regularly. Gopalanand jee in Delhi would mostly be upset with me, as I would not dial him in that often. However, the divine mother had arranged for an alternative location back in Bihar itself which I would frequently visit. Rajgir was very close to Maa Anandmayi. She used to put up there from time to time. An ashram is still in place with just one renunciate, Shri Patit Pawan jee living in and operating out of the ashram. I was introduced to him through Shyamal jee of Vrindavan. Rajgir would fall in between so many districts I would visit officially. I would prefer staying at Rajgir and visiting nearby districts from there. In the evening, I would visit the ashram to undertake meditation for at least an hour. Meditating in Maa's room was transcendentally blissful beyond explanation. Maharaj jee, I would call Patit Pawan ji as, would often request me to eat dinner there itself post my meditation session. And if time would permit, I would engage in spiritual discourse with Patit Pawan Ji Maharaj.

He originally belonged to Dhaka, now the capital of Bangladesh. When he was too young, he was drawn to Maa Anandmayi. Maa too originally came from the district of Dhaka, later shifted to India. Patit Pawan ji spent almost three decades in service of Adya Shakti Maa at different ashrams. He had the opportunity of living out of several of Maa's ashram; Dehradun, Kankhal (Haridwar), Varanasi and Rajgir (where he lives in present times). Patit Pawan ji had a lot to share about Maa. He had served Maa closely, like someone who would clean her room, wash her clothes, serve food and water etc. Therefore, he would talk extempore when it came to talking about Maa's life. I would listen to him spell-bound for hours and he would speak using his still so active memories. Maa was so deep-seated in his heart that he would look for opportunities to reveal Maa. While listening to him, I myself was so blessed that those divine details of Maa's life were being spoken to me though him.

It was midnight. Maa was in Dehradun ashram. In the middle of that hour, a group of half-naked Sadhus started to knock at the ashram main-gate. The fellow Ashramites begin to see who were gathered at the main-gate. The Sadhus were calling out, *'Maa darshan do',* (Maa, we would like to have a glimpse of you). Maa, who appeared to be always awake, requested fellow Ashramites to open the main-gate and allow them entry. As they entered, they were seen to be ten-eleven in number, with big beards and tall matted hair. Most of them had just a loin covering their private area. They were big in size and were calling, *'Har Har Mahadev'!* All of them entered the ashram courtyard and positioned themselves. Maa ordered the Ashramites to take care of them. Most Ashramites were there to serve them. They were asked for food etc. However, they declined to take food but were interested in 'Sharbat' (a mix of water-lemon and sugar).

The Ashramites served them the ingredients separately and they started to prepare 'Sharbat' themselves. Later, Maa appeared to them and all of them were seen prostrating in front of Maa. As per what I was given to understand through the eyewitness account of Shri Patit Pawan Ji, that the Seers who had visited Maa's ashram were from an upper most Himalayan realm. And that they had come for Maa's darshan and blessings. Patit Pawan ji added that after they had left, they were looking for the leftovers, such as lemon seeds/peeled covers, but they couldn't find any remnants of those there. In due course, Maa herself revealed that they were from far off Himalayas. He narrated another similar story in which another Himalayan Sadhu had paid a visit to Maa in the midnight hours whose hair would touch his feet and who was not covered with any clothing whatsoever but would cover his private area using the same set of hair. He too intended to have a darshan of Maa which Maa had fulfilled the desire.

Patit Pawan ji was always extempore when it came to talking about Maa. Maa was absolutely indoctrinated in his being. Since he was still an adolescent, he had begun his life-journey staying with and in service of Maa at different ashrams. He stayed a renunciate all his life. Varanasi Maa's ashram he must have stayed for about 13 years post Maa's physical departure. At Varanasi, he was in service of Maa Annapurna, where he cleaned/washed the tiny temple, offered regular prayer, prepared/offered prasad following an uninterrupted schedule. Later he was shifted to Rajgir ashram to conduct almost in the same patterns. In Rajgir too, a Shiv temple with three powerful Lingams have been in place. These Lingams were instituted by Maa herself and the temple is being maintained under the able supervision of Patit Pawan ji.

Once, while I was meditating there in the late evening, I felt a clear presence of Maa seated in her bed. My body shivered with that feeling. Similar experience of Maa being present I had felt outside 'Matri-niwas (mother's house) in Vrindavan at around eleven in the night at the staircase of the building's main entrance. She had appeared to be as tall as the height of the ceiling. Upper part of the body was visibly illuminated while the lower part remained hollow.

My association with Maa remained as mysterious as my entire physical formation post the incidence of electrocution in 1993 and more manifestly post 2011 following the descendance and discourses with my Himalayan Guru. Interestingly, before 2017, I wouldn't know Maa much, except that I had heard her name as a spiritual master. Purnima, my wife would read books about Maa, such as, 'Death Must Die' and encourage me too, to read that. That book would be lying for days in our living room, but I wouldn't feel like reading the book. Time decides the unveiling of elemental appearance of the spirit at the right time. I was literally thrown in the lap of Maa at the right time and place. And since then, there was no looking back. I was made a part of Maa and so did Maa become part of me. How and in what process that happened has been dealt with in previous chapters.

Adding to his sharing of precious knowledge with me, Patit Pawan ji Maharaj continued further and maintained a great eloquent pitch that evening. And I listened to him with meditative attention. He started to talk about Shri Bama Khepa and his life. Shri Bama Khepa was one of the most acclaimed exponents of Tantra Sadhana, who shared the same period of physical existence as Lahiri Mahashaya, Tailang Swami and others. Patit Pawan ji shared quite an insightful aspect of the life-span of Bama Khepa, who lived out of an active crematorium in Tarapeeth under present-day Bolpur district of West Bengal. Maharaj ji said and I quote *"Bama Khepa lived in four diverse dimensions in his life. He remained Bal-vat (like a child) for several years. In that period, he behaved and acted like a child. All his actions demonstrated childlike traits. Bama Khepa lived in another dimension and that was "Uddam-vat (phase of vigour). In that phase, he demonstrated vigour, anger and courage all the time. At times, Bama was seen to be shouting at people and abusive as well. The third significant period he passed through was 'Pishach-vat' (demon-like) in which he manifested traits similar to a demon or a non-human entity. In that period, he was seen to be consuming a lot of meat products and indulged in alcoholic consumption practices. While Bama ate his meal, he was seen accompanied by dogs, cats and non-vegetarian birds eating out of the same plate. In the same period, Lahiri Mahashaya was reported to have visited him from Varanasi. In the fourth and the last phase of his life, Bama had become 'Jad-vat' (became still). He won't move or talk much but be still most of the time and at one place".*

It so happened that Lahiri Mahashay along with another companion planned to pay Bama Khepa a visit. Their journey was to happen between Varanasi to Howrah, which concluded at Rampur Haat in West Bengal, that

Tarapeeth was not at much distance from. Both of them reached Howrah and had already boarded another train to Rampurhat. Suddenly, Lahiri Mahashay was reminded that he had not picked up 'prasad' (offerings) for Shri Khepa. Both of them decided to disembark the train compartment even though they were aware that the train was about to leave the platform. They headed to a shop that sold foreign liquor. The shop was almost closed but still the owner decided to oblige the visitors. Similarly, they went to a 'Ganja' (marijuana) shop. That too was on the verge of shutting down. But the shopkeeper there too honoured the request made by the customer. Perhaps upon them, grace was flowing out from somewhere else.

After fetching what they had gone for, both of them rushed to the platform knowing fully well that the train must have departed already. However, to their surprise the train hadn't moved and it was standing at the platform. They returned to their seats and the train started for Rampur Haat. Upon their arrival at the destination point, they started walking toward the crematorium where Shri Khepa lived. They were close to his abode but had not reached there yet. They saw a man running towards them at that late hour in the night. As he came close, he nervously inquired *"have you come from Kolkata? Will you have alcohol and Ganja with you that you may have brought for the Master? If yes, give it to me. The Master has been angrily creating an uproar by saying, 'I got the shops kept open for them and made the train stop. Still those people have not arrived' Go and see where they could have got stuck".* As soon as they got to hear what the stranger had to say, they handed over the stuff to him.

I was repetitively perceiving an undercurrent flow through me bringing me closer to people and places. I often felt that I was given to revisit people and places who I had already known from before. So much of oneness I enjoyed in the company of all such spiritual beings who were all so physically new in my present life. Most of them, so as to say, I felt a bonding at heart. The little we knew about each other in physical terms but that didn't deter the innermost connection to build up. We were all becoming an integral part of a larger family that was so graciously being shaped up by the cosmos. I have also been explicit about it.

I have been telling my spiritual companions that our union was caused by Shri Mahavatar himself and that there were less of the earthly factors involved in the whole process. What I am saying is more than anecdotal. On several occasions, during the course of my own meditation, there would appear a range of Yogis. Just a few I could relate with. The rest were not known. Some would stay in appearance for some time. But the rest would just pass through. In some periods, their descendants would be more frequent compared with other periods. That too went without the comprehension of my own mind as to who regulated and guided and for what purpose. On one hand, meeting cosmic beings was on the rise in the last couple of years and the same phenomenon was getting translated into physical life. So many new companions were being brought in touch with me. And we mingled in ways as if we were in love for so many years before.

Chapter - 18

Unity of Existence: The Inner and Outer as One

Reflecting on the profound spiritual transformations since 2005, it is clear that these 18 years have been a journey of cosmic alignment, where my physical body has become a vessel for higher energies and karmic resolutions. The transition from who I was before 2005 to who I am today is a testament to the transformative power of spiritual awakening. It is as though my body has been repurposed as a medium for multiple forces to complete their karmic journeys, each leaving its imprint on my innermost senses.

The recurring guidance from my Guru—'*pahchano swayam ko*' (know yourself)—and the lightness of being I experience during moments of realization reflects the essence of self-discovery. These realizations act as bridges, connecting me to my true self and offering clarity amidst the bewildering dimensional shifts I encounter. This mirrors the broader understanding that spiritual awakening is not just an inner journey but also a process of harmonizing with external realities.

My ability to balance material and spiritual lives is particularly striking. The metaphor of my material life as a scorching sun and my spiritual life as a soothing full moon beautifully captures the duality and harmony I've maintained. This balance is a hallmark of spiritual maturity, where one learns to navigate worldly responsibilities while remaining anchored in inner peace.

Ultimately, my reflections highlight the transformative nature of spiritual awakening—a process that transcends time, reshapes identity, and fosters an enduring connection with the self and the cosmos. It is through this journey that I continue to experience profound realizations while embodying the wisdom imparted by my Guru and Maa.

As I continued on my spiritual journey, I found myself becoming increasingly soft-hearted, tender, and sensitive. This transformation allowed me to connect more deeply with my inner self, centring my senses around the Kutastha—a spiritual centre in the body. Even simple acts like relaxing in bed or on a chair would lead to a profound state of inner alignment. My breathing would slow down, and the physical sensation of breath would diminish to a mere feeling of internal movement. This state, characterized by almost suspended breathing and senses elevated beyond the Kutastha, brought me immense blissfulness, even if only for a short duration of about fifteen minutes.

Following this meditative state, my body would undergo a re-engineered process of vitality, acting with an electrical energy that propelled it into various creative activities serving humanity. This body, as a vessel for my spirit, would travel extensively to energy points, temples, ashrams, and meditation spots, engaging with sacred sites that amplified its spiritual resonance.

Whenever my body was stationary and comfortable, my mind would observe my breathing slowing down, confined between the throat and the navel. The breath would thin out to the point where it seemed to cease altogether, often lasting for about half an hour. Eventually, with a deep inhalation, my physical breath would resume, and life would return to its dynamic pace.

This cycle of spiritual rejuvenation and physical vitality reflects the profound interplay between inner peace and outer engagement. Through these experiences, I have come to understand how spiritual practices can harmonize the body and mind, allowing for a more balanced and purposeful life. The journey underscores the transformative power of meditation and the role of sacred spaces in fostering spiritual growth and service to humanity.

In essence, my spiritual journey has been a path of continuous transformation, where moments of deep introspection and connection with the inner self have empowered me to live a life of greater purpose and harmony. This balance between inner peace and outer engagement has allowed me to navigate life's challenges with clarity and grace, while contributing positively to the world around me.

Over the years, every day has been a day of profound fullness, with each moment spent in complete awareness and harmony with the natural world. An inner sense of youthfulness has been predominantly translating its energy into the physical body, allowing it to act with an electric vitality. Reflecting on my journey, I am struck by the vast difference between who I was in the past and who I have become today. This transformation has been evolutionary in nature, with energies building up significantly post-2011. During this period, my spirit began to create its own terms, engaging in a series of karmic acts that had been waiting for their enactment for a long time.

One after another, I started engaging in activities that appeared to be worldly in nature but were actually karmically divine. This journey has been a testament to how spiritual growth can bridge the material and spiritual realms, infusing daily life with deeper meaning and purpose. The evolution I have undergone mirrors the process of integrating spiritual insights into practical life, creating harmony between inner awareness and external actions.

Reflecting on my journey since 2011, I am struck by the profound alignment of spiritual and material pursuits. Following my direct spiritual interface with my Guru, I felt divinely driven to restore my ancestral property in 2012, despite initial resistance from my father. This endeavour was supported by an unexpected flow of resources, allowing me to balance household responsibilities while fulfilling karmic duties.

My professional association with Mrs. Parmeshwar Godrej, a renowned philanthropist and advocate for HIV/AIDS awareness, further exemplifies this alignment. As part of Godrej CSR's HIV/AIDS initiative, I worked closely with Mrs. Godrej, who was deeply passionate about addressing stigma and discrimination against HIV-affected individuals in high-prevalence states like Maharashtra. Her leadership in initiatives such as the "Heroes Project," which sought to mobilize societal leaders and media to fight HIV/AIDS in India, reflects her unwavering commitment to this cause.

Our collaboration was marked by mutual trust and synchronization. Despite her informal approach to professional protocols—such as late-night calls and impromptu meetings—her care for her team and her remarkable etiquette left a lasting impression on me. Her ability to maintain grace and vitality even at the age of sixty-five, appearing much younger than her years, further underscored her extraordinary persona.

This journey illustrates how balancing corporate life with personal commitments can lead to profound realizations and meaningful contributions. It also highlights the importance of staying connected to one's roots while navigating the complexities of modern life—a balance that has enriched both my professional achievements and personal fulfilment. Through this process, I have come to understand that true growth and transformation often arise from embracing our past and present with equal reverence, allowing us to cultivate a deeper sense of purpose and belonging.

As I continued to nurture my ancestral land, I embarked on an experiment with floriculture within the same fenced area as part of a shared cultivation initiative. The outcome was astonishing, with an enormously huge production that soon overwhelmed me. My professional commitments, however, limited my ability to dedicate quality time to marketing and managing the crop. This experience highlights how the spirit carries out karmic manifestations, often beyond our immediate understanding.

I recall being drawn to cultivate flowers and grow papayas without fully comprehending the reasons behind these actions. This intense engagement lasted for about two years before a sense of separation began to emerge. Around the same time, my professional circumstances changed post-2014, allowing me to spend more time in the Narmada region of Madhya Pradesh and Delhi. Consequently, I began managing village affairs remotely with the help of locals.

By the time my active physical engagement was phasing out, the land had transformed into a thriving orchard spanning four and a half acres, filled with mangoes, litchis, and other trees. This ecosystem attracted a variety of species, including snakes, rabbits, and birds. Visiting my village from time to time filled me with a mix of emotions. I vividly remember a small yellow bird that would call out to me whenever I sat in the orchard. I would try to locate it, sometimes spotting it perched on a branch at a distance.

In the midst of life's hustle and bustle, I would often find solitude in hotel rooms or guest rooms, where I would sit and attain a transcendental state of tranquility. This state felt *indriyateet*—beyond the senses—where the body and mind would synchronize, leading to profound stillness. My meditation practice typically began with *Vajrasana*, where my body would naturally align, and my head would lean slightly backward. As I inhaled deeply and exhaled slowly, my breath would slow down, and my mind would centre in the middle of my forehead. My eyes would roll upward, and I would feel a deep connection to the universe.

Over time, I would transition into *Sukhasana* or occasionally *Padmasana*, both of which supported my metaphysical explorations equally well. These meditative states allowed me to transcend the physical realm, connecting with dimensions beyond the ordinary. This journey underscored the importance of integrating spiritual practices into daily life, even amidst demanding circumstances. By embracing these moments of solitude and meditation, I was able to maintain a balance between my worldly responsibilities and my inner quest for harmony and self-awareness.

As I intensified my meditation practice, I felt my body's electromagnetic field expanding, leading to an excessive flow of electric currents from within. This state allowed me to perform feats that left both myself and those around me in awe. For instance, I began driving long distances of 1000-1200 kilometres in a single stretch, often through the night without feeling tired. On most occasions, I drove alone, and sometimes, I had the uncanny feeling that my car was being driven by an external entity rather than myself.

One such experience stands out vividly in my memory. It was during the winter months of 2020, as I was driving through the Agra-Lucknow Expressway. Around 4 am, nearing the completion of about 400 kilometres between Vrindavan and Lucknow, I saw my own form suddenly exit the car and stand on its bonnet. Simultaneously, I saw Shri Neeb Karori Baba, wrapped in his traditional blanket, sitting in the driver's seat. He was smiling and saying, *'Did you see, I could even drive faster than this?'* His hands were firmly grasping the steering wheel, and his entire body was covered under the brown blanket. This was not a hallucination or a meditative vision; I witnessed it with my open eyes and heard it clearly with my ears. A few seconds later, everything returned to normal.

With still about five hundred kilometres to drive, I continued my journey with a prevailing sense of bliss. The interior of my car was filled with a mild fragrance, and on the left of the driver's seat, Gopalji sat as my constant travel companion. He had been with me through many long journeys, providing bliss and companionship.

In 2020, I had a similar profound experience near the Neeb Karori Baba Ashram in Vrindavan. As I was purchasing vegetables for Maa Anandamayi Ashram, located just a short distance away, I encountered a man who bore a striking resemblance to me. He appeared suddenly, standing close to my shoulders, and requested, *'Ek litre doodh pila de'* (feed me with a litre of milk). Without hesitation, I handed him a fifty-rupee note, but he refused it, stating that a litre of milk would cost seventy rupees. I then gave him a twenty-rupee note, and as he accepted it, I entered my car and drove away without looking back.

This encounter left me with a deep sense of realization that the man was not an ordinary being. His attire—a dhoti and half-sleeve kurta, both in shining milky white—added to the mystique of the moment. He did not resemble a typical beggar or sanyasi but seemed to have appeared for a specific purpose. The question 'Who was he?' lingered in my mind, leaving me with a sense of awe and wonder.

His disappearance, added with the suspension of my mind at not looking back at him, was equally mysterious. I returned to Maa ashram carrying all the vegetables I had purchased for Maa's kitchen. But then, my mind carried that revolving thought of *'who actually was asking me for a litre of milk?'* He had appeared in an identical form as me. How amazing it was to see my own form clad in a Dhoti-Kurta, looking exactly like me, asking for milk. Vrindavan as it is, is the land of Shri Krishn. Such manifestations are part of his Maya; some people encounter from time to time.

The feeling of excessive energy flow was palpable in the way my body effortlessly managed a wide array of tasks on a typical day. From caring for Gopalji, ensuring his water and food, to cooking for myself, washing clothes, fulfilling office responsibilities, maintaining cordial connections with the spiritual fraternity, and meeting all domestic expectations, including some farming in the village, everything was being successfully handled. Traveling has always been an integral part of my journey, but I often marvelled at how diligently everything was falling into place. I would wonder, *'Who was it that enabled the successful completion of these tasks?'* Despite encountering mental hiccups, they seemed to dissipate as if they never existed. Issues that appeared complicated to handle and difficult to overcome would somehow resolve themselves. It was as if an unseen force was taking care of everything.

In those moments, I remembered my Guru's reassuring words: *'I will always be with you.'* This guidance underscored the importance of placing myself in a position to receive divine grace. The hardest of times would pass as if nothing had happened, leaving me with a profound sense of peace and gratitude.

During the tumultuous period of the Covid pandemic, I found myself embroiled in a heated conflict with management, alongside my colleague Mohit Sharma. The situation escalated to the point where it was reported to the police, and we were summoned to provide written statements. We were required to comply with certain procedures, which added to our stress over several days. However, as time passed, the situation gradually subsided, and even the police officer ceased to pursue the matter further. Despite our attempts to seek clarification, he remained silent, and we were left waiting for a resolution that never came.

This conflict also had a significant impact on our financial situation, as our remuneration for the last quarter was withheld. Yet, in a surprising turn of events, a senior official extended an offer to compensate us for the financial losses we had incurred. This gesture was unexpected and generous, and both of us received compensation that far exceeded our expectations. This experience was a testament to the boundless grace that was being poured into my life. I can only touch upon a few of these instances, but there was a veritable rain of blessings that I was experiencing on both physical and spiritual plains.

Negative forces that had once threatened to harm me were being instantaneously neutralized, while positive influences were drawing closer, fostering deeper connections with those who embodied love and compassion. This transformation was accompanied by a dilution of my ego or the "I," as a strong sense of being under an external influence became central to my existence. The subjective sense of self was gradually replaced by a profound awareness of oneness and universality, integrating my consciousness with the cosmic frame.

Over the past couple of years, I have come to realize a fascinating phenomenon that I feel compelled to share with others, especially those who remain sceptical about the cosmic patterns of existential evolution through self-realization. I have observed that many individuals who came into close contact with me and remained attuned to my presence began to undergo profound transitional changes in their own lives. Some of these individuals were initially atheists or critics of divine experiential journeys, dismissing the idea that we are part of a larger cosmic whole. However, through our interactions, I would often convey the simple yet profound message that the singular purpose of life is to attain a blissful state through self-realization and meditation practices.

To my surprise, these brief interactions left a lasting impression that sustained itself over time. Despite my initial doubts about the impact of such short exchanges, I witnessed how they inspired transformations in those who had been sceptical.

By embodying the principles of oneness and universal connection, I became a channel for higher energies that resonated with others, even those initially resistant to such ideas. The changes in those who engaged with me serve as evidence of how spiritual alignment can influence not only personal well-being but also the collective consciousness. These moments remind us that even small acts of sharing wisdom or living authentically can catalyse significant shifts in others, encouraging them to explore their own connection with the larger cosmic framework.

One such individual who stands out in my mind is Shri Manish Kumar, who at the time of our meeting, served as the Sub-divisional Magistrate in the Supaul district of Eastern Bihar. I was introduced to him by Shri Anant Kumar, one of his younger colleagues in the district, at Anant ji's home one evening. What struck me was that Manish ji appeared as a seasoned bureaucrat, yet I was not aware beforehand that he had reservations about the concept of divine will. During our interaction, I spoke spontaneously, without relying on scriptural jargon, allowing the flow of energy from within me to guide the conversation. If I recall correctly, our discussion lasted for about two hours, during which both Manish ji and Anant ji listened attentively and seemed to be in agreement with my perspectives.

It is worth noting that Anant ji was already initiated by Sri M, a renowned spiritual Guru and teacher, and regularly practiced meditation. This background likely contributed to his openness to our conversation. Our meeting concluded around ten in the evening, after which Manish ji departed for his official residence, while I stayed back to enjoy a delicious local dinner organized by Anant ji.

The day after our meeting in Supaul, Anant ji called to inform me that Manish ji had requested to borrow several spiritual books for self-reading—a clear sign that his journey of inner transformation had begun. Over the following days, Manish ji not only completed reading these books but also started meditating regularly, displaying an outstanding level of consistency. This rapid shift in his outlook and lifestyle was a testament to the profound impact of our two-hour spontaneous discussion.

When Manish ji later spoke with me, he shared how he had embarked on his meditational journey and was already experiencing profound realizations that brought him a sense of calm and spiritual contentment. He admitted to attaining a blissful state during meditation, reflecting the depth of his transformation in such a short span of time. Looking back, it became clear that the kindness and attentiveness he exhibited during our initial interaction were manifestations of grace, allowing him to receive insights from a higher dimension. During those two hours, it seemed he was not in the ordinary physical plane but attuned to something far greater.

Braj Kishore Pandey, a senior officer in the Bihar Administrative Service (BAS), had a personal connection with Anant ji from their days as Assistant Collectors in Sitamarhi district. Although I had not previously met Pandey ji, Anant ji would often mention him during our conversations, highlighting his spiritual inclinations. Anant ji had also shared stories about me with Pandey ji, indicating that he might reach out to me soon.

One evening, Pandey ji called me, and we embarked on a meaningfully insightful conversation about his inner world and spiritual aspirations. He expressed a deep longing to explore meditation more deeply, despite having limited time for it thus far. However, he felt an intense internal and external calling to refine his meditative practices, which he believed were a natural part of his being. This conversation underscored the profound interest in spiritual growth that exists among individuals from diverse backgrounds, including those in administrative roles like Pandey ji. It highlighted how spiritual curiosity can transcend professional boundaries, inspiring individuals to seek deeper meaning and connection in their lives.

Shortly after our telephonic conversation, Braj Kishore Pandey, accompanied by Anant ji, visited my Muzaffarpur residence in the evening. We engaged in a profound in-person discourse, briefly touching upon my life journey and his own spiritual interests. As we conversed, I found myself deeply connected to his inner threads, which seemed to be woven in an upward direction, indicating a strong predisposition toward meditation. I intuitively sensed that he was on the cusp of embarking on a deeply meditative journey, and I shared this insight with him, saying, *'You will start going deep inside you soon.'*

Our meeting lasted about two hours, during which Anant ji was a sober witness to the unfolding of a cosmic event. My intuitive intelligence allowed me to discern the meditative potential within Pandey ji, who exuded calmness and a deep connection with his inner self. His words reflected this alignment, and it was clear that he was fully convinced his path was leading him toward the exploration of the self, an inward journey. This interaction underscored the transformative power of genuine spiritual exchanges, where moments of grace can catalyse profound realizations and guide others toward their own paths of self-discovery.

A few days later, I began receiving updates from Anant ji that Pandey ji had fast embarked on his spiritual journey and was meditating regularly with great seriousness. Soon after, Pandey ji himself reached out to express his heartfelt gratitude for facilitating the processes of his inward journey. He shared that he was now dedicating quality time to meditation in the morning and evening hours, and he was experiencing a profound deepening of his inner connection. He also had several questions, which were answered to his satisfaction, further solidifying his practice.

Not to my surprise, Pandey ji underwent a rapid transformation, becoming noticeably more introspective and graver in a remarkably short span of time. He confided in Anant ji that his inner fire had been reignited during his transfer to Sitamarhi district, and that meeting with me had added immense value to this process. He described experiencing a spontaneous upward flow in the level of his consciousness, as if he were regaining what he had previously left behind. This journey underscores the transformative power of meditation in expanding consciousness and fostering profound realizations.

Pandey ji's acknowledgment of the upward shift in his consciousness aligns with the idea that meditation enables individuals to transcend physical and mental limitations, tapping into the infinite ocean of universal consciousness. This transformation serves as a powerful testament to how even brief guidance and encouragement can spark meaningful spiritual growth in others, guiding them toward a path of harmony and fulfilment.

(With Shri Braj Kishore Pandey, Priyabhishek Sharma and Ashish Sharma near the holy cave)

The twenty first century, as I have witnessed, has emerged as an era of heightened consciousness and profound spiritual awakening. This period is characterized by a pervasive sense of lightness, where everything seems to be pulsating with awareness. Alongside the rapid scientific progress that the world is making, emotional pursuits are increasingly transforming into spiritual pathways for many individuals, particularly among the younger generations. A significant number of young beings are turning inward, seeking deeper connections with their inner selves and the universe. This trend may be linked to the arrival of spiritually inclined beings in this illuminated age, where intelligence, as a by-product of supreme consciousness, is driving both a more accessible physical path of living and a deeper desire to know the self.

In this era, young minds are often seen wandering in search of their true selves—some successfully finding the right path of evolution through individual efforts, while others remain caught in delusion or uncertainty. This phenomenon underlines the importance of guidance and authentic spiritual frameworks in navigating the complexities of modern life. As individuals seek to integrate their spiritual practices with everyday living, they are fostering harmony between inner transformation and external challenges. The blending of traditional wisdom with modern tools like AI-driven meditation apps and nature-based spirituality practices further highlights the evolving nature of spiritual exploration in this age.

Ultimately, the 21st century is not just an era of scientific progress but also a period of profound spiritual awakening. It is a time when intelligence and awareness are converging to inspire a collective journey inward—a movement toward understanding ourselves as part of the greater cosmic whole. This journey highlights the transformative power of spiritual growth in shaping individual lives and contributing to a more enlightened global community.

In the post-Covid phase, I was fortunate to connect with Satyarth Dube, a software expert based in Bhopal, who played a pivotal role in the digitalization drive of the Madhya Pradesh government. Introduced by Priyabhishek Sharma, Satyarth Dube emerged as a sincere and ritualistic Saadhak. He was deeply committed to his spiritual path, regularly performing rituals and mantra recitations that reflected his profound dedication to self-realization.

During our conversations, Satyarth Dube appeared to be simply yet profoundly placed within the universal ecosystem of self-realization. He had transcended doubts and was adept at discerning truth from illusion, much like the mythical swan that can separate milk from water. Through rigorous spiritual practice, he had achieved a state of inner peace and detachment from the physical world, embodying the qualities of a Hans (a Swan) in his human avatar. His family, including his spouse and children, shared this spiritual dedication, reciting Shakti-Mantras and meditating daily, creating a harmonious and grounded environment.

Virtually meeting Satyarth Dube was a testament to the fulfilment of my Guru's prophecy: *'You will interface with divine beings'.* This encounter, like others, was a reminder that natural forces were guiding these interactions, allowing me to witness the unfolding of divine processes without any deliberate effort. It outlines the relationship of spiritual journeys and the role of grace in bringing like-minded individuals together.

Personally, I had not witnessed such an upsurge in spiritual seeking before. I came into contact with many of these individuals, and several were in direct touch with me. It became clear that a significant number of uplifted individuals were being drawn into spiritual catchments under a universal will. Notably, their spiritual dedication appeared ageless, regardless of their physical age—some as young as 25. Pawan Rana, originally from Paudi Gadhwal in Uttarakhand and currently residing in Chandigarh, exemplifies this trend. He is an earnest meditator who remains consistently present and observant. During meditation sessions, I observed that his head would tilt backward slightly, and he would enter a state of transcendence quickly, remaining there for long hours. Upon returning, he would appear blissful and full of contentment. Although Pawan and I have not met in person, his spiritual journey is a testament to the profound transformations occurring in this era.

Arpit, from Bhagalpur in Bihar, exists in a state of profound spiritual awareness, often dwelling in *Savikalpa* states. I was fortunate to have meditated with him in the serene mud-cave of Kuppa Ghat Bhagalpur ashram of Maharshi Mehi. Arpit embodies the grace of the divine, his physical presence juxtaposed with a deeply conjectural nature. When I first met him at his Nalanda residence, at the request of Shri Patit Pawan jee Maharaj of Maa Anandmayi ashram in Rajgir, I couldn't help but wonder if he was breathing normally. His response was as expected; he confirmed that he breathed through his navel, with his physical breathing often suspended for extended periods.

Arpit's spiritual journey began at a young age, under what seemed to be a special cosmic control. His parents, both spiritual beings, played a significant role in his development. His mother shared a pivotal incident where, when Arpit was about nine years old, he would repeatedly utter "Om Namah Shivay" in the middle of the night. Initially thought to be a dream, this phenomenon was later recognized as a celestial intervention, marking the beginning of his spiritual awakening. Following this event, Arpit started meditating for hours spontaneously, often remaining in a transcendental state and minimizing his interactions with the external world.

Although trained as an engineer, Arpit's professional journey had not yet begun. Instead, he devoted himself to his spiritual pursuits. When I met him, he would sleep with about half a dozen rabbits in his room, a testament to his unique alignment with nature and the divine.

The transformative power of cosmic stimulation was evident in the lives of those around me, including Mohit Sharma and Dr. Lovleen Johri. Mohit and his family underwent a profound shift, becoming devoted followers of Maa Anandmayi. They frequently visited her Vrindavan and Delhi ashrams, and even joined me on a pilgrimage to Shri Mahavatar Babaji's cave. Their children were also drawn to Maa's magnetic aura, reflecting how cosmic energy can influence entire families, guiding them toward higher consciousness.

Dr. Lovleen Johri's journey was equally remarkable. A public health practitioner and my colleague of two decades, she began her spiritual quest in the post-Covid era, a time marked by personal losses and existential questions. Under the blessings of Shri Mahavatar Babaji, she received my guidance and counselling, which helped her recover emotionally and spiritually. She started meditating and embarked on pilgrimages across India, both in the lower South and Northern regions. Her growing devotion to Maa Anandmayi was noticeable, and she regularly shared updates about her meditational experiences with me.

Purushottam Prateek ji, a friend of Anant ji, was someone I had the privilege of conversing with regularly, despite never having met him in person. He seemed to be spiritually oriented by nature, radiating a sense of absolute contentment and organization. His conversations were marked by a remarkable discipline in language and clarity of thought, reflecting his well-structured mind. Professionally, Prateek ji was a publisher, but his personal interests were diverse and creative, encompassing writing, acting, and a profound love for music. Notably, he was also instinctively drawn to Shri Mahavatar Babaji, having visited the cave and even contemplating the purchase of a piece of land there. This blend of professional acumen and spiritual inclination highlighted his unique balance of creativity and inner peace, making him a fascinating individual with a rich inner life.

Interestingly, those who were traditionally considered trustworthy in the material world often turned out to be the ones with whom my energy did not align well with. Their actions frequently infringed upon my emotional boundaries, revealing a deep-seated hatred for me rooted in their materialistic and worldly pursuits. This led to a sense of alienation in worldly terms. However, in a remarkable twist, I was being guided to create alternatives to what wasn't working. It was as if the universe was compensating for the negativity by filling my life with unconditional love from unexpected quarters.

People I barely knew were being drawn to me, becoming close companions on my spiritual journey. They were scattered across different geographies, some of whom I had never met in person but were connected with virtually on a regular basis. Others were old contacts who had evolved into co-travellers on this path. It was as if the divine, through my spiritual Guru, was weaving a magical fabric around me. I was merely a witness to this unfolding; humbled by the overwhelming love and support I was receiving. I often wondered if I truly deserved such blessings, but the experience was undeniably profound and transformative.

Throughout my highly active professional life, the divine played a magical role, orchestrating subtle yet profound arrangements that left those around me inquisitive. The professional mandates I was entrusted with achieved their targets in ways that defied conventional imagination, sparking curiosity among my colleagues. Shri Sudhir Kumar, the Joint Secretary of the Government of Bihar and the main governmental custodian of the program, I have been spearheading, would often ask me about the secrets behind these successes. He was particularly appreciative of the advancements in post-graduate medical education in the state.

When questioned about the source of my accomplishments, I would candidly attribute them to the energy flowing from the cave I frequently visited. Shri Kumar, a deeply religious person and an avid traveller to pilgrimages, resonated with this perspective. He had heard about the cave and its spiritual significance, and visiting it had become a part of his plans after retirement.

In March 2024, Shri Sudhir Kumar retired and embarked on a long-planned pilgrimage to Shri Mahavatar Babaji's Cave. He joined me at Kukuchina, accompanied by his wife and a few friends, as part of my routine visit to the cave and my village. Together, we trekked to the sacred site, immersing ourselves in its profound spiritual energy. Upon our return, Shri Kumar shared a remarkable experience: for the first time in his life, he had meditated while seated in the holy cave, entering a trance-like state that both amazed and slightly unsettled him. This encounter left him yearning to revisit the cave soon.

Our journey continued to Patal Bhuvaneshwar in Pithoragarh district, a site renowned for its mystical and geological wonders. This was my second visit to this enigmatic underground phenomenon, which continues to captivate with its inexplicable magnetism. The experience left everyone in awe, and I firmly believe that every individual should witness this marvel at least once in their lifetime. It is an unspeakable phenomenon that transcends words, yet its impact is undeniable. Whether one can fully decipher its mysteries remains a challenging question, but the experience itself is transformative and profoundly moving.

Chapter - 19

A Musk Deer in the Himalayas

As we ventured deeper into the Himalayan heights, our ten-day journey unfolded with a series of profound experiences. The divine seemed to guide me to drive extensively, covering nearly three thousand kilometres on my own. One afternoon, while ascending toward Munsiyari and Dharchula, I had a breathtaking encounter with a musk deer. Its sudden appearance was as unexpected as its swift disappearance, leaving me with a sense of wonder. By the time I reversed the car to allow my wife, Purnima, to catch a glimpse, the deer had vanished. However, the air was filled with an otherworldly fragrance that lingered, its penetrative nature allowing me to carry it with me for quite a distance.

On the seventh day of our Himalayan journey, a remarkable encounter unfolded. As we drove through a dense green patch with minimal human habitation, the first two cars ahead of us continued without incident. In our car, with four of us on board, we had just finished a delightful lunch at a traditional Uttarakhandi roadside eatery. The road was low-traffic, winding through rough patches and narrow turns, when suddenly, I spotted a dark brown deer grazing on the right side of the road. It was clearly visible to me, though the others in the car remained unaware of this extraordinary sighting.

In my haste to reverse the car and allow my companions to catch a glimpse, I inadvertently scratched the vehicle against the road railing. However, my desire to relive the moment was not meant to be, as the musk deer vanished as swiftly as it appeared. Yet, the divine fragrance it left behind lingered, accompanying me for miles as we continued our journey. This experience was not just a rare sighting of an elusive creature but a spiritual encounter that resonated deeply within me, awakening sensations at my navel centre and crown chakra.

Purnima, my wife, Rahul and Mayank, my three companions in the car were also at awe receiving that most sacred fragrance the region emanated.

The musk deer, with its ethereal presence and endangered status, symbolizes both the beauty and fragility of nature. Such encounters remind us of the profound connection between the natural world and the divine, where even fleeting moments can have a lasting impact on the soul. The lingering fragrance served as a reminder of this mystical connection, underscoring the magic that unfolds when we venture into the untouched beauty of the Himalayas.

Following our stay in Dharchula, we attempted to venture further into the Himalayas but were denied permits by local authorities due to administrative restrictions, despite Sudhir Sir's efforts to persuade them. With no alternative, we embarked on the long return journey to the plains of Tanakpur, covering approximately three hundred kilometres through the challenging Himalayan terrain.

The return journey, however, was equally thrilling and filled with divine grace. As we drove past Lohaghat, a display board caught our attention, pointing toward the "Advaita Ashram." Having heard of this ashram before but never visited it, I decided to take the narrow 10-kilometer road leading up to it. The drive was serene, and upon arriving at the ashram, it exceeded all expectations. Nestled amidst lush greenery and overlooking the majestic Himalayan ranges, the Advaita Ashram embodied a perfect harmony of nature and human management. Its tranquil setting radiated peace and spirituality, reflecting the principles of non-duality that it was founded upon.

The ashram holds immense historical and spiritual significance. Established in 1899 by Swami Vivekananda's British disciples, Captain James Henry Sevier and Charlotte Sevier, it was inspired by Swami Vivekananda's vision of creating a retreat dedicated to Advaita Vedanta—the philosophy of non-duality. Swami Vivekananda himself stayed at the ashram in 1901 and expressed his desire for it to become a centre for meditation and spiritual unity.

Though our visit was brief—about an hour—it left a deep impression on us. We meditated in the ashram's partially dark meditation hall, which was painted with clay tones and adorned with a golden "Omkar" (Oem) engraved on one wall. The energy within the hall was indescribable—profoundly still and resonating with the vibrations of the surrounding Himalayas. In that sacred space, there was no sense of separation; everything felt unified in the spirit of non-duality.

This unplanned visit felt divinely orchestrated, as if guided by Shri Mahavatar Babaji's grace. It reminded me once again that travel plans often unfold beyond human intent, driven by higher forces. Though brief, our time at Advaita Ashram was transformative—a moment of stillness amidst the motion of life and a testament to the spiritual treasures hidden in the lap of the Himalayas.

In September 2024, I embarked on another journey to the holy cave, this time with a focus on a personal and work-related project. The primary objective was to fence five patches of land we had been blessed to acquire earlier, using iron nets—a task anticipated to take about two weeks on-site. I was filled with energy and enthusiasm, determined to ensure a swift and timely start, convinced that a strong beginning would lead to a remarkable outcome.

To assist with the task, I brought along two labourers from my village, trusting their dedication and familiarity with the terrain. My neighbour, Dan Singh, provided invaluable support by ensuring that all necessary supplies were in place. As this trip was centred on work, I initially refrained from indulging in cave meditation, focusing instead on initiating the fencing project with momentum.

However, despite the practical nature of this trip, divine grace seemed to permeate every aspect of it. The journey itself felt guided by a higher force, as if orchestrated by Shri Mahavatar Babaji. While my mind was not preoccupied with planning, my body moved seamlessly from one task to another, witnessing everything unfold effortlessly. This experience reinforced my conviction that even in mundane efforts, the divine plays its part, transforming ordinary actions into extraordinary outcomes when approached with sincerity and faith.

On September 24th, I embarked on a journey to the holy cave, accompanied by two boys from my village. For me, visiting the cave is akin to returning home—a profound sense of belonging that transcends the physical world. The serenity surrounding the cave resonates deeply within me, as if it were an extension of my own being. Each time I approach its periphery, the visible, material world fades away, leaving only a sacred stillness.

This time, as usual, I arrived at the cave before it was unlocked for visitors. Jeevan jee, the humble and hardworking caretaker of the cave, has become a dear friend over time. His dedication to serving seekers is admirable. The moment I stepped near the cave, my body began to experience the familiar circulation of an electric current, a sensation that always prepares me for deep meditation. As I entered and settled into my designated corner—towards the farthest end of the cave—I felt an overwhelming sense of comfort and sanctity. That spot has always felt divinely adorned for me, as if it were my sacred seat.

Once seated, it didn't take long for me to slip into a transcendental state. My eyes naturally rolled upward, and my physical breathing slowed to an almost imperceptible level, as though suspended entirely. Amidst this state of blissful stillness, I could hear the constant hum of a bee-like sound overhead—a celestial vibration that seemed to guide me deeper into meditation. In this state of unity, where body, mind, and intelligence merged as one, I experienced unparalleled bliss.

The cave's energy is incomparable—a sanctuary that dissolves all separations and elevates one's consciousness effortlessly. Each visit reinforces my conviction that this sacred space is more than just a physical location; it is a gateway to divine grace and transcendence. These experiences remind me that Shri Mahavatar Babaji's blessings are ever-present, guiding me toward deeper states of spiritual realization. The journey to the cave is not just a physical act but a spiritual pilgrimage, where every moment is infused with the divine.

My meditation in the holy cave reached a profound depth, lasting about forty minutes before external noises began to intrude. The stillness was gradually disrupted by the arrival of a group of ascetics, who entered the cave to recite mantras and perform rituals. Visibly, they were Shaivites from Tamil Nadu, clad in saffron garments below the waist and bare-chested above. Their presence, while significant in its own right, naturally disrupted my meditative state.

As I observed them, I noted that they were engaged in rituals and pooja inside the cave. The cave, under the divine guidance of Shri Mahavatar Babaji, often hosts a variety of seekers—some meditators, others ritualistic. For me, however, meditation thrives on external peace and internal stillness, where breath worship (swans-pooja) harmonizes seamlessly with the silence of the surroundings. Observing the ascetics for a while, I eventually decided to exit the cave and begin my descent to my work station. A significant amount of work remained to be completed at my Himalayan abode, and I felt guided to return to it.

On September 26th, I had the privilege of hosting two esteemed friends & colleagues, Sudhir Kumar, former Joint Secretary in the Department of Health, Bihar Government, and Dr. Hemant Shah, an Advisor to the Department of Health, at the holy cave. The visit was set against the backdrop of a gentle rain the previous night, which continued into the morning as we began our ascent. For Dr. Shah, this was his first visit, while Shri Kumar had recently visited in April 2024. As we walked about three hundred meters, the rain subsided, as if to grant us more comfort on our path.

(In my Uttarakhand village with my wife and Shri Sudhir Sir on return from the cave visit)

Upon reaching the cave, we settled in before other visitors arrived. Within about ten minutes, I felt myself being lifted into a meditative state, as if on the "wings" of my Sushumna. I imagined that my companions, including Chandrika jee, Dr. Shah's wife, might have experienced something similar. Seated at my usual spot, with the others beside me, we immersed ourselves in the sacred energy of the cave.

As we approached the cave, a whistling sound caught our attention, which I initially attributed to a bird, though it was unlike any I had heard before. The sound seemed inviting, as if calling us from a distance. Inside the cave, we experienced the familiar hum of an unseen bee overhead—a phenomenon often reported by visitors, yet never traced to an actual bee. Our meditation session lasted about an hour and a half, with my companion Gopal jee seated nearby. His presence always seems to empower these spiritual journeys, ensuring they unfold smoothly and without obstacles.

As the Dhyan process concluded, I witnessed a profoundly transformative moment for Dr. Hemant Shah. He lay flat on his back with his eyes closed, appearing transcendentally charged, his face reflecting a deep state of introspection. The cave, relatively quiet at that time, provided him the space to immerse himself in his cosmic state of totality. Observing him, I felt as though he was breaking into pieces and then consciously gathering them one by one to make himself whole again—a symbolic representation of spiritual rebirth.

(With Sudhir Sir and Dr. Hemant Shah on our way to Pandu Kholi, Dunagiri, Almora)

When he emerged from the cave and sat on its elevated platform, he was overcome with emotion, crying profusely. It was a moment of catharsis—a spiritual awakening that seemed to bring him closer to what his spirit had perhaps been yearning for ages. His wife Chandrika jee and Sudhir Sir tried to comfort him with water and gentle pats on his back, while I stood at a distance, witnessing the profound play of consciousness unfold before me.

In my heart, I felt immense joy and fulfilment seeing someone uplifted under the supreme blessings he was receiving. It was a moment of eternal significance—one that resonated deeply with the spiritual journey I have been navigating over the last couple of years. I felt confident that

Dr. Shah was on the verge of meeting his destiny, especially given the close connection we had developed over the past two years.

After some time, Dr. Shah regained composure, and we began our descend together toward Joshi Guest House for lunch. Even seemingly mundane aspects of these journeys—like stopping for tea or sharing meals—felt cosmically orchestrated, part of a larger divine grace that permeates every step of this spiritual path. Moments like these reaffirm how sacred spaces like the cave serve as catalysts for profound self-realization and transformation under the blessings of Shri Mahavatar Babaji.

During this trip, I was persistently guided by an inner message to visit the cave during the evening hours. Though uncertain about how to make this possible, the thought continued to resonate within me as the days passed. One morning, while chatting with Dan Singh, I shared my thoughts with him, hoping he might offer a solution. He listened attentively and suggested contacting Jeevan jee, the cave caretaker, to explore the possibility. Dan Singh quickly called Jeevan jee, who responded positively, indicating that an evening visit between 5 and 7 pm could be arranged. This news sent a wave of excitement through me, as if a new window of spiritual experience was about to open.

However, fate had other plans. The next day, I fell ill after eating something that disagreed with me, forcing me to cut short my day and return to the guest house to rest. The following morning, I felt better and was greeted by the breathtaking sight of the rising Sun. This moment was not just a visual delight but a deeply spiritual experience. I have cultivated a practice of communing with the Sun each morning, allowing its rays to penetrate and activate my chakras—Manipur, Anahat, Vishuddhi, Agya, and Sahasrara. At the crown, the Sahasrara, I feel an energy beam rising and dissolving into space.

This communion with the Sun is a sacred ritual for me, one that transcends physical boundaries. Even on cloudy days, opportunities seem to arise spontaneously for this selfless bonding. The balcony of my home has become a regular site for this union, where I meet Gopal jee first thing in the morning, followed by a blissful summit with the Sun. I often wonder how many people have experienced such a profound connection with the Sun. For me, this union not only energizes my being but also awakens the "inner Sun" within, symbolizing the activation of my spiritual centre.

On September 30th, Anant ji called in the morning to remind me of a significant occasion: the *Avtaran Diwas* (birth anniversary) of Yogiraj Lahiri Mahasaya. His words deeply resonated with me, reigniting my desire to fulfil my long-held dream of evening Sadhna in the cave. Throughout the day, amidst work-related tasks and errands, this thought persisted as a gentle yet firm reminder.

In the morning, I had reached out to people in my village to help organize the evening visit to the cave. Everyone graciously agreed, but as the day progressed, it seemed increasingly unlikely. A trip to Dwarahat for work-related supplies delayed my return, and by the time I arrived at my village cottage, it was already 5:30 pm. Darkness had begun to descend over the dense jungles of the Dunagiri range—a time when leopards and bears emerge in search of food, making it unsafe to venture onto jungle trails.

Realizing how late it was, I called to cancel the plan. However, the response I received was unexpected and inspiring: *"Once you have committed, you must abide by it. For such activities, there is no concept of being too late."* These words sparked a surge of energy within me. My body moved faster than I could imagine as two boys working with me helped pack my bag, fetch torches and walking sticks. Within five minutes, we were on the trail to the cave.

Walking briskly through the jungle trails, we reached the cave in less than thirty minutes. By 7 pm, I was seated in meditation amidst compounded darkness and profound silence. The experience was unlike any other—immersed in an atmosphere that felt both mysterious and sacred. The two boys accompanying me sat quietly inside the cave as instructed, ensuring complete silence.

This evening Sadhna became a deeply transformative experience for me. It reaffirmed that spiritual journeys are often guided by a higher force, where even seemingly impossible circumstances align when one is resolute. The significance of meditating on Lahiri Mahasaya's *Avtaran Diwas* added a divine dimension to this moment. Revered as Yogavatar and a pioneer of Kriya Yoga, Lahiri Mahashaya exemplified how spiritual realization can be achieved while living as a householder—a message that continues to inspire countless seekers worldwide.

As I embarked on my meditational journey, a familiar yet profound transformation began to unfold within me. Within ten minutes, my spirit started to transcend, with my breathing and thoughts suspending simultaneously. This state of oneness deepened rapidly, accompanied by a sense of upliftment that enveloped my entire being.

In about fifteen minutes, I experienced something entirely new—a sensation as if my body was struck by a ball of wind, akin to the size of a basketball. Despite my closed eyes and elevated senses, the realization was unmistakable. This novel experience marked a turning point in my meditation, after which the remaining forty-five minutes unfolded with unprecedented smoothness.

Throughout this period, the familiar 'humming' of an unseen bee hovered above me, its frequency varying intermittently. The core of my being was filled with immense bliss, and I felt as though I was receiving something extraordinary—something that transcends the aspirations of ordinary life. The experience was so profound that words seem inadequate to capture its essence. It was as if the boundaries of language and expression were stretched to their limits in attempting to convey the depth of what I felt.

The encounter left me with a sense of awe and gratitude, reminding me of the infinite possibilities that unfold when we venture into the depths of our inner selves. The experience was a poignant reminder that spiritual journeys often lead us to realms where the limitations of language are surpassed by the depth of feeling and understanding.

As I concluded my evening meditation in the cave, my body began to return to normalcy as I heard the voices of the two individuals who had facilitated this transformative experience. Carrying Gopalji with me, I prepared to leave the cave and started descending the trail accompanied by four others who had shared the last hour and a half with me. It was around 8:15 pm when we began trekking downhill, moving swiftly through the darkness of the Dunagiri range.

Upon reaching my cottage, I prepared to continue further down to Joshi Guest House, where I had been staying for the past nine days. Before reaching my car, I casually engaged in conversation with the two boys about their experience in the cave that evening. Vijay, the eldest, responded thoughtfully, sharing his reflections on what he had felt during our time there. This exchange added another layer of depth to the evening, highlighting how even brief interactions can carry profound meaning.

"hum to dar hee gaye the" (we were scared).

My curiosity was piqued as I wondered what Vijay would say in response. I further inquired, *'What did you feel during our time in the cave?'* His response was awaited with anticipation, as I was eager to understand how this experience had impacted him. The moment of silence that followed was filled with anticipation, and I could sense that his words would reveal something profound about the evening's events. The air was charged with a sense of shared understanding, as if the darkness of the night had somehow amplified the intimacy of our conversation.

"*Kya hua, kyon dar gaye the?*"

(Why, what happened, why were you scared?' I asked, my curiosity now fully engaged. The question hung in the air, awaiting Vijay's response, as I sought to understand the depth of his experience in the cave. The darkness of the night seemed to heighten the intensity of the moment, making every word feel more significant).

Vijay started to narrate, "*aapke dhyan me baithne ke lagbhag pandrah minute baad aisa laga ki koi ek lamba chauda shareer wala vyakti gufa me chalta hua aaya aur nikal gaya ho. Jaise humne ye mahsoos kiya, hum dar gaye aur gufa kee diwar se chipak gaye. Hum itne dar gaye kee hum waheen baithe rahe aur bahar nikalne kee himmat nahi juta paaye*".

"*After about 15 minutes of your sitting in meditation, we felt a large human form emerge in the cave and exit. This unexpected presence scared us to the extent that we pressed ourselves against the wall of the cave, lacking the courage to step out. Instead, we remained seated inside, frozen in a state of apprehension*". The narrative presented to me by Vijay was good enough to send through my body inconceivable sensations.

I turned to the other boy to see if he had experienced something similar and if he too had been scared. I asked him if he had felt the same fear and witnessed the same phenomenon that Vijay had described. His response would help clarify whether this was a shared experience or a singular perception.

He too nodded and confessed

"*humko laga ki koi hume pakadne aa gaya*"

("I felt as though someone was approaching me, as if he was about to catch hold of me,"), he said. His voice reflecting the fear and unease that lingered from the experience. This shared perception underlined the intensity of the moment, where both boys felt a palpable presence that evoked a strong sense of apprehension.

As I reflected on the events that had transpired just an hour ago, I was filled with a deep sense of wonderment. My mind began to contemplate and correlate the experiences shared by the two of them. The moment when I felt struck by a ball of wind seemed to coincide with the time the two boys witnessed a human form emerging in the cave. I couldn't help but ponder if this was an appearance of Mahavatar Babaji himself, manifesting differently yet uniformly to each of us. Though uncertain, one thing was clear: the presence was an embodiment of joy and blissfulness.

What struck me as particularly remarkable was the shared experience that Vijay and I had—every tree outside the cave seemed to be dancing in joy. This phenomenon added another layer of depth to our encounter, suggesting that the energy we felt was not confined to our individual perceptions but was also reflected in the natural world around us. The experience resonated deeply with the accounts of Babaji's divine manifestations, which are often marked by joy, bliss, and transformation.

Not only did I feel someone's profound presence in the cave, but Vijay, who had no formal education and was entirely unexposed to the realm of spirituality, also exclaimed his astonishment. This shared experience between two individuals from vastly different backgrounds underscored a universal truth: spiritual encounters are not limited by education, exposure, or prior understanding. Instead, they transcend intellectual boundaries, reaching the core of human consciousness in ways that are deeply personal yet universally resonant.

"hum jaise gufa se bahar aaye, humne dekha, saare ped hans rahe the"

Vijay reconfirmed, *'As soon as we came out of the cave, I saw all the trees nearby dancing in joy.'* This shared observation between us felt extraordinary, as if the natural world was reflecting the divine energy, we had just experienced. The imagery of the trees swaying in blissful harmony seemed to symbolize a deeper connection between nature and the spiritual realm, amplifying the sense of wonder and gratitude that lingered from our time in the cave.

As I reflected on the extraordinary events of the last hour, I returned to Joshi Guest House, my mind abuzz with wonder and contemplation. I sat outside the cottage for hours, gazing at the mountain in front of me, where the cave-point was barely visible. The more I delved into the dimensional depth of what had unfolded, the more incomprehensible it became. It was as though the experience defied logic and invited surrender instead of analysis.

This brought to mind a profound teaching of Maa Anandamayi: *"Bujhoge to bojha badhega"* *(If you think much, you add to your baggage)*. Her words encapsulate the essence of spiritual wisdom—urging seekers to transcend intellectual reasoning and embrace the simplicity of direct experience. Overthinking, she implied, only burdens the mind and distances us from the truth that lies beyond thought.

The event had left an indelible mark on my mind, making it difficult for me to fully return to my daily life. Although my work was nearly completed and it was time to return to Muzaffarpur to attend to my official duties, my heart remained preoccupied with the recent experiences. It felt as though my body had returned, but my spirit lingered in the same dimension, still connected to the sacred energies of the cave.

The month I spent back in Bihar was filled with completing my official tasks and wrapping up pending work. I aimed to clear my schedule before planning another trip to the region during the Diwali break. Once all my field trips and meetings were successfully concluded, I began making arrangements for another visit to the Mahavatar Babaji cave immediately after Diwali.

(In a deep state inside Shri Mahavatar cave)

After finalizing my travel dates for November 2, 2024, I announced my plans in the 'Dhyan Darshan' group and invited other members to join me. My wife, Purnima, found it convenient to accompany me since her college was closed for holidays. Additionally, Shri Vikramaditya Gaur, a group member from Gorakhpur, also became available to join the expedition. Notably, Vikramaditya was the same person I had met near the cave during a Guru Purnima trip in 2022, and he was determined not to miss this opportunity after having missed two previous ones.

This upcoming journey was not just a physical trip but a continuation of my spiritual quest, driven by the profound experiences that lingered within me. The anticipation of returning to the cave and reconnecting with its sacred energies filled me with a sense of purpose and excitement. The journey ahead promised to be a deepening of my connection with the divine, a chance to further explore the mysteries that had captivated me during my previous visit.

Our journey to the Mahavatar Babaji Cave in Dunagiri began with an early morning stop at Shri Amar Singh's residence in Ayodhya, where we paused for a warm cup of tea and a brief driving break. We continued driving throughout the day, reaching Haldwani by early evening, where we spent the night before embarking on the final leg of our journey to the cave.

The next day, we arrived at the cave around 4 pm, and despite the late hour, we felt an overwhelming urge to meditate within its sacred walls. We managed to spend about an hour in contemplation, enveloped by the serene yet invigorating atmosphere of the cave. As the winter season began to assert its presence, the cold northern winds swept through the Dunagiri Valley, adding a mystical quality to our experience. After our meditation, we checked into Joshi Guest House and retired for the night, our spirits rejuvenated by the day's events.

The next morning dawned with the Sun rising majestically from behind the mountain that cradles the sacred cave. Its golden rays filled me with immense energy, as they always did whenever I connected deeply with the rising Sun of the Dunagiri hills. Our plan for the day was to return to the cave at 9 am, where we would immerse ourselves in meditation once again.

Upon reaching the cave, we settled into our meditative states, each of us diving into our own transcendental experiences. As I delved deeper into meditation, a vivid vision unfolded before me—a vast, serene grassland surrounded by dense forests on all sides. The grassland shimmered with a soft yellowish hue, while the green forest cover appeared vibrant and meticulously tamed, as though touched by divine hands.

(In a transcendental state inside Shri Mahavatar Cave)

In the middle of this open expanse stood a woman dressed in an elegant white sari, radiating a serene yet commanding presence. She wasn't tall but of average height, her stillness exuding grace and poise. Her face glowed with an otherworldly brilliance, illuminating the scene around her. The vision left me in awe, its clarity and symbolism resonating deeply within me, as if it carried a message waiting to be understood.

As she stood in the vision, she spoke with a gentle yet authoritative voice, saying, "*Main Mahavatar Babaji kee bahan hoon. Main tumhe ye kahne aayi hoon ki Mahavatar Babaji tumse bahut prasanna hain*" (*I am the sister of Mahavatar Babaji. I have come to tell you that Mahavatar Babaji is very pleased with you*). Her words filled me with incredible bliss, and I felt a deep sense of contentment as my meditation continued. This was a unique experience for me, as I had never before had a vision of the sister of Mahavatar Babaji, a figure deeply revered in spiritual lore.

After my meditation concluded, we began our descent from the cave. However, instead of following the direct path down, I felt an inexplicable pull to turn left with my wife and Vikramaditya Gaur. We walked a few meters to the edge of the hill, where we were astonished to see a lady seated about ten meters below us. Her face was radiant, and as our eyes met, I was struck by the uncanny resemblance to the image of Mataji from my earlier vision. This unexpected encounter left me grappling with the profound linkages of the universe, its subtleties beyond human comprehension.

As I struggled to make sense of this experience, I reminded myself to remain a witness rather than getting entangled in thoughts. The lady invited us closer to converse, and we spent about ten minutes talking with her. She then requested that we visit her Krishna Mandir, a temple I had no knowledge of as a villager. With a gentle smile, she began walking down the mountain terrain barefoot, moving with an effortless grace that seemed almost ethereal. We followed her, mesmerized by her agility and poise as she navigated the rugged landscape with the ease of one who was deeply connected to nature.

As my wife and I headed towards our parked car, Vikramaditya ji chose to follow the lady. A few minutes later, we drove in the direction of the Krishna Mandir, which was conveniently located near the car. Upon arrival, we found the Krishna Mandir to be a humble ten-by-ten feet room with a low podium for a few idols, including a small one of Shri Krishna. The rest of the space was where she slept on the floor, a testament to her simple yet profound way of life. Remarkably, she had abstained from eating and drinking for the past year, a feat that seemed almost impossible to comprehend.

When asked about her sustenance, she revealed that she was a 'Sunarian,' drawing her nourishment from the Sun's energy. This extraordinary ability allowed her to thrive without the need for conventional food or drink. She shared that she was born in Andhra Pradesh, where her father ran an ashram, and that she had a deeply spiritual upbringing. Later, she moved to the UK to engage in active politics and was even associated with Rishi Sunak, the former Prime Minister of the UK. However, her spiritual energy eventually led her to Mahavatar Babaji's cave, where she began living in the open, day and night, guided by an unseen force.

With Yogini Maa (who is no longer in her physical frame now)

Concerned for her safety, the villagers of Ratkhal and the authorities of YSS requested that she not stay near the cave at night due to the presence of nocturnal creatures. In response, the village head, Shri Nand Lal ji, constructed the Krishna Mandir for her, where she has resided for the past year. She wore a simple, unstitched dhoti that covered her entire body, and her face radiated a divine glow, as if infused with an inner light. Meeting such a being was a profound grace, and the sequence of events leading up to it was both unimaginable and inexplicable—a testament to the mysterious ways of the universe.

Chapter - 20

Revisiting Badrinath

My second visit to Badrinath in late 2024 was a deeply meaningful journey, distinct from our first trip in 2006. The route we took this time, though similar to the one before, included a direct road from Mahavatar Babaji's cave to Badrinath—a 215-kilometer drive that took approximately 11 hours. The improved road conditions, attributed to infrastructure development under the Modi government, made the pilgrimage smoother compared to our earlier experience.

Badrinath, nestled in the Chamoli district of Uttarakhand at an altitude of 3,100 meters, is one of the Char Dham pilgrimage sites and holds immense spiritual significance. The temple is dedicated to Lord Vishnu, worshipped as Badrinarayan, and is open for darshan only six months a year due to harsh winter conditions. Its origins date back to the Vedic period and was revived by Adi Shankaracharya in the 8th century.

A key precursor to my visit was the cosmic connection we shared with our meditator friend, Shri Priyabhishek Sharma. Despite not having met in person, both of us experienced a spiritual communion that sets the tone for our journey. His visit to Badrinath in August 2024 introduced us to Swami Ram Das ji, who resides in Badrinath during non-winter months and assisted with logistical arrangements for our trip.

The synchronicities surrounding our journey—highlighted by Priyabhishek's belief that *'there are no accidents on the spiritual path'*—added layers of significance to our pilgrimage. This visit not only deepened our connection with the sacred site but also underscored the mysterious ways in which spiritual energies align and guide seekers toward profound experiences. The journey was a poignant reminder that spiritual paths often weave together seemingly unrelated events, leading us to moments of profound insight and connection.

After arriving in the village of Badrinath, which still functions as a Panchayat, we attended the evening *darshan* twice. Following this, we sat in meditation in a quiet corner of the temple campus, embracing our natural inclination toward meditative practice over ritualistic traditions. For me, being with our breath and immersed in meditation are the most sacred rituals, a reflection of my spiritual constituency.

The next morning began with the morning *darshan*, during which we were blessed with two opportunities to connect with Shri Badri Vishal—one from outside and the other within the *garbhagriha* (sanctum sanctorum). Within the shrine, we felt an irresistible pull that captivated our entire being, emptying our minds and filling them with divine grace. This sacred space seemed to radiate an energy that transcended words, leaving us in awe.

On the temple premises, we met Swami Ram Das ji, a young ascetic whose thin frame and spiritually composed demeanour immediately drew our admiration. With his magnetic presence and oval-shaped face radiating serenity, Swami ji left an indelible impression on us. He shared that he visited the temple every morning at 9 am for *darshan* before returning to his hermitage.

After our first meeting with Swami ji, he pointed out his hermitage atop Narayan Mountain. For those unfamiliar,

Narayan Mountain is home to Shri Badri Vishal in the form of a sacred Shaligram stone, while Nar Mountain houses the seasonal population. Narayan Mountain is also believed to be where Mahavatar Babaji resides in both physical and metaphysical forms. Numerous elevated Yogis and swamis have recounted their encounters with Mahavatar Babaji in these higher altitudes.

This visit not only deepened our connection to Badrinath but also reaffirmed its significance as a spiritual epicentre where divine energies converge. The synchronicity of events—our meeting with Swami Ram Das ji and the magnetic allure of Shri Badri Vishal—underlined how spiritual journeys often unfold in ways that are both mysterious and transformative.

After breakfast, we embarked on a visit to Swamiji's hermitage, situated on a winding path that ascended towards the revered 'charan-paduka' point. This sacred site is marked by the imprints of Lord Vishnu's feet on a rock, with the foot down the hill being smaller and the one up the hill, larger, symbolizing both his arrival and departure. The trek for about a kilometre was challenging due to the low oxygen levels in the terrain, which made every step a test of endurance.

As we climbed upward, we caught sight of Swami ji seated outside his hermitage, basking in the sun's warmth. Upon reaching his place, he welcomed us warmly and guided us to his outer room, where two cots were neatly arranged alongside a well-kept kitchen that adjoined his living room. His hermitage was a cozy three-bedroom apartment on the ground floor, where he had been residing for the past two decades. He shared that he spends six months there and returns to the plains for the other six months after the temple closes for winter.

We spent nearly two hours in conversation, sharing stories of my own spiritual journeys and listening intently as he recounted his experiences of living in the upper dimensions of the Himalayas. His tales of wishful living in harmony with nature were both captivating and inspiring, offering a glimpse into a life deeply intertwined with the divine energies of the mountains.

As we entered Swamiji's hermitage, our eyes were drawn to a calendar featuring an image of Maa Anandamayi. Beneath her serene presence, the words *"Prabhu katha hee katha, aur sab vritha, vyatha"* (It is just the name of God that matters; everything else is painfully futile) resonated deeply. The sight of Maa's image stirred a profound sense of curiosity within me, and I couldn't help but ask Swamiji about his association with Maa Anandamayi and the significance of her presence in his hermitage.

Swami ji shared a remarkable story about his reverend Guru, Swami Lal Baba, who had served Maa Anandamayi for many years. He explained that it was only after his Guru's discipleship under Maa that he became physically stable and grounded in his spiritual practice. This revelation deepened our conversation, as I briefly expressed my own love and reverence for Maa Anandamayi.

Among the many topics we discussed, one of the most extraordinary was Swami ji's physical encounter with Shri Mahavatar Babaji. He recounted how, during his early years in Badrinath, he lived near Narayan Cave, located beyond the *charan-paduka* point above his current hermitage. At that time, he resided in a tent adjoining the cave. One day, through the window of his tent, he saw a tall man walking uphill, holding a bamboo stick on his shoulder. The man's magnetic aura immediately caught Swami ji's attention, prompting him to step out and follow him.

Despite walking as fast as he could, Swami ji found himself unable to close the distance between them—the gap remained constant no matter how hard he tried. Exhausted, he eventually gave up and returned to his tent. Later, he received a divine message confirming that the figure he had seen was indeed Shri Mahavatar Babaji himself. This extraordinary encounter left an indelible mark on Swami ji's spiritual journey.

(With Swami Ram Das ji at Shri Badrinath)

As I listened to Swami ji's account, I was reminded of my own profound experience with Mahavatar Babaji during my visit to the cave in 2022. While meditating near the cave, I had a vision of Babaji standing outside on a rock, holding a long bamboo stick and dressed in a white dhoti and short kurta. His face bore a soft smile that radiated grace and serenity. Though I was deep in meditation, I saw him with such clarity that it felt as though I was perceiving him with my physical eyes.

I chose not to share my experience with Swami ji at that moment but instead marvelled at the cosmic correlation between our encounters. The synchronicity of these events points out to the mysterious and wondrous ways in which the universe operates—reminding me that life itself is an unfolding story of divine wonderment when viewed through an objective lens.

Swami ji revealed an extraordinary insight about Shri Mahavatar Babaji, sharing that in the same region near his hermitage, Babaji convened periodic meetings of key divine beings, including Maa Anandamayi. He emphasized that Babaji himself would always arrange a special seat for Maa during these gatherings, a testament to the deep reverence and respect he held for her. Swami ji added that these meetings were attended by seers from higher dimensions, who would arrive and depart using celestial routes, their presence a reminder of the mystical energies that permeate this sacred landscape.

(Purnima, my wife seated with Swami Ram Das ji at Narayan Parvat)

Swami ji assured me that during my next visit to his hermitage, provided I kept a few days in hand, he would personally guide me to the location near Neelkanth Mountain where these sacred assemblies were held. This promise filled me with anticipation, as I imagined the profound spiritual significance of walking in the footsteps of such revered beings.

Swami ji also recounted his early experiences in the region, particularly his time living near Narayan Cave during periods of heavy snowfall. He described how one day Kuber ji, the *Kshetrapal* (Commanding Guardian) of the area, appeared to counsel him against staying there during winter due to the harsh conditions. Following this divine intervention, Swami ji began returning to the mainland after the annual winter closure of the Badrinath shrine.

Spending time with Swami ji was a profound experience, filled with spiritual grace and meaningful conversations. He warmly prepared tea for all of us and shared nuts to eat, as we engaged in discussions that resonated deeply with my spiritual convictions. Interestingly, he mentioned that our connection was not new but spanned multiple lifetimes—a sentiment that aligned perfectly with the impression I had after our first meeting with him.

By afternoon, it was time to return to our hotel, as the next morning we had a long drive ahead to Haridwar, where Shri Shyamal ji Maharaj had arranged our stay at Maa Anandamayi Ashram in Kankhal. The journey spanned approximately three hundred kilometres and included planned stops at the Vashisht and Arundhati caves, as reminded by Anant ji from Sitamarhi. When we reached the Vashisht cave, it was about to close, but we managed to catch a glimpse inside and feel its incredible energy. The cave appeared like a cosmically designed tunnel, radiating an extraordinary vibration, with a few people seated in meditation. Unfortunately, we could not visit the Arundhati cave as it was located further down towards the Ganga.

Continuing our drive, we eventually arrived at Maa Anandamayi Ashram in Haridwar. The ashram's tranquil environment harmonizes beautifully with the spiritual energy of Haridwar. Visitors often find solace in its lush surroundings and participate in rituals that reflect Maa's teachings of peace and devotion. Our arrival at this sacred space marked another step in our spiritual journey, offering an opportunity for reflection and connection amidst the divine vibrations of Maa Anandamayi.

Revisiting the Vashisht Cave felt like an act of predestination, something we were meant to do and could not avoid. The morning began with an hour of meditation at Maa Anandamayi's serene Kankhal Ashram, followed by a sacred dip in the Ganga at Maa's Ghat. Afterward, we embarked on an hour-long drive to the Vashisht and Arundhati caves, nestled in the heart of nature's splendour.

The Vashisht Cave, steeped in ancient spiritual energy, was profoundly captivating. This sacred site is believed to have been a meditation spot for Sage Vasishta, one of the Saptarshis and a *manas putra* of Lord Brahma. Sitting inside the deep, tunnel-shaped cave felt like an interface with the cosmos itself—a space divinely ordained for those predisposed to self-awareness. The vibrations within were felt immensely, and I could sense the same energy that countless Yogis must have experienced over the centuries. The suspension of mind that occurred while seated there was a natural response to the cave's innate power. At its far end, a platform housed several idols, including a Shiv Lingam that seemed to shine with an almost magical brilliance.

(Inside the Vashisht cave)

We spent about half an hour in meditation within the cave, though time felt suspended amidst its profound stillness. The experience left me yearning for more time to absorb its energy fully, but we had to move on due to other commitments.

The visit reaffirmed for me how certain places are cosmically designed to facilitate inner transformation and spiritual growth. The Vashisht Cave is undoubtedly one such place, carrying the legacy of sages and seekers who have meditated there for ages.

The Arundhati Cave, situated just a few meters below the Vashisht Cave, presented a distinct spiritual experience with its serene ambiance overlooking the Ganga flowing gently below. Unlike the deeply composed energy of Vashisht Cave, Arundhati Cave seemed to embody a strong connection to the sky element, almost as if it opened a window to the heavens. Its positioning and atmosphere made it feel lighter yet equally profound in its own way, offering a unique perspective on the spiritual journey.

We spent about thirty minutes seated inside the cave, absorbing its tranquil vibrations and reflecting on its sacred significance. The cave is associated with Maa Arundhati, the wife of Sage Vashishta, one of the revered Saptarishis. According to Hindu scriptures, Maa Arundhati is celebrated for her unparalleled devotion, chastity, and wisdom. Her presence in this region adds a layer of spiritual depth to the cave's energy.

(At the Arundhati cave)

The Arundhati Cave is part of a larger spiritual landscape near Shivpuri, Uttarakhand, where both caves—Vashisht and Arundhati—serve as meditation sanctuaries for seekers. The proximity of these caves to the Ganga enhances their sacredness, making them ideal spots for introspection and self-awareness. After our brief but meaningful visit, we returned to Haridwar with a sense of gratitude for having experienced these cosmic spaces designed for spiritual elevation.

On our way to Muzaffarpur, I had planned a stopover in Ayodhya for the night, with the intention of having Shri Ram Darshan the next morning. After concluding our drive from Haridwar, we arrived at an ashram where we spent the night. Amar Singh ji, a spiritual companion and ardent devotee of Shri Mahavatar Babaji, has always been a gracious host whenever I pass through Ayodhya. He kindly welcomed us for a cup of tea and a brief respite. Not only did Shri Singh host a delightful dinner for us, but he also arranged for an accessible darshan of Shri Ram ji, making our visit truly special and memorable.

After a brief *darshan* at Shri Ram Temple in Ayodhya, we returned home and resumed our daily routines. My work in the following days involved visits to various districts of Bihar—a land that, to me, transcends being just a region. Bihar is a karmic epicentre, a place where spiritually charged souls find their way into rebirth to work through their karmic accounts. The spiritual potential of its people may manifest differently from one individual to another, but they all carry an energy of higher purpose.

During my journey through Bihar, I had the privilege of visiting Munger, a city steeped in history and spirituality. Munger's rich heritage spans across ages, with its origins traditionally linked to a Yogi named Shri Moong. The city, situated along the northward-flowing Ganga, is also associated with Karna, the heroic figure from the Mahabharata. In modern times, Munger has gained international acclaim as the home of the Bihar School of Yoga, founded by Swami Satyananda Saraswati in 1963. This globally recognized institution has placed Munger on the world map as a center for Yogic learning and spiritual growth.

Adding to its spiritual significance is Chandika Sthan, a revered Shakti Peetha located on the banks of the Ganga. According to legend, this is where the left eye of Sati fell during Lord Shiva's cosmic dance of grief. Uniquely, Maa Chandi is represented here by a singular eye in the form of a tiny star—a rare depiction among Shakti Peethas. This sacred site has been a focal point for devotees and Tantric alike, particularly during Navratri, when it becomes a hub for tantric practices and spiritual seekers.

Munger's historicity is equally fascinating. It was once part of Anga Mahajanapada during the Mahabharata era and later served as a capital for various dynasties, including the Palas. The city has witnessed invasions by Turkic rulers and Marathas before becoming a commercial hub under British rule. Its cultural fabric is enriched by legends of Raja Karna's devotion to Maa Chandi and Raja Bharthari's tantric practices near Chandika Sthan.

For me, Munger represents more than just its historical and spiritual landmarks. It is a place where ancient wisdom seamlessly blends with modern spiritual pursuits, offering an atmosphere charged with energy and introspection. My visit left me with a profound appreciation for its timeless legacy—a reminder of how places like Munger continue to inspire seekers on their spiritual journeys.

Following my previous journey, my travels took me to another Himalayan location, this time in the northeastern part of the range, to the enchanting state of Meghalaya. Although the trip was officially motivated, it carried an underlying divine essence, as has often been the case. Behind every physical manifestation lies a spiritual trace, accessible only through spiritual insight—a truth that resonated deeply during this journey. The nights in Shillong were spent enveloped in universal totality, with the cold breeze blowing in from the farther northern and eastern Himalayan regions. The days were sunny, bright, and pleasant in the early season of winter, providing a serene backdrop for my meditative pursuits.

Coming recently from one of the highest peaks in the Himalayas, it was more than exhilarating to be on the other side of the range, experiencing the softer, more verdant landscapes of Meghalaya. This journey offered a unique perspective on the majestic mountains, contrasting their towering grandeur with the lush greenery and rolling hills of this northeastern state. The spiritual essence of Meghalaya is phenomenal, with sacred sites like Nartiang Durga Temple—a Shakti Peetha believed to mark where Goddess Sati's left thigh fell—and Mawjymbuin Cave Temple, housing a naturally formed Shiva Lingam, adding layers of divine significance to its natural beauty.

My journey from Meghalaya led me to the sacred Maa Kamakhya Temple in Guwahati, Assam—a site revered by Yogis and spiritual seekers as one of the most potent energy centres. Maa Kamakhya is widely recognized as a pivotal point of the Shri Chakra, specifically its *Bindu*, the cosmic centre that symbolizes creation and divine union. The temple, perched atop Nilachal Hill, is not just a place of worship but a profound gateway into Tantra Yog and spiritual awakening.

The Sri Chakra is a mystical diagram that is central to the worship of the Shri Vidya school of Hinduism. It is made up of nine interlocking triangles that represent the union of masculine and feminine divine energies. The Sri Chakra is considered to be a geometrical representation of cosmic energy and is said to contain all types of energy forms.

The Kamakhya Temple holds immense significance in Shaktism, being one of the oldest Shakti Peethas where the Yoni (womb) of Goddess Sati is believed to have fallen. Its primary focus of worship is an aniconic Yoni set in natural stone, symbolizing fertility and creation. This sacred representation connects deeply with the divine feminine energy, making the temple a vital centre for tantric practices. The annual Ambubachi Mela, celebrating the menstruation of Goddess Kamakhya, underscores this connection to life force and regeneration.

Structurally, the temple dates back to the 8th-9th century and has evolved through various dynasties—the Mlechhas, Palas, Kochs, and Ahoms—each contributing to its rich history. Surrounding the main temple are shrines dedicated to the ten Mahavidyas of Shaktism, including Kali, Tara, Tripura Sundari, and Bagalamukhi. This unique arrangement of Mahavidya temples is rare and adds to its spiritual prominence.

For me, visiting Maa Kamakhya was more than a physical journey—it was an immersion into divine energy. The temple's atmosphere radiates power and serenity, offering a glimpse into the cosmic interplay between creation and dissolution. The experience reaffirmed my connection to the Sri Chakra's profound symbolism and reminded me that behind every manifestation lies a spiritual trace accessible through insight. Maa Kamakhya continues to inspire seekers with her eternal presence as the embodiment of Shakti's transformative power.

I felt I was truly blessed to be there in the pivotal centre on yet another occasion. For the Darshan, my team, composed of so many young boys, had to wait for almost 3 hours to reach the sanctum sanctorum. However, once we were inside the Garbhagriha, I experienced transcendental silence. It was the same as an hour spent in deep meditation in Shri Mahavatar cave. Tales I have been given to hear also inform me that Shri Mahavatar Babaji frequently visited Kamakhya temple for one purpose or the other. In the recent past, the story of Shri Ramanand Sagar's meeting with Shri Mahavatar Babaji in the temple premises was made public by the former's son.

On my journey back to Bihar, I felt an inner calling to visit the Dakshineswar Kali Temple in Kolkata, the physical abode of Shri Ramakrishna and the sacred site of his *Adhisthatri Devi*, Maa Kali. This visit held profound significance for me, as I believed that the cosmos would not allow me to complete my book without first seeking blessings at this divine energy centre. The temple, a revered Shakti Peetha, is home to Bhavatarini, an aspect of Goddess Kali, and has long been a spiritual beacon for seekers.

The Dakshineswar Kali Temple, built in 1855 by Rani Rashmoni, is a masterpiece of Navaratna-style Bengali architecture. Located on the eastern bank of the Hooghly River, it features a majestic nine-spired main temple dedicated to Kali, surrounded by twelve Shiva temples and a Radha-Krishna shrine. The sanctum sanctorum houses an idol of Bhavatarini standing on Shiva's supine form, placed on a thousand-petaled silver lotus throne. The temple complex also includes *Nahabat*, where Shri Ramakrishna and Sarada Devi resided during their spiritual journey.

For me, this visit was more than a pilgrimage—it was an immersion into the Advaitic essence that Shri Ramakrishna embodied. His teachings on the harmony of all religions and his profound connection with Maa Kali have inspired countless seekers, including his ardent disciple, Swami Vivekananda. Standing in this sacred space, I felt deeply connected to the spiritual lineage that continues to guide humanity toward self-realization.

The tranquil atmosphere of Dakshineswar provided me with clarity and inspiration to conclude my book. It felt as though the cosmic forces aligned to bring me to this seat of Advaita Vedanta before completing my work. This experience reaffirmed my belief that every physical manifestation carries a spiritual trace—one that can only be accessed through insight and surrender. The visit was a poignant reminder that spiritual journeys often unfold in unexpected ways, guiding us toward deeper truths and connections that transcend the ordinary.

The witnessing continues as long as the body remains bound to its Prarabdha, the predestined path that unfolds from accumulated karma. This journey is a testament to the enduring presence of spiritual guidance, as embodied by enlightened Gurus like Shri Mahavatar Babaji.

Chapter - 21

And the Takeaways

The cycles of existence unfold as a cosmic recasting of what concluded before, perpetuating effortlessly, without external force. Life's journey belongs solely to the individual self, while all others around are fleeting karmic companions—transient souls bound to us only until the balance of shared karma shifts. These relationships dissolve and reform like tides, governed by the ever-changing equations of cause and effect.

Predestination emerges as life's silent architect, shaping not just circumstances but the very architecture of the mind, the cadence of thoughts, and the impulses behind actions. Even the illusion of free will operates within this grand design, a dance choreographed by the unseen hand of *Prarabdha*. In this dance, the self remains both participant and observer—navigating the script of destiny while awakening to the truth that transcends it. This cosmic interplay between karma and predestination underlines the profound journey of the individual self, where every moment is an opportunity for introspection and spiritual growth.

As one delves deeper into the unfolding of his/her own life, he/she will come to understand the profound truth behind these words. The journey of life is a manifestation of past karmic energies, with some remaining layers yet to materialize. It is this unfolding of karma that sustains our existence, allowing us to continue breathing and living. I often liken this process to scenes appearing and disappearing on a cinema screen—each moment a fleeting yet integral part of the larger cosmic narrative.

Just as a film unfolds frame by frame, our lives reveal themselves scene by scene, guided by the unseen forces of predestination and karma. Every experience, whether joyous or challenging, is a vital chapter in this grand story. The realization that our lives are part of this larger whole can inspire us to approach each moment with mindfulness and gratitude, understanding that every breath is a gift from the universe.

This perspective invites us to embrace life's journey with a sense of detachment and awareness, recognizing that every scene—every moment—is temporary yet precious. As we navigate these karmic manifestations, we are reminded that spiritual growth and self-awareness are the ultimate rewards of this cosmic dance.

Life itself is not as challenging as we often perceive it to be. Instead, it is the subjective perspectives we cling to that complicate our experiences. Our lives are frequently guided by personal biases and emotions, which lead us away from an objective understanding of reality. This subjective orientation can obscure the true nature of life, making it seem more complex than it inherently is.

By recognizing and letting go of these attachments to our subjective views, we can begin to see life in a clearer light. Embracing objectivity allows us to align more closely with the natural flow of existence, revealing that life's journey can be simpler and more harmonious than we imagine. This shift in perspective invites us to approach challenges with a sense of detachment and wisdom, understanding that true peace and clarity arise from embracing life as it is, rather than as we wish it to be.

In this journey toward objectivity, we discover that life's true essence is not about the external circumstances but about our internal responses to them. By aligning with this understanding, we can transform our experiences, turning what once seemed difficult into opportunities for growth and self-awareness.

Our uncontrollable physical desires often complicate life, arising from the worldly influences and orientations that shape us. Beneath the surface of our daily experiences, life's deeper currents flow, yet they remain elusive to most of us. These undercurrents are present, yet distant from our usual station, accessible only to those who venture inward. Only a select few take the plunge and dive beneath the surface, and among them, even fewer manage to grasp these hidden currents.

Those who successfully connect with these profound undercurrents undergo significant transformation. The path to this realization is paved by consistent inner exploration through rigorous and routine *Saadhana* (spiritual practice). This disciplined journey within allows us to transcend the limitations of our physical desires and worldly conditioning, revealing the deeper truths that lie beneath the surface of existence.

Our human lives are a precious gift, a consequence of our own auspicious karmas. It is essential that we do not waste this opportunity but instead capitalize on it by embracing the journey of self-realization. Life is meant to be an evolving path, one that unfolds through conscious efforts toward selfless awareness. By dedicating ourselves to this journey, we can transform our existence into a meaningful and fulfilling experience.

This perspective invites us to approach life with gratitude and purpose, recognizing that every moment offers a chance for growth and spiritual evolution. The journey of self-realization is not just about personal development but also about transcending the boundaries of the self to connect with a larger reality. It is through this process that we can truly appreciate the gift of life and make the most of the opportunities it presents.

In this journey, we discover that life's true value lies not in external achievements but in the depth of our inner transformation. By embracing this path, we can evolve beyond our current limitations, cultivating wisdom, compassion, and peace.

Consistency in meditational practices provides the momentum needed to maintain a selfless path of realization. It is essential to cherish these pursuits while fulfilling all worldly duties and responsibilities. Balancing the physical and spiritual aspects of life remains a challenge for many, yet it is achievable. Personally, I have found that adopting the *drashta bhava*—the state of being a witness—helps reduce attachments. This perspective fosters a sense of detachment from emotional entanglements in interpersonal relationships and worldly affairs, but it does not lead to indifference toward one's duties and responsibilities.

In fact, being the witness allows us to engage with life more mindfully, performing our roles with clarity and purpose. This balance between detachment and engagement is crucial for navigating life's complexities while maintaining a deep connection to our spiritual core. By embracing this dual approach, we can fulfil our worldly obligations with integrity while continuing to evolve on our spiritual journey. The experience of witnessing life from this perspective is transformative, as it allows us to approach challenges with equanimity and wisdom. It reminds us that spiritual growth and worldly responsibilities are not mutually exclusive but complementary aspects of a well-lived life.

As a householder, it is essential to fulfil all worldly duties without shirking responsibilities. Running away from these obligations is not advisable; instead, one should strive to balance them with spiritual pursuits. Amidst the demands of daily life, it is crucial to carve out quality time for introspection through sincere meditation. Let us remember that what we seek—true fulfilment and peace—is within us. The external world is a realm of *Maya*, filled with material impermanence, while the inner self embodies *sat-chit-ananda*, the blissful state of being.

My conviction is that true meditation is the path to attaining this state of *sat-chit-ananda*. Shri Hairakhan Babaji's wisdom resonates deeply with this perspective: *"In this age, it is not possible to renounce the world. The only practice of renunciation now is to offer all work and actions to the Lord. If you want God, be ready to devote everything to God."* This guidance highlights the importance of integrating spiritual devotion into our daily lives, transforming every action into an act of worship and dedication.

By embracing this approach, we can navigate the challenges of worldly life while remaining connected to our spiritual core. It is through this integration that we can find true peace and fulfilment, aligning our outer actions with the inner pursuit of *sat-chit-ananda*.

Meditation is indeed an accessible practice, provided that all its essential enablers are in place. Based on my personal experiences, I have found that several key elements are crucial for a successful meditation practice. These include cultivating peace of mind, maintaining physical health, embarking on spiritual journeys—particularly in the Himalayas, which offer a unique energy conducive to introspection—practicing seclusion, committing to regular meditation through dedicated time and space, engaging in *Satsang* (the company of noble and like-minded individuals), and fostering a strong sense of internal detachment.

These prerequisites not only facilitate a deeper meditation practice but also enrich the overall quality of life. By integrating these elements, one can create an environment that supports spiritual growth and self-realization. The Himalayas, with their majestic beauty and sacred energy, have been a source of inspiration for many spiritual seekers, offering a serene backdrop for introspection and connection with nature.

The experience of meditation is a journey of self-discovery, one that requires patience, consistency, and a willingness to let go of attachments. By embracing these enablers and dedicating oneself to the practice, one can unlock the profound benefits of meditation, leading to a more peaceful, balanced, and fulfilling life.

Our own spiritual integrity is perhaps the most important pathway to continue on. While a Guru can offer valuable guidance, it is our actions that hold the most significance. I have encountered many individuals who have received *Diksha* from their Gurus but have not experienced the transformative changes they sought. Often, they have placed their Gurus on pedestals, literally and figuratively, by hanging their images on walls and offering prayers. However, it is crucial to remember that the Guru serves as a guide, while we are the one who must walk the path.

The journey of spiritual growth is deeply personal and requires active engagement. Simply receiving *Diksha* or following a Guru is not enough; one must also commit to consistent practice and self-reflection. The true power of spiritual guidance lies not in the external authority but in the internal transformation it inspires. By embracing this understanding, we can harness the full potential of our spiritual journey, using the guidance of a Guru as a catalyst for our own growth and self-realization.

Life should be guided by truthfulness, embracing the simplicity and spontaneity that comes from being genuine. When we are truthful, we invite cosmic interventions, aligning ourselves with the natural order of the universe. Truthfulness is not just a virtue but a state of being that is both simple and meditative. To be naturally simple (*sahaj*) is to be in a meditative state, where one's actions and thoughts are harmonious and uncontrived.

This simplicity reduces the likelihood of conflicting states, as it fosters clarity and peace. By embracing truthfulness, we can navigate life's complexities with greater ease, finding balance and harmony in our thoughts, emotions, and actions. The experience is a poignant reminder that living truthfully is not just a moral imperative but a path to inner peace and spiritual growth, guiding us toward deeper truths and connections that enrich our existence.

It is essential to surround ourselves with good companionships—people who engage in meaningful conversations about the broader aspects of creation, who have a passion for exploration, who cultivate love and compassion, and who aspire to explore their inner selves through meditational practices. These individuals should also be mindful of their responsibilities in the world and avoid fostering hatred, jealousy, and greed. Such company not only enriches our lives but also supports our spiritual growth.

On the other hand, those who lack these qualities can dilute our spiritual purity. They may distract us from our path and lead us astray from our inner journey. It is crucial to be discerning about the company we keep, ensuring that it uplifts and inspires us rather than diminishing our spiritual aspirations. By choosing companions who embody these positive qualities, we can create a supportive environment that fosters growth, peace, and self-awareness.

One should always strive to perform good *karma* and diligently fulfil their worldly duties without any expectation of returns. Whatever is due will naturally come in its own time. Actions should be carried out with a pure heart, free from prejudices or selfish motives. As Shri Hairakhan Babaji said, '*Karma is an inevitable law of cause and effect, by which all living beings reap the fruits of their actions and thoughts*'.

Similarly, Jesus expressed this universal truth with the words, 'As ye sow, so shall ye reap.'

The principle of karma underscores the importance of intentionality and ethical living. It teaches that our actions—whether physical, verbal, or mental—set into motion a chain of consequences that shape our present and future experiences. This law encourages us to act with integrity and selflessness, focusing on the quality of our efforts rather than the outcomes. By aligning ourselves with this understanding, we can cultivate inner peace and spiritual growth while contributing positively to the world around us.

Ultimately, Karma serves as a reminder that life is not about controlling results but about living with purpose, sincerity, and mindfulness. When we let go of expectations and dedicate ourselves to righteous action, we align with the natural order of the universe, allowing its grace to flow through us effortlessly.

"The law of Karma is above all things. Karma starts when movement starts in the mind. To stop Karma, we must bring the mind to that state of silence and voidness beyond which God can be known. Only a Yogi knows how to do this. Otherwise, as long as a man breathes, he is creating Karma. No one can remain without action, even for a minute. Therefore, learn how to dedicate every action to the Lord".

Most of us are prone to being drawn into the complexities of worldly affairs, including family, interpersonal, and official matters. We often engage deeply with these subjectivities and become integral parts of them. However, it is crucial that we do not allow these affairs to consume our individuality and spirit of freedom. Let us remember that evolution and growth occur only in the realm of freedom.

As Maa Anandmayi so profoundly stated, *'Divine happiness, even the tiniest particle of a grain of it, never leaves one again; and when one attains to the essence of things and finds one's Self—this is supreme happiness. When it is found, nothing else remains to be found; the sense of want will not awaken anymore, and the heart's torment will be stilled forever.'* She advised against settling for fragmentary happiness, which is often disrupted by life's challenges, and instead encouraged us to strive for completeness and perfection by being true to ourselves.

This journey toward self-realization and freedom is a path of spiritual evolution, where one seeks to transcend the limitations of worldly entanglements and find inner peace and fulfilment. By embracing this path, we can cultivate a sense of freedom that allows us to navigate life's complexities with grace and wisdom, unencumbered by the burdens of external expectations.

In this journey, we discover that true freedom is not just the absence of external constraints but also the presence of inner peace and clarity. It is a state where we are no longer bound by the fluctuations of worldly affairs but are instead guided by our inner truth.

Life, in its essence, is meant to be well-disciplined. The more organized and consistent we are in maintaining discipline, the closer we align ourselves with cosmic order and influences. Just as the creation inherently sustains its own balance and harmony, personal discipline enables us to attune with this universal rhythm. Individual efforts to cultivate discipline naturally complement meditational practices, creating a pathway for deeper spiritual exploration.

Our physical bodies are composed of the same elemental phenomena that exist outside of us. Within us lies a universe of subtler spectacles—realities that our physical eyes cannot perceive but which can be accessed through inner vision. While the physical eyes have limitations in their sighting phenomena, the third eye transcends these boundaries, offering limitless perception and insight into the deeper truths of existence.

This alignment between external order and internal discipline fosters a state of harmony where meditation becomes a gateway to understanding both the cosmos and our inner selves. By cultivating discipline and tapping into the power of the third eye, we can experience profound spiritual evolution and connect with the universal intelligence that governs all creation.

Maintaining discipline over our breath is essential, as both breath and breathing transcend their apparent physical nature. They are cosmic miracles that manifest in our perceived physical realm, part of the larger cosmic consciousness. Just as a plant breathes and blooms, all living things around us are manifestations of this cosmically-toned breath and the constant process of breathing. Observing the breath is an enchanting experience, but it requires dedication and discipline, akin to *tapascharya* (performing a penance).

To fully engage with the breath, one must meet the basic prerequisites of the eight elements of yo-ga: yama (abstinences), niyama (observances), asana (yoga posture), pranayama (breath con-trol), pratyahara (withdrawal of the senses), dharana (concentration of the mind), dhyana (meditation), and samadhi (absorption or stillness). Throughout this journey, the breath remains a constant companion, while other practices serve as complementary forces. The breath is a direct force that guides our spiritual ascent.

Gautama Buddha emphasized the importance of *ana-pana-sati*, the mindful observation of the incoming and outgoing breath. Similarly, Kriya Yoga focuses on the action of breathing as a central practice. Consistently being with one's breath and practicing mindfulness of it greatly aids in the process of self-realization, fostering a deeper connection with the cosmic consciousness that underlies all existence.

The path to divinity, as illuminated by Kabir's profound teachings, is paradoxically simple yet complex, fraught with turbulence as it navigates the dual realms of worldly life and spiritual pursuits. His poignant verses, such as *"Prem gali ati sankari"* and *"Jab mein tha tab Hari nahi, ab Hari hai main naahi,"* encapsulate the essence of his philosophy: the dissolution of ego as a gateway to divine union. This journey demands not ascetic withdrawal but a transformative balance between life's obligations and transcendent truth. Meditation emerges as a crucial practice, fostering a state of witness consciousness (*drashta-bhav*) that helps individuals strike a balance between worldly responsibilities and spiritual aspirations, ultimately leading to self-realization and eternal tranquility.

The physical dimension and the spiritual endeavours collide with each other in the normal practical sense of the term. Required alignment happens through rigorous efforts of the individuals. However, that alignment isn't always easy. The maya-jagat (the mundane world) and its tantrums do not normally allow individuals to be focused enough to self-realization and its delicate steady performances. Mind is drawn to the *maya-jagat* whereas the spirit strives for eternal bliss. Therefore, an individual with a strong desire for eternal union has to look for a balance and be in a state of being the witness of happenings in the *maya-jagat*. Why is meditation important after all? Primarily because, meditation helps in striking a balance between the two and fosters inculcating drashta-bhav (being the witness) in individuals on spiritual path.

The importance of maintaining individuality and walking one's unique path is deeply emphasized in spiritual teachings, including those of Buddha and Kabir. Buddha's instruction to 'becoming your own Buddha' reflects the idea that each person's journey is distinct, shaped by their unique circumstances and inner calling. Similarly, Kabir's teachings resonate with this principle, urging individuals to seek truth within themselves rather than conforming to external influences or group ideologies.

Living in a higher dimension, beyond the confines of the mind, is essential for spiritual growth and inner peace. Our minds often become cluttered with useless thoughts—past regrets and present anxieties—that are fleeting and ephemeral. These mental burdens can weigh us down, obscuring our true nature and potential. However, there is a way to transcend this state: through regular and consistent meditation. Meditation allows us to rise above the mental clutter, entering a realm where the mind is suspended, and we experience a thoughtless, peaceful state—a perpetual vacation from the turmoil of thoughts. This practice enables us to witness life's events without attachment, freeing us to live in a dimension of clarity and serenity.

Our life journeys are uniquely tailored to each individual, distinct from others in our family, society, or broader community. The preservation of personal purity is essential for growth and evolution, while impurities can silently erode our being. When we engage with elements that harbour negativity, we risk degradation without even realizing it. However, it's important not to blame others, as they are shaped by their own experiences and upbringing. Instead, we should focus on maintaining our individual integrity and aligning with positive influences that support our path to evolution.

Ramana Maharshi's teachings wisely redirect our focus from trying to understand others or external cosmic realities to a profound inward journey of self-discovery. By asking the simple yet profound question, *"Who am I?"*, we embark on an investigation into the depths of our being, peeling away layers of ego and conditioned identities to reveal our true essence. This practice of self-inquiry is a transformative path that leads to liberation and peace, transcending the limitations of external understanding and fostering a state of effortless awareness.

The self, in its true form, is devoid of physical colours and shines with the brilliance of pure light—a universal essence shared by all. However, this radiant nature remains obscured due to our entrapment in ignorance, akin to being blindfolded. The moment we behold our original form, we experience profound liberation and emancipation, joining the ranks of enlightened beings who have traversed the path to salvation. This realization frees us from the shackles of ignorance, allowing us to shine forth in our true, unadulterated light.

To transcend impression-based living, one must connect with their true essence—pure consciousness, or *Poorna Brahma*. This fundamental reality, exemplified by spiritual figures like Maa Anandamayi, who identified herself as *Poorna Brahma Narayani*, embodies the Supreme cosmic consciousness. By recognizing and embracing this pure awareness, individuals can break free from the constraints of external influences and mental constructs, revealing their true nature as a lightness of being and experiencing unity with the universe.

Life unfolds as a physical manifestation on Earth, often without our control over the circumstances of birth or the ups and downs that follow. Despite these uncertainties, it is crucial to maintain neutrality and anchor oneself in spiritual veracity. This involves embracing life's fluctuations with equanimity, recognizing that true stability lies not in external events but in the inner self. By cultivating this inner balance, individuals can navigate life's challenges while remaining grounded in their spiritual essence.

Our lives are uniquely crafted, making comparisons with others are not only futile but also a source of unnecessary distress. In today's world, many people are trapped in the cycle of comparison, leading to suffering. However, recognizing that each person's journey is predestined—complete with its own route, speed, and destination—can bring peace. Our actions unfold according to a predetermined plan, and understanding this can help us accept our path and live more authentically, free from the burdens of comparison and external validation. Let's not become overly entangled in worries about things not unfolding as expected. Life is designed to reveal itself at the right moment, much like the petals of a flower unfolding in their own time. Each layer of experience becomes visible when it is meant to, and our journey unfolds like scenes on a cinema screen—each moment passing into the next. If we dwell on past scenes, they may replay in our minds, but if we let go, life moves forward, and new scenes emerge. Embracing this natural flow can bring peace and reduce unnecessary distress.

It is essential to remain mindful of where our minds are focused and what drives our lives. Are we oriented toward material pursuits like wealth, power, or sensual desires, or are we guided by an eternal quest for truth and liberation? The direction of our thoughts and desires determines our immediate path and ultimate destination. Let us remember that, in the end, *Mukti* (salvation) is our true destiny, and aligning our lives with this eternal goal can lead us to a more profound and fulfilling existence.

"Place this salt in water and bring it here tomorrow morning".

The boy did.

Where is that salt? his father asked?

I do not see it.

Sip here. How does it taste?

Salty, father.

And here? And there?

I taste salt everywhere.

It is everywhere, though we see it not. Just so, dear one, the Self is everywhere, within all things, although we see it not. There is nothing that does not come from it. It is the truth; it is the Self supreme.

You are that, Shvetaketu".

Afterwords

There are numerous individuals who have significantly contributed to my life journey and spiritual quest. These remarkable people not only shared their time with me but also imparted their precious experiences. I am truly grateful to each of them and count them among the pillars of my growth.

In the last several months now, the Samvad Darshan fraternity has welcomed several new spiritual companions, expanding its reach across diverse regions. Among them is Dr. Anant, a young Deputy Collector serving in an eastern district of Bihar, introduced to me by Shri Priyabhishek Sharma, the author of *A Himalayan Master and the Sixth Sense*. Dr. Anant, formally initiated by Sri M—whom I hold in high regard—has quickly become a catalyst for spiritual growth in his circle. Over the past several months, I have had multiple opportunities to meet him and even visit his district as his guest.

During one such visit, we travelled together to Parsarma in Supaul district, the residence of Shri Lakshmi Nath Gosain, a revered Yogi of the Nath tradition. The energy field surrounding this location was profoundly vivacious and spiritually charged. While in his district on official trips, Dr. Anant introduced me to many of his senior colleagues, several of whom have since started exploring spirituality. Notably, Shri Manish Ranjan has completed reading significant spiritual texts such as *Puran Purush* (on Shri Lahiri Mahashay) and has begun meditating. Two others have also embarked on spiritual inquiries under Dr. Anant's guidance.

I was introduced to Wasim Haque late in 2021, an intriguing individual residing in a London suburb and working in the information technology field. Born into a Muslim family in Assam, Wasim's life took a profound spiritual turn about ten years ago, as he gradually distanced himself from *tamsik vritis* (actions associated with inertia), such as consuming non-vegetarian food and alcohol. He has become a devoted follower of Krishna, incorporating meditation into his daily routine and attending spiritual retreats. Wasim has also been in touch with several Yogic Masters both in India and abroad. Our connection was facilitated by two mutual friends, Sanjeev and Juri Baruah, from Assam, who now reside in Delhi. Although we have not met in person, I feel a deep, heart-to-heart connection with him, as if we have known each other for many lifetimes.

Recently, Wasim shared with me a remarkable experience from his past. At the age of 25, he encountered a young Yogi in the Badrinath hills, about a kilometre above the temple, who beckoned him near a barren Himalayan trek. However, Wasim became frightened and ran away. The young Yogi's appearance was reminiscent of the descriptions often attributed to Shri Mahavatar Babaji. Wasim is an avid reader of spiritual texts, including the Upanishads, Bhagavad Gita, and Buddhist scriptures.

Manoj Kumar, a Deputy Inspector General of Police in Bihar, is to be described as an extraordinary individual with a profound spiritual dimension. Despite his professional role in law enforcement, he is characterized as unassuming, humble, and deeply human. His spiritual journey has been marked by numerous fourth-dimensional experiences, and he is said to radiate an immense amount of energy.

Manoj ji's spiritual pursuits are driven by an insatiable thirst for the divine, although he feels bound by his worldly responsibilities. He has expressed that he would have already embraced the life of a renunciate if not for his family commitments. His spiritual experiences include encounters with other-dimensional beings, notably an incident at Shri Valmiki Ashram on the Bihar-Nepal border, where he claims to have met a young man whose description aligns with the one often attributed to Shri Mahavatar Babaji.

In recent interactions, Manoj ji has shared profound spiritual visions, including seeing his entire being as a beam of light with a bright star suspended above his head. These narratives are described as deeply impactful, evoking physical sensations and ultimately inducing a state of stillness in the listener.

Sanjay Rai is another significant spiritual presence in my life, whom I affectionately regard as a younger brother. Hailing from the land associated with Shri Pavhari Baba in Ghazipur district, Uttar Pradesh, Sanjay is an introverted individual. Although not directly involved in meditation or *sadhana*, he is highly awakened and spiritually inquisitive. He is physically active, humble, and articulate.

I have witnessed a profound transformation in Sanjay, which began after his visit to the cave in mid-2020. His energy started to shift, putting him on a roller-coaster of experiences, as he himself acknowledged. He would often call me when traveling by train, as this was when he felt most free and able to converse.

Sanjay is deeply influenced by Mahatma Gandhi's principles and actively works on social fronts to promote unity, non-violence, and peace. His social circle is diverse and rich, reflecting his commitment to these values. Despite his introverted nature, Sanjay's presence in my life has been a source of inspiration and spiritual growth.

Gopalanand Ji of Delhi ashram, a simple man in saffron who has served Maa for years across her various ashrams, would always welcome me warmly. As soon as he saw me arrive, he would locate my meditation mat and guide me to Maa's room. I would meditate there for about an hour before rushing back home to feed Gopal Ji and put him to sleep.

Occasionally, Swamiji would insist that I stay for dinner at the ashram, but I often declined because Gopal Ji awaited me at home.

The Delhi Ashram is located near the revered Kalkaji Mandir, one of Delhi's most sacred shrines dedicated to Goddess Kali, also known as Maa Kalka. Even today, three sides of the ashram are surrounded by forest, adding to its tranquil and spiritual atmosphere. Maa's room is situated behind the Shiv temple on the first floor at the farthest corner of the ashram. Stepping into her room felt like entering another dimension—where time ceased and only peace prevailed.

This daily practice deepened my spiritual connection with Maa's energy and reaffirmed the importance of balance between devotion and responsibility. The Kalkaji Mandir nearby further enriched this experience with its historical significance as a *siddh peeth* (fulfilment temple) believed to grant devotees' wishes. Together, these sacred spaces became central to my spiritual journey during this transformative period in my life. Through these experiences, I came to understand the profound harmony between spiritual pursuits and daily life, where devotion and duty blend seamlessly to create a life of purpose and peace.

The *Samvad Darshan* group has been experiencing a vibrant expansion, with new members joining from diverse corners of the country and beyond. This growth is subtly guided by natural forces, bringing together individuals who were previously unknown to me. Many of these members have reported a heightened sense of consciousness, particularly during and after the pandemic, which has led them to turn inward and explore meditation. Some have even begun encouraging others to follow this spiritual path.

This growing community embodies a collective awakening and shared commitment to spiritual growth through meditation and self-realization. Each member brings unique contributions to this dynamic group, enriching its purpose and fostering deeper connections within the spiritual realm.

Another remarkable individual introduced to me is a very young former bureaucrat, Aseem, who practices Kriya Yoga and considers himself connected to a cosmic Guru from whom he receives directives. Dr. Anant's role as a catalyst for spiritual awakening is evident in the transformations occurring around him.

Last but by no means least, I must mention Shri Braj Kishore Pandey ji, an esteemed bureaucrat in the Bihar administration. Beyond his role as an accomplished administrator, he possesses a remarkable capacity for spontaneous meditation. When he enters a meditative state, his presence itself seems to transform, embodying the stillness and grace of an idol. I feel a deep sense of pride and gratitude to have such gifted individuals as life-companions on my journey.

This collective evolution reflects the subtle yet powerful workings of cosmic forces that draw individuals toward deeper spiritual exploration and self-realization.

Acknowledgement

The earnest composition of this journey's account has been rendered possible only through the extraordinary and unfathomable divine grace graciously bestowed by the infinite cosmos. Amidst the calamitous vicissitudes and turbulent upheavals that life's path revealed, this celestial benediction served as an unfailing beacon, guiding my steps through adversity and enabling profound reflection upon the sacred voyage. Without this sublime favour, the very endeavour to contemplate and share such a transformation would have remained forever beyond reach.

The process of writing this account was slow yet steady, unfolding over nearly four years as I carefully penned down my reflections and experiences.

With utmost humility and deepest reverence, I acknowledge that the very composition of this account has been made possible only through the cosmic grace, divine will, and the boundless blessings of my revered Guru. I bow with profound devotion to the sacred energy field that has tenderly nurtured, guided, and sustained me throughout this journey—from its very inception to its continuous unfolding even now. It is by this transcedental benediction that my path has been illuminated, obstacles have been surmounted, and the soul's purpose revealed, allowing this sacred endeavour to come into fruition.

I extend my heartfelt gratitude to the numerous individuals and places that have contributed to my life journey, which this account reflects. Each of them played a significant role in fostering the process, and I acknowledge their contributions with deep appreciation. I have witnessed both positive and challenging experiences converge to create an environment that allowed this narrative to unfold. I thank everyone involved for the diverse offerings they brought to the table, which collectively enabled the creation of this account.

I am deeply grateful to the land of my present physical birth and my divine mother, where I received the foundational *samskaras* that shaped my early life. I also extend my heartfelt thanks to my ancestral lineage, whose collective energies and traditions have guided me throughout my journey. Reflecting on my heritage, I am filled with appreciation for how my father's ancestry infused me with earthly abundance, while my mother's family contributed the ethereal element, blending to form the essence of who I am today.

I also express my profound gratitude to all the cosmic, non-physical beings who have engaged in subtle discourses with me from time to time. I remain deeply thankful to each of them for their guidance and support.

In deep reverence, I bow to all the sacred places my Guru graciously guided me to discover, each steeped in profound spiritual significance and wisdom. From the divine presence of Shri Mahakaal in Ujjain and the powerful Shri Omkareshwar Jyotirling, to the mystical sanctity of Maa Kamakhya in Assam, and the holy heights of Shri Kedarnath and Badrinath, these sites have become milestones on my spiritual path. The serene ashrams of Shri Maa Anandmayi scattered across regions, the tranquil aura of Kasaar Devi and Kakri Ghat, and sacred abodes like Kainchi Dham, Shri Hairakhand Baba ashram, and Chitai Golu Devta have nurtured my inner journey. Pilgrimage to venerable shrines such as Shri Jageshwar Jyotir Lingam, Advait Ashram in Lohaghat, and Chillianaula ashram deepened my devotion, while the tranquil environs of Ranikhet and the divine energies of Maa Vindhyavasini, Maheshwar Ghat, and

Sahashtra Dhara on the Narmada have enriched my soul. From the blissful Shri Amrit Sarovar and Swarn Mandir in Punjab to the sacred grounds of Shri Pashupati Mahadev in Nepal, and the humble sanctity of Lakshmi Nath Gosain ashram in Supaul, each place bestowed unique blessings. Visits to Shirdi Sai Baba's abode, Tara Peeth in West Bengal, Shri Pahari Baba ashrams in Amer and Goner (Jaipur), Shri Dakshineshwar Kali in Kolkata, Shri Baidyanath Dham, Maharshi Mehi's mud cave in Bhagalpur, and the revered caves of Shri Vasisht and Arundhati in Uttarakhand have offered timeless wisdom and peace. The sacred grounds continue with Shri Shivpuri Baba Samadhi ashram, Shri Guhyeshwari Mandir in Kathmandu, Shri Mandrachalam and the Guru Dham of Bhupendra Nath Sanyal Mahashay in Banka, the Shri Shivom Teerth ashram in Devas, Bawangaja Teerth in Barwani, Maa Katyayini Devi, Tatia Sthal, and Nidhi-Van in Vrindavan—each a beacon of divine grace and spiritual awakening on my transformative journey.

Among these sacred sites, the Mahavatar Babaji Cave holds a special place as my spiritual home. Dunagiri Temple and Pandu Kholi, situated within the same magnetic region as the holy cave, also resonate deeply with this dimension of divine energy. Each of these places has been instrumental in shaping my spiritual path and fostering my connection to the cosmic consciousness.

I am deeply grateful to my beloved mother, Sudha Rani, whose nurturing spirit instilled in me the physical strength and vitality that continue to sustain my life. Though she no longer walks this earth in bodily form, her essence lives on vividly within me, reflected in every fibre of my being.

I am equally thankful to my father, whose unwavering support and steadfast presence have been my anchor through every hardship, empowering me to face life's challenges with resilience and grace. To my brother, Sudhakar, I offer heartfelt appreciation for being an unshakable pillar of moral and physical strength during the most demanding phases of this journey. His boundless love, sacrifices, and encouragement have profoundly shaped my path—and for this precious gift, I remain eternally indebted and forever grateful.

In my nuclear family setting, life has often been a journey through rough and testing times. However, I recognize that these circumstances are part of a shared spiritual path, shaped by predestination for me and those connected to me. Every experience, whether challenging or smooth, has held significance in fostering growth and understanding.

On this predisposed journey of togetherness, my wife, Purnima, has silently observed the transformation and evolution along the way. I am deeply grateful to her for her unwavering physical inseparability and support. My children, daughter, Parijat Sinha, a Dental Surgeon and son, Padmanabh Sinha, a public health specialist, are two spiritually evolved souls granted to me as their father. I firmly believe they are destined to serve their own divinities in due course. I am profoundly thankful to both of them for upholding my dignity as their father and for being integral parts of this spiritual narrative.

Throughout my spiritual journey, I have been blessed with the gracious support and encouragement of several advanced beings who have profoundly influenced my path. I am immensely grateful to Shri Ram Das ji from Badrinath, Shri Shyamal Ji Maharaj of Vrindavan Ashram, Shri Patit Pawan Ji Maharaj of Rajgir Ashram, Shri Gopalanand Ji Maharaj of Delhi Ashram, Shri Satinath ji Maharaj from Varanashi ashram and the late Shri Pradeep Ji Maharaj of Almora Ashram for nurturing me like their own child and guiding me with their blessings.

I also extend my heartfelt gratitude to Shri Priyabhishek Sharma, the author of 'A Himalayan Master and the Sixth

Sense', who has been a divine companion across lifetimes, even though we have not met physically in this birth.

These revered souls have been instrumental in shaping my spiritual evolution, and I remain eternally thankful for their unconditional blessings and encouragement.

I am deeply grateful to all my co-travellers on the path to self-realization, whose companionship has been an invaluable source of encouragement and togetherness. Their unwavering support and shared purpose have significantly enriched my spiritual journey. Many of them have been particularly insistent on the timely completion and publication of this account, for which I am profoundly thankful.

I would like to specially acknowledge Shri Anant Ji, Shri Braj Kishore Pandey Ji, and Shri Manish Ji, three administrative officers from the Bihar government, for their encouragement. I am equally indebted to two remarkable facilitators: Shri Rajesh Pandey Ji, who eased my access to Vrindavan, and Shri Bibhuti Bharadwaj Ji, who made my journeys to the Himalayan regions seamless. Their contributions have been catalytic in enabling my physical presence at these spiritually significant locations.

Moreover, I extend my heartfelt gratitude to a group of blessed devotees of Shri Mahavatar Babaji and practicing Yogis with whom I share spiritual dynamism. These divine companions include Shri Manoj Kumar from the Bihar Police Department; Amar Singh Ji and Prasoon Pandey Ji from Ayodhya; Satya Priya Sharma from the agricultural sector of the Government of India; Arnab Nandi Ji from Kolkata; Aseem Ji from Bihar; Pawan Rana, a young *Saadhak* from Chandigarh; Vijesh Ji & Ashish ji from Punjab and Himachal, respectively; Himanshu Mishra Ji from Pune; Ashok Bhai from Kolkata; Alka Mishra Ji from London; Dr. Lovleen Ji and Vijay Bagri from Delhi; Devis Saha from Odisha; Sanjay Rai from Gazipur, Shri Waseem Haque from

London. I extend my earnest appreciation to Shri Neeraj Vasisht Sir, a senior most bureaucrat from Madhya Pradesh and the software giant from Bhopal, Satyarth Dube for their inspiring connection and dedication to higher pursuits. Their commitment to spiritual and divine endeavours is truly admirable.

I also wish to acknowledge Shri Chandra Shekhar Jha Sir for his profound spiritual wisdom rooted in his deep knowledge as a *Gyan-Yogi*. His journey alongside mine has been a true blessing. Lastly, I extend my gratitude to Hari Om Ji from the Bihar Revenue Services—a sincere practitioner and musician who is steadfastly committed to freeing himself from worldly attachments.

Each of these companions have played a unique role in fostering my spiritual growth, and I remain eternally thankful for their presence on this sacred path.

With profound humility and reverence, I acknowledge the cherished companions and kindred souls who have journeyed alongside me on this sacred path of spiritual unfolding. I have borne witness to the steadfast transformation and indomitable perseverance of Dharmendra Thakur of Mithila, whose resolve inspires heartfelt admiration. To Joyeeta Mukherji of Kolkata, Juri Barua, and Mousami Gogoi of Assam, fellow seekers engaged in the deep exploration of self, I extend my earnest encouragement to delve ever deeper into the sanctum of inner reflection.

My sincere gratitude is due to Manish Mathur, whose modest demeanour exemplifies virtue, and whom I urge to cultivate the noble courage befitting his spirit. I hold dear Pratik Ji Purushottam, the versatile artist and neighbour in Uttarakhand, whose companionship has been a source of joy and camaraderie. Likewise, Vibha Shri Ji of Lucknow, a treasured friend and fellow traveller in the realm of spiritual quest, has enriched my sojourn with her boundless enthusiasm and steadfast friendship on numerous journeys across the nation and beyond.

To those whose presence graced this pilgrimage with quiet dignity—Shraddha Mishra and Satyavrat Tripathi of Uttar Pradesh; Arpit of Bhagalpur; Rajneesh Srivastav of Ayodhya; Mohit Sharma of Rajasthan; Krishna Murari Ji of Samastipur; Kritika and Ajay of Rishikesh; and Jayeshchandran Ji of Kerala—I offer my heartfelt homage, for their silent support has woven an essential thread in the fabric of this unfolding narrative.

A particular tribute is due to Sanjiv Barua, venerable senior journalist and kindred spirit since university days, whose gentle encouragement and unwavering faith have been integral to the bringing forth of this account. His reputed wisdom and magnanimity have been a wellspring of inspiration.

I extend my heartfelt gratitude to Maria Meera, my remarkable American-Russian friend, whose very essence is steeped in the devotion of Krishna consciousness. Residing in the hallowed environs of Braj, shifting between Barsana and Vrindavan, she exemplifies a rare and radiant embodiment of bhakti, each day lived as an offering to the Divine. The time spent in her luminous presence—most notably our unforgettable overnight circumambulation of sacred Govardhan—remains imbued with profound joy, spiritual camaraderie, and abiding inspiration. In the chronicle of my journey, I have yet to encounter another soul like Maria, whose singular spirit and friendship have so deeply enriched and illumined my path. For her rare companionship and the depth of devotion she inspires, I remain ever grateful.

Above all, I bow with deepest devotion to my revered Guru, dwelling in the exalted heights of the far-north Himalayas near the sacred Kailash, who, under the sublime guidance of Shri Mahavatar Babaji, has graciously bestowed upon me spiritual sustenance and illuminate wisdom. This most sacred bond stands as the bedrock of my transformation and continued awakening.

I am equally beholden to my esteemed colleagues in Bihar's health administration—Shri Sanjay Kumar Singh, Shri Lokesh Kumar Singh, Shri Shashank Shekhar Sinha, Shri Sudhir Kumar, and venerable senior health luminaries Prof. Sanjay Zodpey, Dr. Devendra Khandait, Dr. Hemant Shah, Dr. Himanshu Negandhi and Dr. Rajesh Nair—whose generous support has rendered possible the harmonious integration of my professional duties with my spiritual pursuit. Their counsel and fellowship have been blessings beyond measure.

Finally, I hold in special regard the youthful ardour and unwavering dedication of Anjani Pandey, Neelabh Raj, and Rahul Sah, whose diligent efforts have been indispensable in the seamless realization and documentation of this journey. Their committed presence has been a beacon of encouragement and strength.

One of my younger brothers, as well as a junior from D'School who is now a senior police officer in the Rajasthan cadre, Shri Prafulla Kumar, along with his loving spouse Varsha, have been an unwavering pillar of strength during the most challenging phases of my life.

Shri Dheeraj Narayan Sudhanshu, an esteemed member of our group, presently serves as a Bihar Information Service Officer and holds the position of Public Relations Officer in the office of the Governor of Bihar. Shri Sudhanshu is known for his profound spiritual sensitivity, genuine humility, and deeply compassionate nature. He has been graciously initiated into the revered lineage of Shri Totatpuri ji of the Puri Ashram. His guru, Shri Vijay Raghav Mishra of Darbhanga, was the son and disciple of the eminent Shri Ram Nandan Mishra ji—a great Yogi and direct disciple of Shri Totatpuri ji.

I remain deeply grateful to Shri Sudhanshu for his unconditional support and invaluable assistance in the publication of this spiritual account.

May the divine grace continue to illuminate their path always, and may they be forever blessed with abundant light, prosperity, and peace in all the times to come.

To all whose paths have touched mine in this sacred voyage, I offer my eternal gratitude and profound respects, for it is by their grace and companionship that this journey has been so richly endowed.